BEYOND THE BOYCOTT

D0875010

BEYOND THE BOYCOTT

LABOR RIGHTS, HUMAN RIGHTS, AND TRANSNATIONAL ACTIVISM

GAY W. SEIDMAN

A Volume in the American Sociological Association's
Rose Series in Sociology

Russell Sage Foundation • New York

Library of Congress Cataloging-in-Publication Data

Seidman, G.
  Beyond the boycott : labor rights, human rights, and transnational
activism / by Gay W. Seidman.
      p. cm. — (American Sociological Association's Rose series in sociology)
  A study of the impact of the Sullivan Code in South Africa, the Rugmark
social labeling effort in the Indian handwoven carpet industry, and the
COVERCO monitoring of the Guatemalan apparel industry.
  Includes bibliographical references and index.
  HB ISBN 978-0-87154-761-3   PB ISBN 978-0-87154-762-0 (alk. paper)
  1. Employee rights—Developing countries—Case studies.   2. Labor
movement—Developing countries—Case studies.   3. Human rights
monitoring—Developing countries—Case studies.   4. International
business enterprises—Developing countries—Management—Case studies.
5. Social responsibility of business—Developing countries—Case
studies.   I. Title.   II. Title: Labor rights, human rights, and transnational
activism.
  HD8943.S44 2007
  331.01'1—dc22   2007009609

The paper used in this publication meets the minimum requirements of American National Standard for Information Sciences—Permanence of Paper for
Printed Library Materials. ANSI Z39.48-1992.

Text design by Suzanne Nichols.

RUSSELL SAGE FOUNDATION
112 East 64th Street, New York, New York 10021
10   9   8   7   6   5   4   3   2   1

The Russell Sage Foundation

The Russell Sage Foundation, one of the oldest of America's general purpose foundations, was established in 1907 by Mrs. Margaret Olivia Sage for "the improvement of social and living conditions in the United States." The Foundation seeks to fulfill this mandate by fostering the development and dissemination of knowledge about the country's political, social, and economic problems. While the Foundation endeavors to assure the accuracy and objectivity of each book it publishes, the conclusions and interpretations in Russell Sage Foundation publications are those of the authors and not of the Foundation, its Trustees, or its staff. Publication by Russell Sage, therefore, does not imply Foundation endorsement.

Previous Volumes in the Series

Forthcoming Titles

Good Jobs, Bad Jobs, No Jobs: Changing Work and Workers in America
Arne L. Kalleberg

Morality by Choice: Politics, Personal Choice, and the Case of Covenant Marriage
Scott Feld and Katherine Rosier

The Production of Demographic Knowledge: States, Societies, and Census Taking in Comparative and Historical Perspective
Rebecca Emigh, Dylan Riley, and Patricia Ahmed

Race, Place, and Crime: Structural Inequality, Criminal Inequality
Ruth D. Peterson and Lauren J. Krivo

Repressive Injustice: Political and Social Processes in the Massive Incarceration of African Americans
Pamela E. Oliver and James E. Yocum

Re-Working Silicon Valley: Politics, Power and the Informational Labor Process
Seán Ó Riain and Chris Benner

Who Counts as Kin: How Americans Define the Family
Brian Powell, Lala Carr Steelman, Catherine Bolzendahl, Danielle Fettes, and Claudi Giest

Setting Out: Establishing Success in Early Adulthood Among Urban Youth
Frank Furstenberg, Jr., Julie Kmec, and Mary Fischer

"They Say Cutback, We Say Fight Back!": Welfare Rights Activism in an Era of Retrenchment
Ellen Reese

The Rose Series in Sociology

The American Sociological Association's Rose Series in Sociology publishes books that integrate knowledge and address controversies from a sociological perspective. Books in the Rose Series are at the forefront of sociological knowledge. They are lively and often involve timely and fundamental issues on significant social concerns. The series is intended for broad dissemination throughout sociology, across social science and other professional communities, and to policy audiences. The series was established in 1967 by a bequest to ASA from Arnold and Caroline Rose to support innovations in scholarly publishing.

DOUGLAS L. ANDERTON
DAN CLAWSON
NAOMI GERSTEL
JOYA MISRA
RANDALL G. STOKES
ROBERT ZUSSMAN

EDITORS

Contents

═ About the Author ═

Gay Seidman is professor of sociology at the University of Wisconsin, Madison.

Acknowledgments

Like most comparative projects, this one took me to places to which I could not have traveled on my own. Without the generous help of Padma Priyadarshini and her family, I could not have conducted research in India. Padma's analytic and practical skills allowed me to negotiate a reality I could never have understood on my own. Landy Sanchez accompanied me on several trips to Guatemala and commented on draft chapters; her intellectual and practical contributions to this project are enormous. I am deeply grateful to Padma and Landy, as I am also to César Rodríguez-Garavito, who helped orient my fieldwork in Guatemala and commented on the manuscript.

This book would not have reached completion without Dan Clawson. As one of the American Sociological Association's Rose Series editors, Dan nudged the book to press, commenting carefully on repeated drafts. In the course of finishing the book, I found in him a generous and insightful colleague and friend.

Ruth Milkman and Peter Evans, as outside reviewers for the Russell Sage Foundation Press, offered wonderful suggestions that greatly strengthened the final product. Joya Misra, Naomi Gerstel, Bob Zussman, and their fellow editors for the ASA's Rose Series generously read and discussed a rough draft. Allen Hunter's thoughtful comments on chapters helped me think through some complex questions. Andrew Schrank—a great traveling companion as well as constructive critic—also patiently read through several drafts and caught some embarrassing errors (although doubtless more still lurk in the text). The final book is far better for all their advice, questions, and challenges.

Many activists granted interviews, but I am especially grateful to Abby Nájera and Homero Fuentes from COVERCO, who were so open, welcoming, and insightful that getting to know them turned out to be an unanticipated benefit of fieldwork in Guatemala. John P. John, editor of India's *Labour File*, and Scott Nova, executive director of the Workers' Rights Consortium, were especially generous in sharing their experiences.

I am grateful to many more people than I can list here, but I must specifically acknowledge my debts to the following: Glenn Adler,

Swami Agnivesh, Shireen Ally, Mark Anner, Richard Appelbaum, Ralph Armbruster-Sandoval, Carmen Bair, Jeff Ballinger, Joe Bandy, Charles Bergquist, Fred Block, Edna Bonacich, Alison Brysk, Sakhela Buhlungu, Michael Burawoy, Jackie Cock, Jane Collins, Lance Compa, Marisol de la Cadena, Jill Esbenshade, David Fig, Archon Fung, Steven Gelb, Gary Gereffi, Carolyn Hamilton, Shireen Hassim, Patrick Heller, Jeff Hermanson, Huberto Juárez Núñez, Bridget Kenny, Margaret Levi, Mara Loveman, Tumi Makgetla, Ivanka Mamic, Phil McMichael, Sheila Meintjies, Devan Pillay, Gerry Pinto, Nancy Plankey-Videla, Anne Posthuma, Raka Ray, Jonathon Rosenblum, Jeffrey Rothstein, Cindy Ruskin, Gershon Shafir, Aseema Sinha, Michael Small, Jackie Smith, Barbara Stallings, Scott Straus, Sid Tarrow, Dave Trubek, Leanna Trunzo, and Eddie Webster. Participants in several seminars at the University of Wisconsin at Madison and elsewhere raised challenging questions and offered suggestions; the final argument is certainly clearer because of their engagement with the material.

The University of Wisconsin's Graduate School and its Latin American Studies program provided funding for several field trips, and the university's Vilas Associate Award provided support during the writing phase.

During most of the time I was working on this book, my twin sister, Neva Seidman Makgetla, served as a policy analyst for the Congress of South African Trade Unions. It was sometimes challenging to have a brilliant labor economist as an interlocutor, but it was also really fun, and the book is much better for her sharp insights.

My biggest debt, of course, is to my husband Heinz Klug and my sons Ben and Matthew, who managed cheerfully while I was away, and who filled my homecomings with joy.

= Chapter 1 =

Citizens, Markets, and Transnational Labor Activism

The press release called it the dawn of a new era: after years of difficult negotiations, multinational corporations, labor activists, and human rights groups had agreed "to work together as equal partners to make significant improvements in labor conditions in garment factories" around the world (U.S. Department of Labor 1998). With footwear and garment factories moving beyond the reach of American law, corporate codes of conduct and independent monitoring offered an alternative strategy that might help workers from New York to Central America, Los Angeles to Southeast Asia.

Despite the internal tensions that plagued it, the Apparel Industry Partnership (AIP) embodied a new approach to global labor rights. In the rapidly integrating economy of the 1990s, policymakers, activists, and scholars hoped that pressure from transnational networks and "global civil society" could create a floor under a competitive "race to the bottom," stopping unscrupulous employers from taking advantage of workers in the world's poorest countries. As sweatshops proliferated in hidden corners of global cities and export-processing zones, could global standards backed by ethical consumers protect workers across borders?

Through transnational campaigns, proponents hoped that "stateless regulation" would improve working conditions in factories everywhere by focusing global pressure on points of corporate vulnerability. Threatened with consumer boycotts, brand-name companies would adopt voluntary codes of conduct and accede to monitoring by nongovernmental organizations (NGOs), which would, in turn, threaten to "name and shame" companies that mistreated employees. Successful campaigns since the 1970s had used new information technologies to appeal for boycotts, and proponents suggested that these ad hoc campaigns could be regularized into new forms of global governance. While companies cared more than ever about their image, advocates pointed out that national states—previously the only building block in mechanisms of global governance—were ever weaker. "Global civil

1

society" offered a new arena for organizing, with transnational campaigns providing building blocks for a new, worldwide strategy.

But what does this brave new world really look like? Most discussions of transnational activism focus on efforts to mobilize consumers, examining how boycott threats can force companies to acknowledge their social responsibilities. Far less attention has been paid to efforts to institute systems of monitoring and certification, especially in the developing world. What happens when companies accede to pressure, adopt codes of conduct, and allow external monitors to examine their facilities? What difference do these transnational campaigns and monitoring systems make to workers' daily experience?

This book represents an effort to explore independent monitoring on the ground as it has played out in some widely cited schemes. Examining three important examples of independent certification—the Sullivan Code in South Africa, the "Rugmark" social labeling scheme in India's handwoven carpet industry, and independent monitoring in Guatemala's apparel industry—I explore how transnational campaigns alter the dynamics of struggles at work. Under what circumstances do companies admit nongovernmental monitors into their factories? How has "naming and shaming" worked to change corporate culture and behavior? How do monitoring schemes support workers' struggles across the globe?

This new approach marks a shift away from the way labor rights have been protected in the past. Historically, labor rights were defined through local struggles, as social movements called on states to protect citizens at work. While labor campaigns have generally emphasized the creation of channels for voice and bargaining power in specific settings so that workers and their unions can represent their own concerns, they have also tried to protect workers who are unable to challenge employers directly by strengthening state enforcement of national labor laws. By contrast, the "stateless" vision of the early twenty-first century draws on experiences from the international human rights movements, appealing to global audiences and universal standards. What does this shift mean for both the practice and content of transnational labor campaigns?

Independent Monitoring as a Strategic Tool

Why does independent monitoring matter? Embedded in most discussions of how transnational campaigns could improve working conditions lies some vision of external monitoring designed to ensure that companies live up to their promises of decent treatment. External monitors, usually local nongovernmental organizations committed to certifying companies' compliance with a voluntary code, would alert transnational networks to violations; those networks would then mobilize consumer pressure against the corporate violator.

The logic is persuasive: private voluntary groups monitoring factories around the world could assure ethical consumers that the goods they purchase were produced under broadly acceptable conditions, guaranteed by external certification. Jill Esbenshade (2003, 9), a sociologist who played an active role in debates about the AIP, summarizes the strategy:

> Codes of conduct created . . . by companies are a public statement of intent. Workers and their advocates can use these as a tool to hold companies accountable. What is needed is a more credible form of certification. . . . Independent monitoring . . . offers a necessary check on a system that is otherwise controlled by the companies themselves.

While some companies would willingly comply, companies that failed to meet the new standards could be publicly "named and shamed" based on independent monitors' reports. If global commodity chains link workers in developing countries to consumers around the world, Jane Collins (2003, 190) suggests, "new international communities of accountability, focused on particular firms and their brands, can support workers in their attempts to negotiate improved conditions."

Without external certification of compliance, voluntary codes are unreliable. In her detailed study of corporate codes of conduct, Ivanka Mamic (2004) finds that managers comply with voluntary guidelines when executives at headquarters are committed to compliance, when they provide resources for implementation, and when they punish subcontractors that violate their codes. Without that central commitment, codes are less effective; cost-cutting pressures may tempt even well-intentioned employers to "play for the gray," reinterpreting or ignoring voluntary standards (Braithwaite and Drahos 2002, 19). Internal company monitoring processes, using internal monitors or accountants, are unreliable—most companies employ accountants rather than trained labor inspectors, and most companies are reluctant to publicize their reports (O'Rourke 2000).

Instead of asking weak national states to enforce national laws, then, proponents of stateless regulation envision pressure from an energetic civil society as a mechanism for enforcement. Independent monitors would alert consumers, and companies threatened by transnational boycotts that might forever tarnish their corporate image would then police their own factories.

Evidence suggests that some consumers are ready to play their part. In telephone surveys, American consumers claim that they would pay a bit more for goods produced under safe, healthy conditions (University of Maryland 2000), and "fair trade" sales have increased rapidly in Europe and North America (Raworth 2004).

In 2002 an ingenious experiment in a Michigan department store offered some empirical evidence for both the promise—and the dangers—of consumer concern. In that experiment, a slight majority of shoppers preferred socks with fair trade labels over slightly cheaper socks without them (Prasad et al. 2004). But that experiment—which involved entirely fictitious labels and completely unsubstantiated claims about working conditions—illustrates a widely acknowledged conundrum. Although consumers may be willing to pay for decent labor standards, they do not always take the time to ascertain what lies behind the label. By themselves, labels are hardly reliable indicators of working conditions (Blowfield 1999; Oxfam 2004, 89). Without external monitoring, claims of corporate social responsibility may simply be a new marketing ploy. In order for consumers to be able to "hold companies accountable," they need accurate information provided by monitors who are not simply working on behalf of the companies themselves (Shamir 2004).

But under what circumstances do companies accede to external monitoring? How are these schemes organized, and what kinds of monitoring is involved? If global governance is to rest on transnational movements of ethical consumers, surely we should look more closely at actual instances in which independent monitoring is said to have worked and examine how that happened.

Logic of Inquiry

What does independent monitoring really entail? Business ethicist Prakash Sethi (2000, 119) notes that although "code development is a growth industry," there are remarkably few studies of how codes have worked in the past, especially in cases frequently cited as successes. Scholars who write about transnational campaigns write about the novelty of long-distance altruism and the importance of business ethics to potential sales, but they have made little effort to examine the kinds of issues that mobilize—or fail to mobilize—broad consumer support, the pressures that have prompted companies to accede to monitoring, or the different approaches embodied in existing monitoring arrangements. Thus, for example, the "Sullivan Principles" governing American companies in South Africa under apartheid are likely to be mentioned in the same breath as the global boycott against Nestlé over its baby formula advertisements or a more recent campaign linking Nike's athletic footwear to sweatshops and labor violations. Similarly, discussions of transnational activism often assume that "fair trade" coffee programs are similar to campaigns to reward good employers, when in fact, most fair trade coffee schemes have focused on the price-per-pound paid to small growers, and do not attempt to monitor working conditions on coffee plantations (Levy and Linton 2003; Talbot 2004, 208-9).

Just as advocates' enthusiasm tends to elide distinctions between stateless schemes, they often overlook the problems raised by the handful of empirical studies that do exist. Recent studies suggest that voluntary, privatized monitoring has had relatively little impact on working conditions in factories, in industrialized countries, or in developing societies (Esbenshade 2004; Mamic 2004). In agriculture there is ample evidence suggesting that NGO monitoring has done more to ensure the quality of fruits and vegetables destined for wealthy-country consumers than to improve the lives of farmworkers (Bain 2006; Guthman 2004; Mutersbaugh 2002; Talbot 2004). Nevertheless, proponents persist in their view, painting voluntary regulatory schemes as the best available option in a world where multinationals seem more vulnerable to wealthy consumers than to weak legal sanctions.

Given the enthusiasm surrounding independent monitoring, it seems worth pursuing the characteristics of successful cases more systematically. The rest of this book examines the actual workings of independent monitoring, trying to tease out common empirical patterns across different schemes and contexts.

In chapter 2, I examine the assumptions underlying visions of stateless regulation. In their efforts to appeal beyond borders, transnational campaigns tend to be most concerned with bearing witness to and seeking protection for vulnerable victims. Does this shift prompt activists to subtly reorient their appeal and redefine their targets in ways that change the character of their goals? What is entailed in the shift from labor rights to human rights, and from national states to the international arena? How does the shift to global audiences shape the appeals, issues, and mobilizing strategies of transnational labor campaigns, and what does it mean for how local workers' concerns are interpreted and redefined?

In chapter 3, I describe what may be the first—and perhaps the most frequently cited—scheme in which multinationals submitted to external monitoring. The Sullivan Principles in South Africa represent an important historical antecedent to corporate codes of conduct; by most accounts, this code altered corporate culture in important ways, changing discussions around corporate responsibility. Like most people who were active in the American anti-apartheid movement, I was deeply critical of the Rev. Leon Sullivan's efforts in the 1970s and 1980s to persuade companies to become "good corporate citizens" in South Africa, yet in discussions of codes of conduct today, Sullivan's approach is described as a key early model. The history of Sullivan's program highlights some important aspects of monitoring schemes—from the characteristics of consumer mobilization to the impact of codes on local managers' behavior to the ways in which local monitors' choices may define corporate social responsibility.

In chapter 4, I look at the use of "social labels" in the Indian handwoven carpet industry, focusing on "Rugmark," a widely cited program that labels carpets as free of child labor. I explore the decision by local activists to focus on a specific issue and industry and the impact of consumer pressure on corporate and local government responses. This case study underscores the persistent tensions between transnational and local activists. However well intentioned, corporate codes of conduct—especially those located primarily within the export sector—can sometimes come into conflict with local efforts to change government policy and may weaken broader national campaigns by focusing only on export-oriented production.

Chapter 5 examines monitoring in the Central American apparel industry through the prism of the work done by the Commission for the Verification of Codes of Conduct (COVERCO), an independent Guatemalan monitoring group that is often cited as a model. COVERCO's success has much to do with the integrity and commitment of its staff and leadership; it also reflects specific characteristics of its local context, especially the failure on the part of Guatemalan state officials to protect citizens. COVERCO's efforts grow out of a long-standing effort by Guatemala's human rights activists to build a "culture of compliance" in a context where impunity has reigned. Rather than seeking to replace state regulatory frameworks with a market-driven logic, COVERCO aims to strengthen and reorient state institutions in order to build a more inclusive democracy.

In chapter 6, I conclude by teasing out points of similarity and difference across these widely varied examples. There are, of course, important differences in the local contexts, in the way monitoring works, in the funding for monitoring schemes, in the density of contacts within transnational activist networks, and, above all, in the relationships between monitors and local states. Nevertheless, the comparison between very different cases reveals some dynamics that are surprisingly similar, even across those very different cases. Tables 1.1 and 1.2 offer a preview of the dimensions that emerge as important through the comparison, including several issues that are rarely mentioned in discussions of transnational activism.

- Transnational campaigns tend to redefine labor issues as human rights issues, generally seeking to mobilize support through broad transnational campaigns around issues of political and social inclusion. Successful international mobilization tends to stress political and human rights, not workplace-based concerns; in the process, local activists' concerns may be subsumed to match those of transnational networks.

- Consumer pressure has been most successful when it is mobilized through institutions, not by appeals to individual consumers making decisions in supermarket aisles. Rather than relying on individual consumers to make ethical choices, campaigns that have forced corporations to accede to independent monitoring have invariably worked through more organized consumer pressure—through church groups, universities, and major stockholders.

- States have played a much greater role in these "successful" campaigns than is generally acknowledged. In each of these schemes, transnational campaigns sought help from politicians and policymakers in importing states, using threats of legal market closure to prompt exporting corporations to let in outside monitors to their factories.

In terms of the actual monitoring process, key similarities emerge from the comparison in terms of funding, tensions between local and transnational goals, and—perhaps above all—in the proliferation of alternative codes that undermine more effective monitoring as companies seek out monitors that will provide a level of oversight that suits their needs. As table 1.2 suggests:

- Monitors have often been heavily dependent on outside funding, usually from the corporations seeking to show their customers that they have responded to pressures. This pattern also creates concerns about the ability of monitoring groups to retain their independence and still gain corporate permission to enter workplaces.

- In each case, relations between monitors and local activists were marked by visible and profound tensions—generally over who made strategic decisions and who represented workers to international activists—reflecting the kind of questions about accountability, representation, and access to global resources that arise in civil society everywhere.

- In each case, alternative codes or interpretations of codes have proliferated, complicating the choices facing even the most alert consumers. In each case, activists and companies alike recognized that this proliferation was driven by corporate efforts to find more lenient monitoring schemes—a dynamic that effectively undermines the long-term reliability of any independent monitoring process.

In my conclusion, I tease out the implications of the similarities and differences between these cases of "successful" independent monitoring, showing how some of the patterns observed in the comparative

Table 1.1 Comparing Transnational Processes

	Specific Aim	Larger Campaign	Organized Consumer Pressure	Role of Exporting State	Role of Importing State
Sullivan, 1977 to 1994	Workplace integration and affirmative action	Anti-apartheid, anti-racism	U.S. churches, students, and pension funds	South African state (during apartheid) viewed as enforcing discrimination	Explicit threat of increased sanctions against South Africa
Rugmark, 1992–94 to the present	To monitor looms, rescue children from carpet industry	Anti-child labor	German churches, UNICEF, and other child groups; U.S. churches and politicians	Indian state viewed by activists as complicit in permitting child labor	Explicit threat of market closure against carpets made with child labor
COVERCO, 1996 to the present	To improve working conditions across Guatemala, including maquilas	Central American human rights concerns *and* globalization of U.S. apparel industry	U.S. student groups and universities	Guatemalan state viewed as non-enforcing, possibly complicit in permitting labor law violations	Explicit threat of market closure if labor law reform not enacted

Source: Author's compilation.

Table 1.2 Comparing Monitoring Schemes

	Monitoring Agency	Funding Source	Local Relations	Alternative Codes
Sullivan, 1977 to 1994	Arthur D. Little, accounting firm	Corporations seeking monitoring of subsidiaries and affiliates	Tensions with unions and anti-apartheid activists	Not for American firms
Rugmark, 1992–94 to the present	Independent NGO	Exporters paying for monitoring subcontractors	Tensions with unions and child labor activists	Several, both private and state-run
COVERCO, 1996 to the present	Independent NGO	Brands paying for monitoring subcontractors; U.S. government programs and labor rights groups	Some tensions with unions; close working relations with human rights groups; now working with Ministry of Labor	Several, both private and through industry coordinating council

Source: Author's compilation.

empirical material seem to reflect not simply local concerns but also characteristics inherent to the approach. Through a comparative lens, I explore the promise and limitations of these efforts to create independent monitoring schemes and suggest that strategies aimed at strengthening democratic state institutions might provide a more powerful mechanism for protecting citizens at work.

Case Selection, Methods, and Comparative Design

Discussions of international monitoring often rest on a flimsy understanding of past cases. In comparing three very different cases—acknowledging their differences in approach, context, and goals—I examine common patterns in order to understand better the kinds of campaigns, networks, and labor activism that have prompted companies to accede to external monitoring; the characteristics of "successful" external monitoring programs; and the questions or issues that confront those schemes over time.

The design of this study follows a common approach for comparative-historical social science: many, if not most, comparative studies select on the dependent variable in the hope of identifying the conditions necessary to produce successful outcomes. Douglas Dion (1998) suggests that, following the tradition of John Stuart Mill's "logic of agreement," this approach might help to identify the conditions necessary to attain that common outcome (while leaving open the question of which conditions might be considered sufficient) and also provide a way to explore the dynamics through which those outcomes might be reached.

But defining "success" proved difficult. I sought broad programs in which transnational campaigns had managed to insist that companies accede to nonstate regulatory monitoring schemes, where transnational activists had effectively mobilized threats of consumer boycotts to persuade employers to accept some form of independent workplace monitoring. I hoped to find common characteristics—of mobilization, appeals, commodities, or monitoring schemes—that had produced widely acclaimed models of global workplace regulation.

As I examined these "exemplary" cases, however, I began to recognize that even this limited understanding of success might be problematic. Comparisons between the campaigns revealed common dynamics not only in the transnational campaigns that produced independent monitoring schemes but also in the difficulties and constraints facing those who tried to make these schemes work. The closer I looked at cases I had initially viewed as success stories, the more I was forced to confront their limitations.

Nevertheless, I chose to persevere, largely because I wanted to counter a trend that has characterized discussions of transnational activism: seeking new promise in "global social movements," accounts of global activism tend to focus only on successful mobilization. As Heather Williams (2003, 528) notes, "Many scholars have resolutely avoided the unpleasant task of examining failed campaigns or spent networks." Whenever journalists or researchers have criticized a specific case of monitoring, scholars, activists, and policymakers tend to drop it from their repertoire, continuing to list only those cases in which they can still claim that a transnational campaign has worked.

Perhaps making a virtue of necessity, I became convinced that instead of looking for new, less problematic cases, it made sense to consider the problems that complicate even successful monitoring efforts. Perhaps a comparison of characteristic tensions would reveal common features. Instead of dropping cases in which success seemed overstated, therefore, I have tried to analyze the positive impact of each effort, while still reflecting honestly on the difficulties faced by well-intentioned activists and policymakers. In exploring a complicated, often messy reality, I hope to offer insights into the constraints as well as the promise of transnational labor monitoring.

Descriptions of the three schemes are based on archival and interview material, as well as on visits to each site and interviews conducted there. Between 2003 and 2006, I traveled repeatedly to South Africa, India, and Guatemala to interview participants directly involved; these individuals ranged from monitors involved in daily factory visits to corporate spokespeople involved in debates about monitoring to Ministry of Labor officials to unionists and nongovernmental activists to factory workers employed in the factories being monitored. In addition, I reviewed as much published and archival material as I could find for each case; most transnational activists and corporate spokespeople are both articulate and self-reflective, and they frequently offer more eloquent and reliable pictures of their strategies and concerns in their own publications and documents than they are likely to sketch in interviews. Finally, I made concerted attempts in each country to interview activists, government officials, and unionists who were aware of monitoring efforts but were peripheral to them, out of a concern that a simple focus on those directly involved in monitoring might present a distorted sense of the schemes.

Although this is a comparative study, each case deals with a specific local context and history and is thus unique. In the empirical chapters, I have sought to develop an historical account that remains conscious of local dynamics, recognizing that "successful" independent monitoring emerged in very different contexts, shaped by local concerns. Each project is unique, having been constructed by real people in very different, but always difficult, circumstances. Thus, in each description I have tried to develop separately a thorough picture of local dynamics, even while also seeking to construct a comparison that not only emphasizes the unique character of each campaign and its result but also draws out those issues that may be common across all three programs.

Lived Experiences

Many discussions of transnational labor campaigns start with accounts of real workers' experiences of being exploited by ruthless employers or challenging authoritarian labor relations; indeed, I suggest in the next chapter that this mode of storytelling may itself be a tactic required by the decision to appeal for international support. This study is somewhat different: like many comparative-historical studies, my cases explore broad social processes, and I leave readers to imagine for themselves what those processes mean for the lived experiences of individual workers.

But if the effort to develop a broad comparative framework requires stepping back from the details of workers' daily lives, it should not be forgotten that discussions of global regulation stem from the poverty and working conditions of real people in real situations. Before turning to abstract questions about global governance, then, I want to offer two anecdotes from my field notes. These accounts may offer some sense of the problems and promises that international labor campaigns embody for workers in situations that can seem hopeless.

In January 2003, Padma Priyadarshini, a graduate student in sociology who made my research in India possible, took me to visit a successful carpet-exporting business in Agra. The two cousins who ran the business offered to show us their entire operation, from the sales office not far from the gleaming spires of the Taj Mahal to the dark sheds in distant villages where carpets destined for sale in New York or Berlin were woven.

One weaving-shed stands out in my memory. We drove down dusty dirt roads that were little more than footpaths, parked in an open space, and walked over to a windowless mud hut where a beautiful young woman worked alone. Like most looms in India's carpet belt, this one was owned by a "master" weaver; the exporters provided the weaver with designs and materials and planned to pick up the finished product after several months. Like most master weavers, this man employed others to tie the hundreds of thousands of knots that make up a hand-knotted carpet.

Sitting on the dirt floor was a young woman, perhaps seventeen years old and dressed in a brilliant red sari, who tied knots so fast that her hands moved in a blur across the loom's vertical strings, the sharp knife she used to cut the threads flashing as she worked. Taken by her smile, I asked her permission to take photographs as she worked—of the loom, of the pile of dried dung used for fuel, of the young woman herself. While I was snapping photos, Padma stood outside with the loom-owner and the exporter, who was telling the weaver to fire the young woman because her knots were not tied tightly enough.

The young woman was not legally underage, but her poverty and vulnerability left her completely helpless—and our visit, innocent as it was, may have made her situation even worse by bringing her work to the attention of the exporter several weeks early, perhaps before she had had a chance to learn thoroughly the skills of knotting threads.

Some six months later I found myself in a situation that seemed painfully similar, reminding me of the powerlessness and poverty that confront so many workers around the world. In a small house in an industrial area outside Guatemala City, a group of women talked about their poverty, their vulnerability, their fear that they would be fired from jobs that paid barely enough to scrape by on. Abby Nájera, an energetic Guatemalan activist, had taken the sociologist Landy Sanchez and me to meet a group of women workers who had organized a union in a foreign-owned apparel factory in one of Guatemala's export-processing zones. The independent monitoring group COVERCO had been monitoring this factory, which produced clothing under contract for various corporations, including Liz Claiborne, and Abby had been involved in helping the group.

These women were clearly desperate and quite despondent. They had struggled for several years to build a union, facing repeated threats and assaults from their employer; one union organizer suspected that an assault on her daughter had been instigated by the company, apparently in an effort to intimidate the unionists. In 2003 the factory was threatening to close, and even the women's coworkers were arguing that the union should keep quiet to save their jobs. Under Guatemalan law, the union's existence depended on the company's survival: if the factory closed, the union would be disbanded, even if the company opened under a different name the following day. It looked as if the only union then registered in any of Guatemala's export-processing zones was about to be closed down and that the union activists were all going to lose their jobs.

In contrast to the Indian weaver, however, these workers' situation was not hopeless. Through Abby Nájera, the Guatemalan workers had access to a transnational network of people who were already aware of the struggles at this particular factory and already concerned about the situation of apparel workers in Guatemala. Within days of our visit, Abby helped the women write letters describing their situation and then sent the letters to a range of activist groups in a network that she and other labor activists in Guatemala had developed over the previous three or four years. Central American solidarity groups in the American Midwest, a group of labor activists in Washington, D.C., and an international union body in Geneva, Switzerland, offered different kinds of help: one individual sent money for a cell phone, while another contacted other organizations around the world—much as one would expect transnational labor networks to behave.

A call from the Geneva-based international clothing workers union federation to unions in Guatemala and its Ministry of Labor eventually provoked the most effective intervention of all. Six weeks after that despairing conversation, the Guatemalan Ministry of Exports threatened to cut off the company's export licenses, and the company responded. Two years later the factory was still operating under its old name, and the union was still stumbling along—still facing endless difficulties, still fearing intimidation and unemployment—but still in place.

If the tale of the Indian worker underscores the vulnerability and voicelessness of many workers in export-oriented industries around the world, the Guatemalan saga gives a sense of how transnational campaigns can help—while still revealing some of the limits to such campaigns. Almost certainly, the young Indian weaver with the winning smile had few choices when she was told to leave the loom; her employer held all the cards. The Guatemalan workers were vulnerable to employer whims, even employer assault. Their links to outside networks were fragile, almost serendipitous, leaving them dependent on the kindness of strangers. Nevertheless, those outside ties—mediated, as is so often the case, by a handful of energetic local activists like Abby and her colleagues, working for NGOs like COVERCO, which serve as key nodes in transnational network activities—helped them reconfigure relations of power within their factory. By bringing outside pressure to bear, both on the Guatemalan state and on the employer, they saved their union, at least for the moment. It is sometimes possible to deploy transnational campaigns, however slowly and in however piecemeal a manner, to create new possibilities and construct channels through which workers can begin to speak for themselves.

Independent monitoring is often cited as the best way to strengthen those possibilities as companies adopt voluntary codes of conduct and monitors ensure that they fulfill those codes. The rest of this book explores what that approach means in practice: under what circumstances, and through what kinds of strategies, have consumer-based campaigns around independent monitoring helped improve workers' ability to organize, to represent themselves, and to improve their conditions at work? Before turning to empirical cases, however, I want to shift gears slightly. A look at the theoretical underpinnings of these debates will suggest some of the issues that are raised as labor struggles move from a national to a transnational arena, and labor rights are redefined as human rights.

= Chapter 2 =

Labor Rights as Human Rights: Regulation in the Context of a "Thinned" National State

What does it mean to redefine labor rights as human rights? Transnational campaigns often try to mobilize global support by invoking universal standards rather than locally enforced labor law. But in the process, labor activists often abandon older labor strategies, which tended to focus on expanding definitions of citizenship and national regulation. In this chapter, I contrast an approach based on the human rights model—using consumer boycotts and privatized, voluntary regulatory schemes to raise labor standards—to the older, more state-centric approach, which emphasizes the construction of national labor law and industrial relations frameworks. What assumptions about power, voice, or targets are embedded in global campaigns to "name and shame" corporate violators, and how do these assumptions change the dynamics of local labor struggles? What has propelled the shift, and to what extent does it redefine the very content of labor campaigns?

These questions underlie a growing discussion among transnational activists about global governance and the construction of independent monitoring processes. In recent decades, scholars, policymakers, and activists have increasingly focused on voluntary regulatory schemes to protect labor rights, but they rarely stop to think through the assumptions involved in the strategy. What are the links between transnational campaigns, consumer boycotts, and new visions of global governance? Why have so many activists turned to stateless regulatory mechanisms rather than seeking to strengthen the national legal frameworks that have historically been the primary mechanism providing protection for citizens at work? What happens when activists turn their attention away from workplace negotiation to focus instead on mobilizing consumers to punish or reward multinational employers?

In an era when most national governments seem weaker than footloose multinational corporations, the international human rights movement and past examples of transnational consumer-based pressure on corporations seem to offer promising new directions for transnational campaigns. In this chapter, I interrogate this promise, hoping not to undermine efforts by transnational activists to find new approaches to organizing workers, but to provoke discussion: in the effort to create new support for workers' struggles, why do so many activists neglect or bypass local institutions designed to protect citizens, and what might be gained or lost as a result?

Citizenship and Labor Rights

Seeking to imitate the successes of the international human rights movement, transnational labor activists generally invoke what Margaret Keck and Kathryn Sikkink (1998) call the "boomerang" of international pressure on local actors. Using new communications and computer technologies to send information rapidly around the globe, human rights activists have brought global attention to local struggles by "naming and shaming" violators and asking international audiences to put pressure on those who abuse innocent victims. Thus, for example, Amnesty International collects information from local groups and transmits that information to groups around the world; those groups, in turn, express their concern to repressive states and call on their own governments to insist in the international arena that repressive states mend their evil ways.

Transnational labor activists generally seek to imitate that pattern, engaging in a boomerang process that parallels the human rights approach. Local activists provide information about working conditions or environmental degradation to transnational activists, who then use that information to mobilize pressure on violators—usually corporations rather than national governments. Global networks of transnational activists use information about local workers' grievances to mobilize consumers across international boundaries, hoping to persuade companies to change their practices through the threat of global boycotts. Based on information gleaned from far-flung factories, transnational activists ask consumers to threaten multinational employers with the prospect of a tarnished image and a damaged profit margin (Bullert 2000; Featherstone and United Students Against Sweatshops 2002; Juárez Núñez 2002).

As Ralph Armbruster-Sandoval (2005) shows in his detailed study of cross-national campaigns in Central American garment factories, transnational labor campaigns have generally mobilized international consumer pressure against specific corporations and manufacturers, leaving the state out of the picture. "Today," Naomi Klein (2002, 338) writes, "more and more campaigners are treating multinationals, and the policies that give them free rein, as the root cause of political injustices around the globe"; anticorporate activists seek to mobilize consumers to support workers' struggles at the point of production. If companies are concerned with protecting their images and brand names, what could be more logical than asking consumers to punish them if they mistreat their workers?

But this stateless vision of consumer-based protection of labor rights marks a crucial shift from the general pattern of human rights campaigns, with important implications for the kinds of issues and concerns driving consumer campaigns. As figure 2.1 shows, human rights activists seek to involve states, mobilizing international opinion against national governments and involving their own national governments to raise human rights concerns in the international arena. In contrast, as figure 2.2 suggests, labor activists tend to emphasize moral pressure against corporate headquarters rather than political campaigns that involve states, whether in exporting countries or in the importing countries that provide markets for transnationally traded goods.

This shift reflects both pragmatic and logical considerations. Corporations are the leading violators of labor rights worldwide, and activists believe that they can mobilize consumer-based campaigns against major brands and labels to mount direct pressure on those violators. Moreover, economic theories and international policies over the past twenty-five years have weakened national states' willingness to regulate multinational corporations, while companies, heavily invested in images and concerned about retaining market share, seem much more vulnerable to consumer action than states could ever be.

Yet the ease of this discursive transformation—from targeting states to targeting multinational corporations—obscures the tensions contained within it, between claims articulated in terms of citizenship and claims articulated in terms of universal human rights or global morality. The philosophical underpinnings of citizenship rights and human rights have very different histories, and different epistemologies. As Gershon Shafir (2004) cogently argues, citizenship claims tend to reflect participation in bounded communities, while human rights discussions evoke the transcultural, transnational commonalities of human experience. Long before the emergence of modern notions of the nation-state, citizens addressed their claims to local governments, seeking protection and support for locally defined rights. Indeed, under feudalism ordinary citizens could sometimes invoke local practice and custom in demanding greater state protection (Somers 1993). By contrast, the human rights perspective is built around universal norms based on common human needs and concerns emerging in the twentieth century as a broad set of rights. Claims-making occurs not within the framework of domestic law, but through appeals to fundamental rights

Figure 2.1   Human Rights "Boomerang"

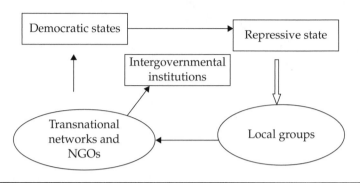

Source: Adapted from Keck and Sikkink (1998).

within a universal community, especially since the United Nations adopted the "Universal Declaration of Human Rights" in 1948.

The dynamics of local struggles over citizenship and international campaigns around human rights differ in important dimensions. Historically, labor campaigns have sought to protect vulnerable members of a local community, often invoking local norms and citing the need to protect one's neighbors; in general, when local labor activists call on their national state to protect "rights" at work, they speak in terms of regulating relationships within an existing community. By contrast, "human rights" are advanced in more universal terms: human rights discourse tends to explicitly reject local variation and instead assert commonalities across contexts, setting an international standard for the treatment of all individuals regardless of their local cultures or traditions. Often drawing on the principles of the European Enlightenment, human rights activists evoke broad moral standards and hold actors up to a set of principles considered constant and global (Sikkink 1993). As an international movement that often appeals to an ill-defined "international community" to enforce global standards (Malkki 1994), the human rights movement invokes a far more universalistic approach than the locally defined concerns of citizenship, and it appeals to broad audiences rather than to policymakers embedded within national governments or specific cultural contexts.

Citizenship is a protean concept allowing local actors to articulate a wide variety of claims shaped to fit local circumstances. Despite that variation, it is important to recognize that for most of the past two centuries, labor rights have been central to citizenship narratives everywhere. Militant labor movements since the mid-nineteenth century have drawn on the language of citizenship as they sought state protection for workers. Especially since T. H. Marshall (1950/1992) published

Figure 2.2   Stateless Consumer-Based Regulatory Vision

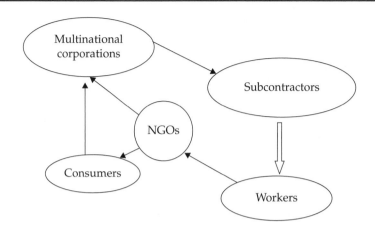

Source: Author's calculations.

his classic arguments about the different stages of citizenship, unions have argued that full citizenship is in fact defined by state protection of citizens' living and working conditions. As social and economic rights have come to be viewed as a logical extension of political inclusion, workers and their communities have voted for politicians who support government policies to strengthen workplace protections and unions' bargaining power, and organized labor takes as axiomatic the idea that states should regulate the workplace and protect the dignity of workers and their families (Somers 2005). By the late twentieth century, democratic citizenship had come to be defined, in large measure, in terms of states that routinely enforced labor laws, through protections for workers backed by inspections, sanctions, and a range of other mechanisms regulating working conditions, employer behavior, and collective bargaining processes. This pattern of political mobilization has had very tangible results. As Dani Rodrik (1999) concluded in a large cross-national study, "democracies pay higher wages"; when citizens vote in democratic elections, workers and their families tend to support a regulatory framework that protects and improves working conditions.

To say that labor rights have historically been defined through local struggles is not, of course, to suggest that unionists are inevitably protectionist or parochial. Indeed, organized labor could be described as one of the oldest transnational social movements, stemming back to the earliest beginnings of industrial unionism. As craft unionism gradually gave way to industrial organization in mid-nineteenth-century Europe, workers seeking a broader base for collective action regularly called on all workers to unite in a single struggle, and the language of an "international" brotherhood of workers resonated even while workers persistently organized along national lines. By the late nineteenth century, labor leaders understood that capital was mobile and argued that unless workers supported each other across national boundaries, capital would always seek out the cheapest, most docile labor, undercutting workers' negotiating power by moving elsewhere. "Workers of the world, unite!" Marx and Engels wrote; and though that slogan has sometimes been distorted by more parochial concerns, most labor leaders around the world have paid at least lip service to the idea that a strong workers' movement requires working-class solidarity across boundaries of nation, race, and industry (Nimtz 2002).

But a century of internationalist rhetoric should not obscure the reality: most labor movements have been defined by national boundaries. Workers' identities are shaped through local communities as well as in terms of structural location; as E. P. Thompson (1963) famously noted, workers' organizations have always drawn on local cultural repertoires, and subjective interpretations of class relations are always embedded in local geographic and historical understandings. Even claims invoking a universal standard—such as demands that employers pay a "living wage" or that they respect workers' basic human dignity—define the substance of those claims through local prisms, reflecting expectations constructed within a local context.

Local histories can of course divide rather than unify. As nationalist and racial conflicts within international labor federations demonstrate, cultural repertoires and local identities can create barriers between workers, excluding immigrant or newly proletarianized workers from membership rather than incorporating them into an imagined community. Far from reflecting universal standards, appeals to local communities are often based on self-interest and exclusion. Few examples are quite as egregious as the 1922 white South African unionists' racialized slogan "Workers of the world, unite! and fight for a white South Africa," but labor activists have often privileged domestic interests over internationalist sympathies. In the late 1940s, for example, American unions tended to view expressions of labor internationalism with distrust, seeing internationalist leanings as a mark of Communist sympathies (Silverman 2000).

But unionists may invoke nationalist sentiments as a strategy for demanding state action. Frequently, labor nationalism involves a strategic component: long viewed by unions as the most effective protectors of workplace rights, states can enforce national labor laws even in sites where workers have been unable to challenge employers directly. Thus, movements defined by global altruism may invoke nationalist sentiments in order to engage state action. For example, in the last decades of the eighteenth century, British antislavery activists first managed to mobilize British public opinion against the slave trade when they called on the British government, not to protect black Africans from brutal European slavers, but to end "the ill treatment of [British] seamen in this wicked trade" (Thomas Clarkson, 1808; quoted in Hochschild 2005, 119).

This pattern is not simply instrumental—states have been central to labor campaigns. Though union rhetoric may often target employers, many labor activists have turned to government regulation as the first step in improving working conditions so that standards can be enforced even on employers who are unwilling to bargain with workers. Responding to community demands, states since the late nineteenth century have regularly intervened at work to demand that employers provide at least minimum protections. As the industrial revolution unfolded, European policymakers turned to public policy to prevent workplace abuse; protective labor legislation marked the inception of what T. H. Marshall (1950/1992) calls "industrial citizenship," a fundamental component of industrial democracies. A century later, in the latter half of the twentieth century, the assumption that states have a crucial role to play in regulating and enforcing market mechanisms was widely accepted. Karl Polanyi (1944/2001, 76) viewed the state's intervention to regulate work as basic common sense: "To allow the market mechanism to be the sole director of the fate of human beings and their natural environment," he wrote, "would result in the demolition of society."

Historically, national systems regulating workplace practices emerged through some shared sense of a common destiny and mutual concern, as vividly illustrated in the aftermath of New York's infamous Triangle Shirtwaist Factory fire, when sympathetic upper- and middle-class New Yorkers called on the state to enact and enforce protective legislation to prevent further tragedies. Richard Greenwald (2005, 140) reminds us that in early twentieth-century New York some labor activists rejected the idea that laws and state enforcement could adequately protect workers, arguing that workers could best articulate their own demands in direct negotiations with employers. But the history of protective labor legislation reveals a growing consensus among elite politicians and unionists alike that governments should intervene to protect vulnerable workers, who are also neighbors and fellow citizens.

Once those laws were passed, factory inspectors were usually mandated to inspect work sites and enforce protective laws; state inspectorates, in turn, often publicized abuses, mobilizing support for further factory regulation. Karl Marx, of course, frequently cited factory inspectors' reports in his description of factory conditions in nineteenth-century Europe, but factory inspectors themselves often publicized abuse, apparently deploying their "expertise" and their status as impartial experts to create public sympathy and to help construct new legal standards for workplace conditions and worker rights. Polanyi (1944/2001) suggests that government inspectors' reports educated the public about conditions inside nineteenth-century factories and mobilized public support for new government intervention; similarly, recent historical work suggests that in the United States, France, and Britain, factory inspectors formed a strong lobby for labor law reform, in some cases helping to design new channels of collective bargaining (Fuchs 2005; Greenwald 2005). Laws may often have been imposed from above, but as E. P. Thompson (1975, 267) persuasively argued, the law "has also been a medium through which other social conflicts have been fought out," providing an arena and resources in which social movements could mobilize and put forward their claims on the state (see also McCann 1994).

After World War II, labor activists in former colonies assumed that new independent governments would protect their citizens from rapacious employers. Throughout the postcolonial world, labor activists viewed national independence and democratization as a crucial first step toward protecting labor rights, by creating the possibility that new democratic states might pass and enforce labor legislation (Cooper 1996; Koo 2001; Rueschmeyer, Stephens, and Stephens 1992; Seidman 1994). Following a similar logic, the International Labor Organization (ILO) for most of its history viewed national states as central to the construction and enforcement of labor protections. Calling on national states to ratify international conventions, the ILO hoped that states would adopt new legislative protections for citizens and then enforce those protections within national boundaries, making labor law part of the basic framework of national governance. Virtually all mechanisms designed to protect workers from abuse—from the specific details of national labor law and the character of labor organizations to practical enforcement tools—are located at the level of the national or provincial state. Industrial relations frameworks are predicated on a vision of national sovereignty and state authority; labor rights have been protected by national states with control over their territory, and business elites have generally acceded to regulation by the state as a normal part of doing business.

But in the 1990s, globalization seemed to undermine that strategy. Following the logic of transnationalism, the ILO shifted from its earlier emphasis on strengthening national-level labor law and labor enforcement to a new focus on promoting "core" labor standards and universal labor rights. Like many frustrated labor activists who believed that global competition to attract investors had created a "race to the bottom," undermining any hope that governments would enforce labor laws, the ILO began to view transnational labor activism as a more promising direction. Before discussing the implications of this new strategy, however, I turn to the underlying arguments for a more global approach. These arguments boil down to the belief that a highly competitive global economy undermines national states' capacity—and perhaps their will—to protect citizens at work.

The "Thinned" National State

By the early twenty-first century, the state's centrality in discussions of labor rights seemed to have been blurred. In an increasingly integrated global economy, many labor activists and policymakers viewed states with skepticism and distrust. When increased capital mobility threatens economic stability and growth, when businesses can realistically threaten to pack up and move to a lower-wage site, and when politicians routinely express the fear that workplace intervention will undermine growth, how can states be relied on to protect citizens at work? This is the puzzle that confronts transnational labor activists: in a competitive global environment, when corporations can move or outsource production and states cannot be counted on, what regulatory mechanisms can be put in place to enforce labor protections?

Since the early 1980s, rapidly changing international economic policies and an increasingly competitive global market have altered the relationship between states, business, and labor, apparently undermining states' willingness to intervene in the workplace. Even in already industrialized countries, these pressures have eroded workers' protections (Bronfenbrenner and Hickey 2004; Golden and Pontusson 1992). In developing countries—where states were notoriously weak and corrupt and politicians viewed labor rights as balanced in a precarious trade-off with job creation and economic growth—what hope could labor activists place in a thinned national state?

From the mid-1970s, changing technologies, changing trade rules, and changing economic orthodoxies transformed corporate strategies, and global supply chains became the hallmark of transnational production. Corporate managers discovered that a more flexible approach to production could cut costs. Instead of owning a subsidiary outright and producing for a single national market, multinational corporations increasingly moved production toward a global assembly line: components of the final product might be made in one region, brought together for final assembly in another, and sold to consumers in still a third. At the same time, corporate managers began to restructure managerial relationships, relying increasingly on buying components from independently owned factories through subcontracting relationships that left the multinationals to emphasize design, advertising, and branding.

The flip side of the global supply chain was brutal competition on the shop floor. Viewing contracts with major multinationals as a way to gain access to wealthy global markets, small firms from Mauritius to Vietnam competed for contracts from big multinational labels—especially in relatively low-skilled manufacturing industries, such as apparel and toys, but increasingly in higher-skilled industries like automobiles and electronics as well (Gereffi and Korzeniewicz 1994; Herod 2001; Kaplinsky 2005; Kapstein 1999; Ruggie 1998; World Bank 1996). Relationships between multinationals, subcontractors, and the workers who actually produced the goods became increasingly attenuated (Collins 2003; Gereffi and Korzeniewicz 1994; Juárez Núñez and Babson 1998; Rosen 2002; Ross 2004). The "runaway shop"—a term originally coined to refer to garment factories that abandoned New York City's heavily unionized garment district for the more pliable nonunionized workers in small-town Pennsylvania (Wolensky, Wolensky, and Wolensky 2002)—now came to refer to factories that moved across international borders, beyond the reach of either union contracts or regulatory pressures.

This pattern was exacerbated by new economic theories and international institutions, which insisted that states in developing countries should seek to attract foreign investors as a strategy for increasing exports. By the mid-1990s, most economists and global policymakers agreed that economic growth required increased exports, and they urged developing countries to liberalize their economies. In the effort to expand exports, many states concentrated on attracting more investment, hoping that increased production would bring more jobs and economic growth (Babb 2001; Biersteker 1995; Evans 1997, 2000; Kapstein 1999; McMichael 2000; Stallings 1995; Stiglitz 2003; World Bank 1996).

The neoliberal "Washington Consensus" of the 1980s and 1990s constrained national governments—especially national governments in developing countries—in ways that have greatly diminished their capacity to regulate and control investment capital or provide social services to their citizens. Threats of capital flight and job loss often persuaded governments to back away from efforts to regulate business and also persuaded workers to accept more "flexible" labor regulations—giving employers greater flexibility to hire and fire workers, which makes any effort to demand collective bargaining rights at work even more risky for individual workers (Cook 2006). Even governments that had developed an institutional capacity to enforce domestic labor law—a capacity lacking in many developing countries—often explicitly waived labor laws for new investors, fearing that the threat of law enforcement might scare away the investors.

This pattern is most clearly visible in export-processing zones around the world, but it can even be seen in advanced industrialized countries. Writing about the United States, Human Rights Watch (2000, 10) concluded that, in the face of global competitive pressures, "workers' freedom of association is under sustained attack . . . and the government is often failing its responsibility under international human rights standards . . . to protect workers' rights."

Of course, increased global trade holds some promise for developing countries as well as dangers. Optimists argue that in the long run the benefits will outweigh the cost: by spreading industrial growth around the world, globalization brings new jobs and skills and ultimately will benefit workers. An increasingly liberalized trade regime, it is argued, will push everyone to adopt more efficient, cheaper production processes; the combined effects of new trade rules and new production possibilities will stimulate countries to be more productive and to seek niches in which they may have a comparative advantage, creating greater economic growth around the globe. Countries that manage to attract new industrial investment may gain jobs for more skilled workers, with new opportunities for high-wage industrial employment and job creation. From this perspective, rigid labor laws could undermine economic growth by limiting countries' abilities to exploit their "comparative advantage"; the "high road" could lead to prosperity as skilled workers join with management to find new productive niches—new efficient production processes, new products, and new international markets. Optimists suggest that skilled and efficient workers will be able to demand higher wages, since employers depend on workers' participation in production, and that gradually the benefits will trickle out to the entire economy (Kapstein 1999; Moran 2002; World Bank 1996).

More skeptical analysts fear, however, that international competition narrows governments' and workers' options. First, economic restructuring—particularly the restructuring resulting from pressure on developing countries to open their markets and increase exports—has routinely involved massive layoffs in the large, often state-owned companies that served as the basis of industrial expansion for most late industrializers, undermining the relatively privileged core of many developing country labor movements (Candland and Sil 2001; Webster and Adler 2000). But even beyond the cold shock of restructuring, globalization could lead to a "race to the bottom" as companies search for cheap and acquiescent labor and developing countries compete for new investments by promising low wages and a stable, cheap workforce (Greider 1997; Lipietz 1987). Industrialized countries may be able to draw on historical assets to retain high-wage jobs—educated workforces, developed infrastructures and labor markets, and easy access to the world's wealthier consumers—but developing countries may have little choice but to offer low wages, low taxes, and limited regulation if they want to create jobs in the private sector (Moody 1997).

How do these new patterns of industrialization change workers' ability to demand better working conditions? New technologies have reorganized the geography of industrial production; they may involve new skills, and they certainly permit new managerial strategies. New technologies have allowed the spread of industrial production to new sites, stimulated the production of nontraditional commodities and products for export, and promoted increasing international competition. But even optimists acknowledge that new, sophisticated technologies have not always strengthened workers' ability to negotiate with employers. Workplaces may be organized to reduce the possibility that even skilled workers could disrupt production, and technologies that in the context of tight labor markets seem linked to greater trust and co-operation—in what is often called "post-Fordism"—may look meaner rather than leaner when embedded in authoritarian and hierarchical workplaces where there is abundant labor available (Juárez Núñez and Babson 1998; Kaplinsky 1995; McKay 2006; Posthuma 1995; Shaiken 1995). Even more importantly, most foreign investment does not involve sophisticated new technology or require skilled workers. Many export-processing zones simply bring old equipment to new, cheaper workers, especially in labor-intensive industries (Cowie 1999; Freeman 2000; Kaplinsky 1993); employers are often more interested in cutting labor costs than in finding cooperative workers.

When national governments are constrained by the threat of capital flight, labor cannot expect much support for expanding the enforcement of local labor law. Global competition seems to "thin" the national state, limiting states' ability to tax corporate profits, regulate corporate behavior, or protect workers from unfair labor practices. High tax rates could chase away investments, while higher wage bills undermine international competitiveness; indeed, global competition may erode state revenues in countries that already lack social services or infrastructures—further undermining any possibility that developing countries will educate workers to give them skills that might increase their bargaining power with employers or create any of the social security programs that characterize what Marshall calls "social" citizenship. When large multinational companies hold out a country's best hope for investment capital or technology transfer, even democratic states find it difficult to set terms or restrictions.

In a competitive environment, governments are often tempted to strike what Judith Tendler (2002) calls the "devil's deal," waiving basic health, safety, and labor rules in the hope that businesses will create jobs for more citizens—a tension especially obvious in thousands of ex-port-processing zones, where government incentives range from tax breaks or export subsidies to explicit waivers of national labor laws and minimum wage levels (International Labor Organization 1997, 2003, 2006). Indeed, many governments put more resources into publishing brochures advertising their citizens' "nimble fingers" than into moni-toring health and safety protections at work (see, for example, Lee 1998; Ong 1987; Ross 2003). From El Salvador to the Dominican Republic to the Philippines to China, governments have found themselves weigh-ing labor law enforcement and corporate tax revenues against their de-sire to attract new jobs and new industries, repeatedly choosing to pro-mote growth rather than protect citizens (Lee 1998; London 2003; Mannon 2003; McKay 2006; Ross 1997).

Needless to say, this "thinning" of the state's regulatory capacity is not what Karl Marx had in mind when he predicted the withering away of the state. But neoliberal development strategies have undermined state capacity for intervention at the workplace by creating a sense that states must choose between job creation and labor law enforcement or tax collection. Fearing that labor law enforcement might frighten away potential investors, states often choose jobs over regulation, leaving workers with few protections. Labor rights, though often written into law, are seldom enforced; inspectors rarely visit worksites and even more rarely impose fines or sanctions against abusive employees. Mea-suring the impact of increased global trade, Nita Rudra (2005, 30) con-cludes that while workers in poor countries "are experiencing greater economic gains (greater employment opportunities), they are not nec-essarily increasing their bargaining power with employers, [much less] with their government. The repercussions may be significant: labor-friendly policies (e.g., higher wages, national welfare programs, em-ployment benefits, political freedoms, etc.) will be inconceivable in poor nations undergoing globalization."

How should organized labor respond? If an increasingly competi-tive global economy has transformed management strategies and lim-ited state capacity for enforcement of national laws, it has also created new dilemmas for unions. If labor militancy might frighten away in-vestors and reduce employment levels, how should unions define or defend their members' interests? Even well-established labor move-ments have struggled to find new bases of solidarity or support to sus-tain union efforts, responding to the threat of capital flight by urging members to cooperate with employers to meet the global challenge (Adler and Webster 2000; Candland and Sil 2001; Clawson 2003; Golden and Pontusson 1992; Gupta 1998; Heller 1999; Milkman 1997; Moody 1997; Silver 2003; von Holdt 2000).[1]

In a context where states back away from protecting citizens and unions worry that strikes might drive away investors and jobs, what can transnational labor activists do? During the 1990s, many labor activists turned away from traditional strategies, looking for new vulnerabilities created by the logic of the global market. In the late 1990s more and more transnational activists turned to nonstate actors in the search for new nodes of pressure.

Boycotts: A Global Strategy

Might a changing global environment offer possibilities as well as constraints? While national states and organized labor may everywhere be weaker than they were in the middle of the twentieth century, the human rights movement offers an inspiring example of how global activism can change national and international policies. In the absence of both international and national mechanisms to prevent abusive work conditions, could a global labor movement imitate the successes of recent human rights campaigns, linking consumers separated by borders and oceans—as well as barriers of language and culture—to those who work in export-processing zones, using consumer pressure to reward companies that comply with basic labor standards and punishing those that fail?

To many labor sympathizers, the underlying problem—global corporate pressure and weak states—suggests an obvious alternative. By the late 1990s, labor activists had begun to explore strategies based in the dynamics of market-driven globalization. Rather than emphasizing citizenship, these transnational strategies sought to find points of entry in the structure of global production, using international consumer pressure to target global supply chains—the complicated networks of suppliers, subcontractors, producers, and retailers through which goods are made, assembled, and sold. Instead of trying to fight global integration, this strategy involves trying to understand—and redefine—the dynamics of globalization itself.

It is worth noting that stateless strategies differ more than many activists recognize from the strategies deployed by international human rights groups. Human rights activists do frequently work outside state systems, mobilizing networks of concerned individuals to provide evidence and write to abusive governments, but states are always crucially involved, both as targets and as instruments of transnational activism. Human rights activists seek to apply direct pressure to authoritarian states through the "naming and shaming" process, and they view democratic states as potential allies, asking these governments to use whatever diplomatic leverage they can muster to put pressure on authoritarian states. In less egregious cases, campaigns to protect human rights on the ground almost inevitably work through national states, seeking to construct democratic national institutions that will protect citizens rather than permit abuse. Although the human rights movement may draw its inspiration and energy from networks of principled individuals, those networks almost invariably work with, and through, national states.

By contrast, transnational labor activists often treat national states, especially in developing economies, as irrelevant and weak, focusing instead on corporations as the key actors of globalization. These activists argue that as production and consumption become geographically divided, and as governments lose any capacity to regulate powerful multinationals, global activism needs to find new points of vulnerability and new sources of pressure.

For many activists, global consumer boycotts appear the most logical way to force companies to respect workers' rights. Consumer boycotts, of course, predate corporate globalization: campaigns to build solidarity beyond the workplace through consumer campaigns have a long history. As proponents argue, successful consumer boycotts have helped make distant grievances visible to broad audiences, creating a community of concern far beyond the local workplace. In the 1790s, British antislavery activists refused to take sugar in their tea while slaves worked on sugar plantations, and perhaps as many as half a million people in England stopped drinking "the blood-sweetened beverage" (Hochschild 2005, 193; Robert Southey, quoted in Hochschild 2005, 194). Some two hundred years later, the United Farm Workers publicized the conditions of migrant workers in California's fields through a national boycott of table grapes; the boycott mobilized widespread support for labor law reform, and American laws were rewritten to give farmworkers basic collective bargaining rights. If the sugar boycott "caught people's imagination because it brought [hidden] ties to light, laying bare the dramatic, direct connection between British daily life and that of slaves" (Hochschild 2005, 194), the grape boycott vividly reminded middle-class Americans of how agricultural workers lived and worked, giving sympathizers across the country an easy way to demonstrate their support with the striking farmworkers.

Appeals to consumers resonate, too, with the history of national labor relations frameworks. Around the world, striking workers have appealed for support from a moral community on the basis of a shared humanity—as, for instance, when a community of Irish peasants refused to pay their rent to an abusive landlord named Charles Cunningham Boycott, giving rise to the noun. Today transnational activists seek to build a broader sense of community, forcing consumers to consider the conditions under which goods are produced, no matter how far away. In an increasingly global market, consumers may need reminding that they share a community with workers spread across the globe. Just as distance allows corporate decisionmakers to ignore the human consequences of cost-cutting policies, it permits consumers to overlook the conditions under which goods are produced. Jane Collins (2003) suggests that transnational activists need to build a sense of "moral accountability" by reminding consumers to consider the lives of the people who produce the goods they consume. By publicizing accounts of unacceptable conditions in far-off factories and appealing to consumers to boycott products made under inhumane conditions, activists hope to make the problem visible. If globalization has stretched the distances between workers and consumers, boycotts can publicize grievances and pressure corporations, helping build new transnational awareness and a sense of shared humanity across borders.

Historically, even famously successful consumer boycotts constitute only one tactic within larger campaigns. Thus, for example, middle-class women called on fellow American consumers in the mid-twentieth century to support workers' efforts to organize, arguing that they had a moral responsibility to help improve the conditions under which the clothes for their families were sewn; organizers were more concerned, however, with raising awareness than with actually enforcing codes of conduct (Boris 2003; Cohen 2003; Frank 1999).

By contrast, many transnational campaigns of the early twenty-first century seem more focused on forcing companies to comply with corporate codes of conduct by exploiting corporate sensitivity to threats to "their most valuable asset: their carefully cultivated brand image" (Rodríguez-Garavito 2005b, 74). Oddly enough, there is surprisingly little concrete evidence that even widely publicized campaigns have a significant impact on corporate profits. For example, because companies refuse to comment publicly, there is no public information about the extent to which sales were affected by either the widely publicized Nestlé boycott of the 1970s (provoked by the company's advertising tactics for its baby formula, which were seen as undermining poor mothers' commitment to breast-feeding) or the 1990s campaign against Nike shoes (provoked by the labor and environmental practices of the company's subcontractors). As Dana Frank (1999) shows in her insightful history of "buy American" campaigns, even active efforts by retailers to attract ethical consumers seem rarely to have altered spending habits.

Most activists recognize that while consumer boycotts place some pressure on corporations, the impact on sales is hard to determine. Some go so far as to suggest that the privatized nature of consumption choices does not lend itself to public acts of protest. James Jasper (1997, 264) writes that consumer boycotts "can express a moral stance. But they never do so very articulately or forcefully. *A silent choice, made alone, in the aisle of a crowded supermarket, is a poor way to sustain a sense of injustice and indignation*" (emphasis in original).

Consumer boycotts are clearly a complicated strategy, one limited in scope and fraught with risks. Consumer pressure tends to be most effective when applied to well-known logos, easily identifiable products, or goods produced in specific countries. Most goods produced in export-processing zones are not easily identifiable and thus are not vulnerable to transnational boycotts. Even ethical consumers—certainly a small part of the global market—balk at boycotts of goods they consider necessities; it is much easier to persuade consumers to support a boycott if the goods involved are luxuries, or ones for which there are easy substitutes, than to ask them to engage in real sacrifice.

Boycotts across borders may be even more complicated. Not only are most goods not vulnerable to transnational consumer pressure, but developing country unionists have repeatedly warned that transnational consumer boycotts could reinforce global hierarchies. Global boycotts work only for some products; most goods—especially those produced in rural areas for domestic markets—are never exported and thus are not subject to transnational campaigns, no matter how bad the conditions under which they are produced. Further, as many developing country activists note, a strategy that puts decisionmaking power in the hands of wealthy consumers in North America and Europe carries the risk that those consumers, rather than workers in developing countries, will make key decisions about which labor rights matter and which factories will be targeted (Ali 1996). Consumer campaigns carry other risks for workers too: wealthy consumers lose nothing if a company goes bankrupt, but workers risk losing their jobs (Ali 1996; Bickham Mendez 2005; Brooks 2007; Esbenshade 2004). Just as corporate executives often worry that a badly researched activist campaign might unfairly punish companies that are energetically trying to improve conditions at a problematic factory, labor activists around the world discuss their fear that a successful consumer campaign might lead to a factory's closing just when workers are on the verge of winning trade union recognition. And, even if international consumers respond to workers' concerns, activists frequently debate when to end a campaign; who should decide whether a situation has improved enough to call off consumer pressure (Bullert 2000)?

Nevertheless, transnational consumer campaigns clearly threaten corporate images—to such an extent that policymakers and scholars have begun to incorporate these campaigns into their thinking about the long-term effects of global economic integration. Most importantly, transnational campaigns can increase global awareness of the conditions under which goods are produced. Campaigns by groups like Oxfam, Global Exchange, and the Ethical Trading Initiative have clearly raised consumers' awareness of the impact of global competition on the daily lives of workers, their families, and their communities. Even economists who firmly insist that increased trade will eventually benefit all regions of the world recognize that transnational campaigns matter. Economist Pietra Rivoli (2005, 214–15), for example, argues that the "moral case for trade [is] even more compelling [than] the economic one," but she ends her discussion of how trade helps by urging an imaginary student activist to continue to publicize corporate exploitation because "Nike, Adidas, and GAP need her to keep watching, and so do Wal-Mart and the Chinese government. . . . Future generations of sweatshop workers and cotton farmers need her as well."

Transnational activists seek to create a sense of moral accountability in order to create global pressure on corporations. In response, some major corporations have made sincere efforts to improve working conditions, either because they fear that transnational campaigns may tarnish their image and hurt their sales, or because they recognize the validity of activists' concerns. But before turning to activist efforts to deploy consumer boycotts as a means to regulate multinational corporations, I want to examine the issues that have attracted transnational consumer attention and compare them to the kinds of issues that have motivated more traditional labor campaigns.

Labor Rights as Human Rights

What rights do transnational activists hope to protect through consumer pressure, and which rights matter most? Through the 1990s, much as feminist activists since about 1980 have viewed international treaties as tools for changing national state obligations toward their citizens (Brown-Thomson 2002), many transnational labor activists viewed campaigns against corporations as a starting point for raising global awareness and sought to redefine international norms against which to measure local conditions. But appeals to international audiences also often involved a subtle shift in the kinds of grievances stressed. To mobilize international audiences, activists cannot emphasize the mundane or prosaic. Dramatic images of child workers and wretched working conditions are meant to provoke sympathy and outrage, persuading consumers that they would prefer to pay more for goods produced in safer, more dignified, more humane conditions.

The appeal for protection of innocent victims has deep roots. From the eighteenth century, David Brion Davis (1992, 23) writes, Western writers popularized "an ethic of benevolence" in which "the man of sensibility needed to objectify his virtue by relieving the sufferings of innocent victims." This ethic required, of course, that beneficiaries of altruistic acts be conceived as victims. Early antislavery activists offered as the iconic image of their campaign a kneeling black man asking plaintively, "Am I not a man and a brother?", evoking sympathy for an injured innocent, Adam Hochschild (2005, 128) notes, rather than offering a figure of heroic resistance or even an African on his home soil. Similarly, Keck and Sikkink (1998, 27) point out that the images that have inspired some of the most outstanding transnational campaigns revolve around the protection of innocent, vulnerable victims, usually from egregious physical harm:

> As we look at the issues around which transnational advocacy networks have organized most effectively, we find two issue characteristics that appear most frequently: (1) issues involving bodily harm to vulnerable individuals, especially when there is a short and clear causal chain (or story) assigning responsibility; and (2) issues involving legal equality of opportunity.

Transnational activists tend to frame appeals in terms of helplessness and vulnerability, insisting that only international intervention can prevent abuses so extreme that any decent human being would accept the need for social change. Most successful transnational labor campaigns of the late twentieth century—the anti-apartheid campaign, the Nestlé campaigns, the campaigns against child labor and against forced or prison labor—have been framed in terms that fit more easily within a discourse of human rights violations and victimization than one that stresses workers' labor rights or making workers' voices more audible. Apparently, appeals to broad universal concerns—often based on vivid, dramatic images of bodily harm to workers or violent repression—evoke far more international response than appeals based on the kind of procedural or detailed grievances that arise in most workplaces over issues like low wages or forced overtime.

By the late 1990s, labor activists seeking to confront globalization responded to the apparent success of the international human rights movement by adopting both its rhetoric and its strategies; activists and policymakers began to talk about "labor rights as human rights," framing labor rights within a human rights paradigm. To most transnational activists this shift is logical and easy, since they view labor rights as fundamental to human rights and see workers' exploitation as egregious. But in seeking to appeal to broader audiences, activists frequently offer workers' "testimonials" bearing witness to egregious violations. Accounts of suffering or deprivation stemming from abuse or the neglect of basic human needs, like hunger, exhaustion, or exploitation in an authoritarian workplace, are far more likely to provoke international support than a dry discussion of labor laws (see, for example, Featherstone and United Students Against Sweatshops 2002; Ross 1997). Seeking international support, transnational campaigns regularly frame appeals in terms that are instantly recognizable: physical violation, discrimination, and coercion are all linked to violations of basic human rights.

Such claims demand redress; international intervention in such circumstances has been legitimized by several decades of changing attitudes toward universal norms.

Campaigns seeking to mobilize transnational networks of sympathetic consumers who are willing to act on information about corporate misdeeds by boycotting products often emphasize workers' victimization rather than the construction of channels for negotiation or bargaining. In her examination of several transnational labor campaigns in the 1990s, Ethel Brooks (2003) argues that reframing workers as victims can become itself a victimizing process, turning activist workers into international symbols for solidarity campaigns. In a more detailed case study, Brooks (2005) suggests that activists in a transnational campaign against child labor in Bangladesh's garment industry recognized that a focus on child workers would appeal to a broad audience; such a focus united diverse interests in a coalition that included people concerned about the exploitation of innocent victims and American activists seeking to protect jobs for adults in the United States; the use of images of child workers avoided some of the thornier problems that plague international labor solidarity.

Does the search for images that evoke international sympathy shift labor's focus from the effort to strengthen workers' voices to the creation of images that demand sympathy? Historically, labor campaigns emphasized workers' dignity and strength; unions have sought to create channels through which workers could articulate their own grievances. By contrast, in the effort to gain international audiences' sympathy for victims, most transnational campaigns present workers as victims who are vulnerable to "global pillage" and dependent on outside support—much as international human rights campaigns have done. Only visible, egregious violations of labor rights are likely to evoke international sympathy or mobilize international audiences. As Brooks (2005) points out, appeals based on protecting victims tend to avoid issues of empowerment; these campaigns often appeal on behalf of the voiceless, claiming protection for victims rather than insisting on the right of citizens and workers to negotiate on their own behalf.

To put it bluntly, in the effort to reach transnational consumers, these campaigns may be more likely to help workers "bear witness" and gain international sympathy than to negotiate with managers on their own behalf. Indeed, many business ethicists view codes in precisely this light—as a way to protect the voiceless. For example, Lisa Nelson (2000, 277) suggests that codes should embody a corporate commitment to protecting the "mute victims—the refugee, the tribesman, and the land itself"; echoing Dr. Seuss's repentant capitalist, the lorax, she asks, "Who will speak for the trees?" It is, of course, easier to imagine intervening on behalf of helpless victims than designing a strategy for creating new collective bargaining processes in far-off regions of the world, but is there a tension between creating a voice for workers and creating global sympathy for their cause? Does speaking out to protect local workers impede the creation of new channels through which they could speak on their own behalf?

In the mid-1990s, the ILO displayed a version of this tension in its decision to focus on "core labor rights," a set of universal labor principles designed to attract global attention to egregious violations of labor rights. For most of the twentieth century, the ILO sought to persuade member states to incorporate labor rights into their legal codes and asked them to ratify the conventions drawn up by international conferences (Charnovitz 2000; Gould 2003; Leary 1996; Weisband 2000). In 1998, however, the ILO turned to a new strategy: constructing a global standard for labor rights that would be simple and universal rather than specific, multifaceted, or enforced through national legal institutions (see, for example, ILO 1997, 1998a, 2001, 2003). Apparently, the ILO's shift came in direct response to concerns that global integration was undermining local labor law enforcement: when a ministerial meeting of the World Trade Organization (WTO) in 1996 refused to include labor standards in trade rules, arguing that labor standards could be used for "protectionist purposes" and insisting "that the comparative advantage of countries, particularly low-wage developing countries, must in no way be put into question" (World Trade Organization 1996), the WTO asked the ILO to develop core labor standards to prevent a race to the bottom.

Thus, the ILO began to develop an internationally recognized, easily understandable set of core labor rights: freedom of association and recognition of a right of collective bargaining; elimination of all forms of forced or compulsory labor; effective abolition of child labor; and elimination of employment and occupation discrimination (ILO 1998a; see also Howse 1999; Langille 1999). In 1998 the ILO conference approved a new "Declaration on Fundamental Principles and Rights at Work," describing the core obligations meant to be binding on all member governments. Imitating a human rights approach that holds national governments up to a universal standard, the ILO also moved away from stressing national ratification of ILO conventions. Because the new declaration suggests that ILO membership entails obligations regarding core labor principles, most international legal analysts agree that the new approach "represents in itself a very significant, if not revolutionary, step" (Francis Maupain, cited in Charnovitz 2000, 8; see also Alston 2006).

Yet the ILO's shift to core labor principles may redirect the attention of labor activists to the kinds of labor violations most likely to appeal to transnational audiences, so as to evoke sympathy and concern beyond the small networks of principled individuals already committed to publicizing labor grievances (Compa 2000). Coerced labor, discrimination, and child labor all involve immediate physical harm to relatively powerless victims. The ordinary workplace grievances experienced more frequently in workplaces around the world are less dramatic and perhaps demand less immediate attention. While the ILO's shift to core principles may strengthen its ability to intervene in extreme cases—such as the 2002 ILO call for global sanctions against Myanmar's military government for its widespread use of forced labor (Olsen 2002; ILO 1998b)—it may also prompt the "international community" to overlook more commonplace labor grievances.

Even where this discursive shift—reframing labor rights as human rights and focusing on egregious bodily harm—does not reduce real workers to victims, it may narrow the definition of labor violations, especially by undermining a historic emphasis on strengthening workers' voices. While the ILO's core labor principles include the right to free association—a right that, if honored, empowers workers to organize their own unions or staff associations, through which they can raise ordinary grievances—the principle remains somewhat ambiguous.

The right to free association is almost as difficult to define and implement as it is to police. Most common violations of collective bargaining rights are relatively invisible and hard to prove: for instance, workers blacklisted for union organizing attempts, employers' failure to permit union elections, or employers declaring bankruptcy (while reopening next door under a different name) to forestall union recognition. None of these violations involve the kind of egregious bodily harm that might attract global attention. Transnational activists acknowledge that the most serious obstacles to collective bargaining generally involve unfair dismissals, especially among employers who blacklist or fire union activists. But when transnational movements seek to mobilize international support, their first step is usually to look for more visible indications of harm, with physical markers of exploitation and abuse. Most workers who are brought to speak to international audiences generally tell stories reflecting more immediate, physical concerns—those revolving around underage workers, coercion, or physical harm. Indeed, it is no exaggeration to suggest that these testimonies often come closer to "bearing witness" to violations of human rights than to discussing strategies for organizing workers in export-processing zones. Just as private corporate codes of conduct are far more likely to mention the ILO's other core standards than to include consideration of collective bargaining rights (Jenkins 2002), labor activists appealing to global audiences may be tempted to stress traumatic violations of the ILO's more human rights–based core principles—bans on child labor, forced labor, and discriminatory practices—than more complicated, less visible violations (see Blanpain 2000).

Finally, transnational pressures sometimes overlook local concerns. Most transnational labor activists are committed to the goals of empowering local workers and forcing multinational corporations to recognize and negotiate with local unions, yet those goals remain remarkably elusive. Examples of transnational campaigns that have successfully strengthened local unions are hard to find. Around the world, local trade unionists express strong suspicions of transnational campaigns, viewing consumer boycotts as potentially undermining local efforts to organize workers. Although this hostility may simply reflect local jealousies and turf battles, the recurrent pattern suggests that something more important is at stake: transnational campaigns may find it difficult to construct viable channels for workers' voices. Indeed, workers' voices are frequently absent from monitoring schemes, and nongovernmental groups rarely create processes through which transnational activists might become accountable to workers (Bandy and Bickham Mendez 2003; Bickham Mendez 2005; Esbenshade 2004, 145–77; Frundt 2005).

Even with the best of intentions, the international community is ill equipped to ascertain the legitimacy of workers' organizations or to distinguish unions that provide real avenues of expression for workers' concerns from authoritarian corporatist bodies that restrict workers' participation; the history of international efforts to support unions across borders is replete with manipulation, tainted by national governments' foreign policy concerns and protectionist impulses (Bergquist 1996; Gordon 2000; Herod 2001). Union-to-union cross-border labor alliances have been complicated by outsiders' multiple agendas: transnational labor alliances often reflect domestic agendas rather than responses to workers' immediate concerns (Khor 1994; see also Ali 1996).

And of course, transnational campaigns become especially complicated when they try to intercede in complex negotiations between employers, unions, and local government officials. All too frequently, when transnational campaigns pressure a single factory or company to recognize a union, the employer simply closes up shop; sometimes the company reopens under a new name, but the original workers are left unemployed. As Heather Williams (2003, 527) concludes, "While much optimism remained among labor and human rights activists about the potential of transnational networks to meet the labor challenges presented by the rapid relocation of manufacturing to ever lower wage markets, a number of stunning and brutal defeats in recent years have served as cautionary notes in drawing conclusions about the direction of citizen action."

Global Governance

Once global attention has been mobilized, how well can it be deployed in support of international labor standards? Can consumer pressure really be used to enforce voluntary codes of conduct? In discussions of global governance, success tends to be defined in terms of enforcement: how can activists construct regulatory schemes that would persuade "bad" companies as well as "good" ones to improve work conditions? What kinds of enforcement across borders might prompt heedless employers to provide better conditions, pay higher wages, or permit workers to organize unions or engage in collective bargaining?

The need for enforcement mechanisms is almost self-evident. Activists, scholars, and policymakers agree that while voluntary systems of compliance may persuade some companies to meet high standards, corporate actors facing a competitive environment are tempted to cut corners. An entirely voluntary enforcement system permits free-riding, and market pressures almost inevitably push corporations to "play for the gray," appearing to comply with standards while effectively avoiding them (Braithwaite 2002). Studies of voluntary regulatory frameworks across companies, industries, and countries have repeatedly demonstrated the limits of persuasion (Ayres and Braithwaite 1992; Esbenshade 2004; Guthman 2004; Mamic 2004). Even if well-intentioned companies adopt and implement voluntary corporate codes of conduct (see, for example, Mamic 2004), there are always some managers for whom voluntary codes are little more than a public relations exercise, a strategy for staving off public pressure. Without some mechanism to monitor compliance, and without some threat that violations will be noticed and punished, actors in a market environment have strong incentives to evade compliance (Compa 2001; Compa and Darricarrere 1996; Posner and Nolan 2003; Schoenberger 2000; Wells 1998).

But who should monitor compliance, and how? Again, most discussions of transnational labor monitoring in the early twenty-first century embrace a vision of workplace regulation that bypasses the national state. Distrusting the contradictory motives of states in a competitive global economy, many scholars and activists assume that mobilized consumers and nongovernmental groups make more reliable allies than governments. If the world is viewed in terms of a dichotomous distinction between states and civil society, the underlying problem—weak states—suggests an obvious alternative. Michael Santoro (2003, 102) summarizes the broad consensus that emerged at the turn of the century among activists, policymakers, and scholars:

> In developing countries the competition to attract foreign capital and corruption both contribute to lax enforcement of local labor laws in a phe-

nomenon that some have called a "race to the bottom." At the same time that national governments have failed to regulate global labor practices of [multinational enterprises, or MNEs], international institutions have yet to acquire sufficient power and global support to do so. . . .

NGOs, along with labor unions, have stepped into the power vacuum to become the most conspicuous and vociferous critics of MNEs on labor and human rights. NGOs, by default, are the primary channel for exerting pressure on MNEs to meet this moral obligation.

Activists argue that as production and consumption become geographically divided, and as governments in developing countries fail to control powerful multinationals, global activism needs to identify new points of vulnerability and new sources of pressure. Especially since the collapse of the statist regimes of Eastern Europe, social movement activists have embraced "civil society" (defined largely by the absence of state involvement) as the primary sphere for citizens' interaction, and they have come to view nongovernmental groups and privatized, market-based programs as more credible, more reliable, and often more effective than governmental institutions (Somers 1999). NGOs gather information and publicize local conditions, holding local behavior accountable to global norms of environmental protection, women's rights, and human rights (Bandy and Smith 2003; della Porta, Kriesi, and Rucht 1999; Guidry, Kennedy, and Zald 2000 ; Khagram, Riker, and Sikkink 2002; Sikkink 2002; Smith and Johnston 2002; Tarrow 2005); transnational activists often assume that protecting global labor rights should be similarly built on nongovernmental processes (see, for example, Hartman, Arnold, and Wokutch 2003; Kidder 2002). Tim Bartley (2003, 441) writes, "As NGOs experienced repeated defeats in international arenas, they put more energy and resources into developing nongovernmental programs"—a shift that dovetailed with "government [support for] private programs that were immune to rules about international trade."

This nonstate approach has attracted prominent critics, of course. Transnational activists frequently note NGOs' limited capacity for monitoring or enforcement, as well as their limited accountability to workers and governments. Labor law experts remind activists that states have historically been central to enforcement of rights at work (Arthurs 2004; Murray 2003), while many activists recognize that nonstate actors have trouble gaining access to work sites. Scott Nova, the widely respected founding executive director of the Workers' Rights Consortium (WRC), suggests that a nongovernmental group like the WRC is better positioned to publicize workers' grievances through international networks than to try to mount a regular monitoring program (Scott Nova interview, 2004). In contrast to many global campaigns, the WRC has taken what is sometimes described as a "fire-alarm" approach: using publicity to raise consumer awareness about abuses rather than claiming to certify that specific manufacturers have complied with global codes (O'Rourke 2003, 19).

Yet in discussions of transnational strategies, the turn away from the state remains a persistent theme. Since the mid-1990s, a series of global initiatives have claimed to provide credible information about global manufacturing conditions. Despite their many differences in standards, reporting, funding, and corporate sponsorship, all these groups—including the Fair Labor Association (FLA), Social Accountability International (SA8000), Worldwide Responsible Apparel Production (WRAP), the Ethical Trading Initiative (ETI), the Clean Clothes Campaign, and the Fair Wear Foundation—reflect deep suspicion of state willingness or capacity to protect workers. Dara O'Rourke (2003, 5) notes the irony:

> Many transnational activists have historically been extremely suspicious of market mechanisms, weakening state roles, and privatized regulation. However, for groups interested in strengthening the enforcement of labor standards, nongovernmental regulation is attractive as a supplemental system of monitoring and enforcement. Increasingly influential NGOs are thus advancing market-oriented, nongovernmental standards and monitoring systems as a supplement to state regulation in countries where it is ineffective and as a new point of leverage over firms operating globally. The turn to "voluntary private initiatives" reflects, in large measure, the realities of international power: lacking a set of global institutions through which to design and enforce new rules, most policymakers and activists emphasize cooperation rather than coercion.

Certainly, many activists and policymakers turn to market-based approaches to labor rights more out of desperation than out of any conviction that consumer-based campaigns offer an easy alternative.

Like social movement activists, many distinguished scholars began in the 1990s to rethink strategies through which businesses might be regulated, even in already industrialized countries. Partly in response to political discussions of deregulation and privatization throughout the industrialized world, a new approach to regulation emerged, stressing the importance of cooperation between "stakeholders" rather than punitive sanctions and coercion. Hoping to avoid the authoritarian excesses that often marred state oversight in the past, while also hoping that regulatory frameworks might be more responsive to rapidly changing conditions, many policymakers sought to replace coercive rules with privatized monitoring frameworks built on flexibility, learning, and responsive regulation rather than punitive measures (Picciotto 2002).

Many of these schemes rested on the participation of nongovernmental groups and private agencies, often viewed as the expression of "global civil society" and vaguely assumed to be acting on more credible information, propelled by more altruistic motives, and holding actors accountable to more universalistic standards than more self-interested national states. Thoughtful analysts regularly remind their readers that "soft" regulatory processes can coexist with more state-centric enforcement processes, but this vision—involving horizontal networks of policymakers, bureaucrats, and transnational activists developing new rules that would transcend national borders and gaining compliance through monitoring and transnational campaigns—became increasingly accepted as basic to a "new world order" (Sikkink 2002; Slaughter 2004). Nonstate transnational networks seemed especially appropriate for regulating cross-border problems, from pollution and deforestation to water rights and agricultural change (Bartley 2003; Commission on Global Governance 1995; Slaughter 2004).

This vision of "soft" regulation-by-monitoring first emerged in discussions of domestic regulation: legal and business scholars suggested that policymakers seek to promote voluntary compliance through a framework that stressed mutual learning and efforts to attain mutually desirable goals. Acknowledging that corporate self-regulation alone has often failed to produce socially responsible behavior, Ian Ayres and John Braithwaite (1992, 101–32) proposed what they called "enforced self-regulation": by enlisting management to write rules, they argued, states could create regulatory systems that would enlist managers' participation to ensure compliance and be more responsive to a rapidly changing business environment.

It is important to note, however, that most discussions of regulation-by-monitoring assume that voluntary self-regulation will be backed by state enforcement in domestic settings. Ayres and Braithwaite (1992, 129), for example, noted that small and medium-sized businesses—more fly-by-night, more vulnerable to competitive pressures, or less visible to consumers—would always have to be policed by national government inspectors, since their low profit margins are likely to tempt them to cut corners. Yet when these schemes are proposed as a mechanism for international regulation, enforcement is left entirely to ethical consumers overseas. When Ayres and Braithwaite propose flexible monitoring for international corporate regulation, their discussion of enforcement seems based on faith rather than evidence. Taking as their model the transnational campaign against Nestlé marketing practices, monitored by transnational activists and enforced by a consumer boycott, they suggest, "With an international regulatory problem and in the absence of an international regulatory agency, [public-interest groups] acted as a proxy for the state to give effect to enforced regulation" (Ayres and Braithwaite 1992, 132).

Like Ayres and Braithwaite, other scholars in the 1990s viewed transnational consumer-based campaigns as the basis for new forms of global regulation. Often citing as positive examples the Sullivan Principles in South Africa or the Rugmark Foundation in India (see, for example, Braithwaite and Drahos 2000, 254–55; Sethi and Steidlmeier 1991; Waddock 2002; Williams 2000a, 2000b), most of these proposals linked corporate self-regulation, independent monitoring by civil society groups, and international consumer pressure. Proponents of this new form of business regulation laid a new stress on corporate social responsibility as business leaders and ethicists began to argue that corporations do best when they incorporate ethical concerns into their business practices.

In the mid-1960s, corporate leaders had frequently insisted that their only concern should be profits and that their only goal should be raising shareholders' dividends. By the late 1990s, in part because of experiences with transnational campaigns like the anti-apartheid movement and the Nestlé campaign, business leaders were much more likely to accept some level of social responsibility in the communities where they did business. That shift in business discourse opened new avenues for cooperation—if managers were more willing to police themselves, and if public pressure could ensure that violations carried real costs, then privatized, voluntary regulatory schemes began to seem more plausible. Further, these proposals reflected a larger epistemological shift, suggesting a prominent role for civil society and nongovernmental organizations rather than a state-centered vision.

Thus, for example, Archon Fung, Dara O'Rourke, and Charles Sabel (2001) suggest that corporate codes of conduct and consumer campaigns could provide the basis for "ratcheting labor standards" upwards by combining independent monitors and international consumer pressure to enforce corporate social responsibility. While major corporations could begin to "benchmark" best practices, they suggest, alert consumers could demand ever more stringent monitors. It is worth quoting from their conclusion at length to give the full flavor of their approach:

> Even as contemporary globalization makes us complicit in terrible abuses of workers, it opens up new possibilities for public action to mitigate these wrongs. These possibilities come from the increasing capabilities of corporations—under the pressure of public revulsion at their social practices—to improve workplace conditions through the same sophisticated management strategies that make them champions of the current globalization in the first place.
>
> We have argued that the best way to exploit these possibilities is through a new kind of labor regulation—Ratcheting Labor Standards—

that relies on information, competition, and the participation of not only regulators and firms but also workers, consumers, journalists, investors, NGOs, and the public at large. RLS promises labor standards that are feasible because they are based on actual best practices, and non-protectionist because they take into account differences in contexts of economic development. These labor standards, moreover, join the limited enforcement power of government to the potentially great disciplinary forces of social pressure and market competition. They aim, finally, not at establishing a minimum fixed set of core workplace rights, but rather at creating a process that makes workplaces as good as they can be and better over time, as companies become more capable and nations more developed. (Fung et al. 2001, 38–39)

Proposals such as this are not simply academic exercises. Searching for new systems of global governance, key international institutions have begun to try to enlist corporate managers and transnational consumers to prevent the race to the bottom. In 1999 Kofi Annan launched a United Nations initiative called the "Global Compact," building on principles much like those embodied in the "ratcheting labor standards" scheme: by bringing together major multinational corporations, trade unions, and nongovernmental groups, the Global Compact hopes "to generate consensus-based understandings of how a company's commitment to [human rights and labor and environmental principles] can be translated effectively into corporate management practices" (Ruggie 2003, 111). These multinationals would teach by example; John Ruggie (2003, 108), a distinguished scholar and active participant in the Compact, suggests optimistically "the adoption of good practices by major firms may exert an upward pull on the performance of local enterprises in the same sector."

Like the Global Compact, international proposals for voluntary regulatory schemes tend to rely far more heavily on social pressure, including monitoring by nongovernmental organizations, than on sanctions or enforcement through external regulatory agencies. Where discussions of regulation within national borders generally assume that internal monitoring schemes will be backed by national state enforcement, that question is left hanging in international proposals. Fung, O'Rourke, and Sabel (2001) point vaguely to large international institutions (primarily the World Bank, with a nod to the International Labor Organization) as potential repositories of information about monitors and corporations; similarly, Braithwaite and Drahos (2000, 255) suggest that corporate monitoring capacities could be linked to the ILO's reporting capacities, but the only concrete enforcement mechanism they suggest involves "taking corporate abuses to mass publics." The UN's Global Compact is perhaps even more voluntaristic; Ruggie (2003, 108) notes that it has thus far depended entirely on consumer pressure, since firms' decisions to engage with the compact are "driven . . . above all by the sensitivity of their corporate brands to consumer attitudes." Ruggie adds: "The Compact is not a code of conduct but a social learning network. It operates on the premise that socially legitimated good practices will help drive out bad ones through the power of transparency and competition" (113).

This stateless vision is echoed in activists' proposals, which regularly invoke independent monitoring as the basis for alerting consumers to corporate misconduct. The call for independent monitoring is reflected, for example, in the campaign against Nike's global production practices. Typically, activists considered the giant footwear corporation's agreement to "include non-governmental organizations in its factory monitoring" and make those monitors' reports available to the public "the most important of [Nike CEO Philip] Knight's promises" in 1998—although some concluded three years later that the company's subsequent monitoring efforts were in fact woefully inadequate (Connor 2001, 2, 44–51). Similarly, in 2004 Oxfam urged consumers to buy fair trade–labeled products, but it also urged consumers to demand that brand names "ensure adequate monitoring and independent verification" (Oxfam 2004, 89).

At the heart of most activist proposals lies active monitoring by civil society; independent NGOs, perhaps working in cooperation with corporate headquarters, would monitor conditions in corporate factories and the facilities of their suppliers, providing information that would allow consumers and activists to "name and shame" abusers and focusing on transnational campaigns as the most realistic source of pressure on multinationals.

Most proposals recognize the limits of voluntarism, but few see any viable alternative. Thus, for example, Fung, O'Rourke, and Sabel (2001, 36) suggest in an aside that perhaps national states could be persuaded to incorporate elements of the "ratcheting labor standards" into their domestic legal systems, but they fail to pursue their own logic. Similarly, Jill Esbenshade (2004) is keenly aware of the flaws of purely U.S.-based voluntary monitoring schemes in the American apparel industry, but at an international level she views independent monitoring as the only option. The best workplace monitors, she notes, are workers themselves, at least in situations where they feel protected enough from victimization to assert their concerns and secure enough in their employment to ignore threats of capital flight. In developing countries, however, where states are weak, unions are repressed, and employers can threaten to move at a moment's notice, are corporate codes of conduct, transnational consumer pressure, and nongovernmental monitoring groups the best route to improving working conditions? Like most analysts who discuss transnational regulatory schemes, she ends by calling for what she considers a second-best option: since states are weak and unions weaker, perhaps voluntary regulation involving corporate codes and independent monitors offers the only realistic approach to protecting workers.

Conclusion

Over the past twenty years, a rapidly integrated global economy has changed the relationship between national governments, businesses, and labor, raising fears that governments may engage in a race to the bottom as they trade away worker protections in the hope of attracting investors and creating jobs. In response, policymakers, academics, and activists have sought new ways to regulate transnational corporations. Modeling their approach on the international human rights movement, activists have targeted logos and regions instead of governments; campaigns have sought to mobilize international sympathy by "bearing witness" to egregious violations and creating nonstate monitoring systems instead of focusing on creating new channels of negotiation and union representation.

The shift is not, perhaps, quite as simple as it appears. As I have tried to show, transnational labor campaigns may redirect attention away from labor's traditional strategies and toward those core labor principles that look most like universal human rights; sometimes this approach emphasizes the protection of victims rather than the strengthening of workers' voices.

But in an era of global economic integration, when governments and international institutions view international investors as their best hope for economic growth and employment creation, the appeal of labor strategies that deploy the logic of global markets to improve working conditions is obvious. If national states lack the capacity, even the will, to enforce labor laws, transnational consumer pressure offers an alternative form of sanction on abusive employers. Most proponents of this approach recognize that transnational labor campaigns are limited, but they hope that even localized or industry-specific interventions will gradually lead to other, more systematic improvements in working conditions around the world by "ratcheting up" labor standards.

How successful have stateless regulatory schemes actually been in improving workers' conditions? Under what conditions can transnational campaigns mobilize pressure on employers, and how does nongovernmental monitoring work in practice? In the chapters that follow, I explore three important examples of transnational campaigns and independent monitoring. There are, of course, enormous variations between the cases in terms of the issues that prompted the campaign, the character of the campaign and the monitoring framework, and the impact that each campaign has had. But they also share important patterns: in the character of the issues involved, in the relationships between local and transnational activists, in the relationships between independent monitors and local labor organizers, and in the responses of corporations and national governments to monitoring processes. By comparing the dynamics of specific campaigns, I hope to provide a more empirically grounded understanding of the possibilities and limits to this approach.

═ Chapter 3 ═

Monitoring Multinationals: Lessons from the Anti-Apartheid Era

One of the most frequently cited examples of transnational corporate monitoring involves labor standards only tangentially: the nearly twenty-year effort to improve the "corporate citizenship" of American companies in South Africa by promoting corporate efforts to undermine apartheid, a system of racial oppression that went far beyond the workplace.[1] But workplace reforms came first, and in many ways such reforms served as the cornerstone of Sullivan's code of conduct. American companies were asked to reconstruct their South African workplaces as beacons of enlightenment, demonstrating that good business practices could start with treating all employees fairly.

Today business ethicists frequently identify the Sullivan Principles as the first "successful" example of independent monitoring. Although the South African program was an unusual one in that it was designed specifically for American companies operating under apartheid, the experience undoubtedly helped shape subsequent approaches to corporate codes of conduct and multinational monitoring, and it continues to resonate in contemporary discussions. From 1977 to 1994, hundreds of American companies with affiliates or subsidiaries in South Africa signed on to a voluntary code of conduct and permitted a nongovernmental organization to monitor compliance, publicly announcing subsidiaries' grades. Managers faced real consequences for failing to comply with the code, and there were efforts to strengthen the code even further through the nearly twenty years it was in force. Importantly, the code was applied in a relatively accessible site where information about corporate behavior was relatively available (Spence 1998), and its signatories were involved in making a wide range of products, from pharmaceuticals to automobiles, computers to agro-industrial goods. Often credited with changing global corporate culture, the code marked the first time multinational executives accepted some "corporate social responsibility" for the communities where global investments were

47

located. The implementation of the Sullivan Principles stands out as a key episode in the spread of stateless consumer-based strategies for regulating global corporations.

To those of us who were involved in anti-apartheid campaigns, the Sullivan Principles' iconic status seems somewhat ironic: most anti-apartheid activists viewed the entire Sullivan process with distrust, believing that corporate executives signed on because they hoped to mute calls for full economic sanctions, not because they truly wanted to undermine apartheid. But thirty years later, it seems worth revisiting the subject. Did anti-apartheid activists underestimate the impact of the principles? Did the Sullivan Principles prompt significant corporate reform?

In this chapter, I suggest that the answers to these questions may be somewhat ambiguous: the code of conduct and the monitoring process provoked real changes in corporate behavior, but not always for the desired reasons, nor necessarily in the direction claimed by the system's advocates. Why did companies accede to outside monitoring, and what does this example of independent monitoring suggest about how voluntary regulatory schemes are constructed and implemented? What kinds of monitoring systems were put in place, and how effective were they in changing corporate behavior? How did the Sullivan Principles evolve over time, and why?

The Sullivan Framework

The Sullivan framework emerged out of three separate developments through the 1960s and 1970s: a growing international movement focusing on economic sanctions as a way to undermine South African apartheid; a movement for what was called socially responsible investing; and a movement to make American corporations more accountable to American communities. From the early 1960s—when South Africa outlawed most political parties that called for an end to apartheid's repressive system of white domination—anti-apartheid activists urged the West to impose international economic sanctions as a nonviolent alternative to armed struggle.

Massive capital flight following the 1960 Sharpeville massacre revealed South Africa's dependence on international finance. Anti-apartheid activists argued that without emergency loans from British and American banks, South Africa would have collapsed. But through the 1970s, the U.S. and British governments routinely vetoed international sanctions, claiming that South Africa's strategic minerals and its control over key sea lanes made the white-minority regime a crucial ally in the cold war. In response, anti-apartheid activists sought to block the foreign loans and investments that they believed shored up apartheid in South Africa, calling for nongovernmental, privatized economic sanctions; they urged multinationals to withdraw their investments from South Africa, thus "rais[ing] the cost of doing business as usual" for the white-minority regime. Jennifer Davis (1995, 177), a prominent activist on divestment issues, writes that many activists viewed these efforts as basically educational; they never really expected to have any practical impact on South Africa's economy. But by making Western economic links to apartheid visible, they hoped to make Americans aware of what was happening on the remote tip of a far-off continent in order to mobilize support for a new American foreign policy toward the region. Other anti-apartheid activists took the economic ties more seriously, arguing that American economic ties to South Africa's military and industries weighed heavily in American foreign policy. As long as the investments remained profitable, they argued, American policymakers would veto international economic sanctions (Danaher 1984; Seidman and Seidman 1977). Either way, anti-apartheid activists viewed Western investments in South Africa as a starting point for mobilizing global anti-apartheid campaigns.

Anti-apartheid activists faced an uphill battle, however. In the early 1960s, most corporate leaders rejected the idea that they could or should use their economic clout to push for reform, in South Africa or anywhere else. Corporate leaders insisted that businesses should be considered apolitical and that profits were the only legitimate business goal. As a Citicorps officer told a congressional hearing as late as 1978, "There is one rule for American multinationals wherever they operate. This rule is: Hands off" (George Vojta, quoted in Rodman 1994, 317). Some went so far as to claim that their South African ties reflected cold war realities. Chase Manhattan, for example, justified its loans to the South African government as strengthening anti-Communist voices, arguing, "It would endanger the free world if every large American bank deprived developing countries of the opportunity for economic growth" (quoted in Sampson 1987, 87). Investing in apartheid South Africa proved almost irresistible; by 1972 nearly three hundred American corporations had established subsidiaries or affiliates there, leading a *Fortune* magazine commentator to remark, "South Africa has always been regarded by foreign investors as a gold mine, one of those rare and refreshing places where profits are great and problems are small. Capital is not threatened by political instability or nationalization. Labor is cheap, the market booming, the currency hard and convertible" (Blashill 1972, 49).

Even though corporate executives appeared deaf to concerns that their investments were supporting apartheid, the idea that companies could use their economic leverage to push for change received a great deal of sympathy from ordinary Americans, especially in the context of the burgeoning American civil rights movement. The anti-apartheid focus on corporate links to South Africa resonated at home: if African Americans in the United States could change department stores' hiring practices by boycotting local merchants, could anti-apartheid activists change apartheid by blocking investments?

In March 1965, Students for a Democratic Society (SDS) organized a demonstration outside a New York branch of Chase Manhattan to protest the bank's loans to South Africa. The demonstration had little immediate impact; responding to a shareholder's question only a week later, Chase's chairman, George Champion, rejected any responsibility for South African apartheid. "We can't be responsible for the social affairs of a country," he said. "Where there's commerce and trade, we feel we should be part of it" (quoted in Massie 1997, 193). But while SDS organizers soon shifted their attention to protests against the spreading war in Indochina, sporadic efforts continued to make American investments in South Africa visible. In October 1970, black workers at Polaroid's Massachusetts factory discovered that Polaroid provided the film used in the passes carried by black South Africans. Publicizing Polaroid's contribution to a key component of apartheid's controls over blacks' movement, these workers forced a change in company policy, blocking all Polaroid sales in South Africa (Kahn 1979, 134).

These moves paralleled more general concerns about the relationship between U.S. corporate leaders and American policy toward southern Africa. In early 1971, for example, Congressman Charles Diggs (D-Mich.) held hearings on U.S. businesses in South Africa in which corporate leaders were asked to discuss their role in supporting or reforming apartheid. University students, unionists, and others took the question of moral complicity in apartheid seriously. In 1968 Princeton students raised the issue of university shares in corporations with South African investments, and the SDS chapter there launched a divestment campaign. In 1972 Randall Robinson, then a Harvard law student, helped take over a building to protest Harvard's shares in companies involved in southern Africa; the protesters specifically objected to continued Portuguese control over Angola.

Over the next two decades, the issue would not go away. Sporadic waves of anti-apartheid activism demonstrated the broad appeal of what activists framed as an effort to "cut economic ties" to a system of racial oppression. Their impact would create a new corporate culture in which "corporate social responsibility" would no longer be considered an oxymoron by company directors. As Robert Massie (1997, 307) writes in his comprehensive account of the American anti-apartheid movement:

> By the early 1970s, the South African divestment movement had begun to affect scores of huge institutions throughout the United States. The effects

were slow and nearly imperceptible at first, confined to panel board-rooms and executive suites, legal consultations and committee meetings. However tedious the pace or imperceptible the steps, the process steadily transformed the logic that underlies American corporate governance. Eventually the leaders of hundreds of elite institutions—from pension funds . . . to religious denominations . . . from philanthropic organiza-tions . . . to universities . . .—would address the morality of investing in companies operating in South Africa. As they did, they found themselves reassessing everything from their organizational mission to the moral le-gitimacy of American capitalism.

Concerns over ending apartheid in South Africa were always inter-twined with a broader discussion about the changing character of inter-national commerce; the widening "global reach" of multinational cor-porations had already raised questions about how states and global institutions might regulate transnational corporations as they increas-ingly spread production across borders. By 1972 these concerns had be-come widespread enough that the United Nations began to develop a code of conduct for multinationals—with a special focus on southern Africa, where developing countries strongly supported UN efforts (Feld 1980).

Alongside this set of practical concerns about corporate regulation, expanded public discussion focused on corporate responsibility to the communities where America's new global investments were located. Perhaps the strongest effort to change corporate behavior came from within mainstream American religious denominations. The debate over "socially responsible investments"—and the sense among these churches that by holding shares they themselves were complicit in global capitalist enterprises—provoked much soul-searching. Church members became increasingly concerned about the ethical responsibil-ity associated with financial investments and with the possibility that their churches were benefiting from corporate profits that might stem from behavior antithetical to their concerns about social justice.

Apartheid in South Africa, of course, presented an extreme case. In 1967 the Episcopal Church convention passed two resolutions, the first calling on the church to use its investments in support of social justice and self-determination, and the second instructing the church specifi-cally to look into any church investments that might be linked to South Africa and apartheid. This stance found echoes in other mainstream de-nominations, and in 1971 a church-linked activist, Tim Smith, per-suaded them to fund the Interfaith Center on Corporate Responsibility (ICCR) to promote ethical corporate behavior globally—with a special emphasis on how churches could vote their shares to promote social change in southern Africa (Massie 1997, 263–332; Morano 1982).

Many church communities accepted Smith's arguments: companies producing goods inside South Africa were morally and often practically complicit in apartheid. Subsidiaries and affiliates of American corporations followed segregationist practices within the workplace, complied with laws prohibiting the hiring of black workers in skilled positions, and supported the migrant labor system, the cornerstone of apartheid's systematic exclusion of black South Africans. Moreover, these companies provided goods and services needed by the apartheid state and military and paid taxes to a repressive state.

Increasingly, church members began to believe they had to act. In May 1971, as three thousand people attended General Motors' annual shareholder meeting in Detroit, a leading Episcopalian bishop presented an ICCR-crafted shareholder resolution to the board—the first shareholder resolution ever calling on a company to withdraw completely from South Africa.

That resolution, as it happens, intersected with a third historical thread, one which brought the Rev. Leon Sullivan into the picture. From the mid-1960s, community groups and civil rights activists had begun to ask large companies to respond to the concerns of local communities around their American factories. As part of that trend, General Motors had been specifically targeted by Ralph Nader and a group of young lawyer-activists demanding that GM appoint some black directors. In late 1970, GM invited on to its board the Rev. Sullivan, an African-American Baptist minister known for his community work in Philadelphia (Massie 1997, 287–95).

Sullivan's first meeting as a director of General Motors happened to be the May 1971 meeting at which the Episcopalian bishop presented the country's first shareholder resolution on South Africa. Surprised, Sullivan gave an impromptu speech about the urgency of the moral issues involved, but the resolution gained support from only 1.29 percent of the shares voted. As shareholders were to discover repeatedly over the next twenty years, corporate managements generally control enough shares to dominate corporate policy discussions.

The event was momentous, nonetheless. Charles Stewart Mott, the ninety-five-year-old patriarch of General Motors, had been attending meetings since 1913. That May 1971 meeting was the first attended by a black board member, and also the first time Mott saw a member of the board vote openly against management. (It was probably also the last; he died two years later.) For the next few months, Sullivan was snubbed by the other GM directors, who apparently turned their backs on him as he sat at their meetings (Kahn 1979, 137; Massie 1997, 295).

Over the next five years, Sullivan shifted to a more gradualist view: instead of beginning by withdrawing completely from South Africa, he suggested, American subsidiaries could start by improving the conditions of their South African employees. This view received some support from inside South Africa, where a strike wave beginning in 1973 had reawakened interest in labor-related issues. In 1975, when Sullivan visited South Africa, American managers and a handful of moderate black leaders suggested that instead of supporting economic sanctions, companies like General Motors could take a "positive stance and call for American companies in South Africa to recognize the same working conditions they employ in the U.S." (GWU General Secretary to Leon Sullivan, 1975, quoted in Sethi and Williams 2000, 12).

Perhaps imitating a parallel British campaign (an effort that eventually resulted in a European Community code of conduct for EC businesses in South Africa), Sullivan began to view a voluntary code of conduct as a potential starting point. In January 1976, he invited the chair of IBM, the CEO for General Motors, and seventeen other top corporate executives to design a corporate code of conduct to improve the behavior of American subsidiaries in South Africa.

Sullivan's suggestion initially provoked great skepticism from business leaders as well as from activists. Although American businessmen hoped to reduce pressures from anti-apartheid activists and to ward off legal limits on investment in South Africa, they insisted that Sullivan could not expect corporations to contravene apartheid legislation— ironically, precisely the point that anti-apartheid activists would make repeatedly over the next two decades as they continued to reject the idea that corporations could realistically hope to reform apartheid from within. Through the late 1970s, corporate spokesmen raised the specter of legal limits to corporate reformism. The CEO of 3M wrote in 1976: *"To the degree that South African law and South African government policy allows*, our subsidiary there has taken aggressive action to conform to these principles" (R. H. Herzog to Sullivan, 1976, quoted in Sethi and Williams 2000, 16, emphasis added by Sethi and Williams). Two months later, the chairperson of Caltex wrote: "Caltex is, as you know, strongly opposed to Apartheid and will continue to seek to [fulfill the principles] *so far as that is possible within the laws of South Africa*" (J. M. Voss to Sullivan, 1977, quoted in Sethi and Williams 2000, 17; emphasis added by Sethi and Williams).

True to this spirit, Sullivan's first set of principles, released in March 1977 after a complicated team drafting process, defined "good corporate citizenship" entirely within the limits of South African law, calling on American companies to desegregate eating, comfort, and work stations, to give equal pay for equal work, to train black employees, and to engage in efforts to improve the quality of employees' lives outside the workplace—but not to break any South African laws in the process. Companies were not asked to ignore South Africa's job reservation rules (which protected skilled and higher-paid jobs for white workers only)—much less to challenge apartheid's migrant labor system or its pass laws. In their first version, the Sullivan Principles did not ask American subsidiaries to recognize trade unions for black workers; Prakash Sethi and Oliver Williams, who advised the Sullivan program over the next twenty years, revealed later that Sullivan had been warned by several important American companies that they would refuse to sign on to the principles if trade union recognition was required (Sethi and Williams 2000, 69).

Even these limited principles, however, caused commotion. Executives warned Sullivan that even limited reformist activities might complicate ordinary business life. Repeating what would become a constant theme, the signatories agreed at the board meeting in 1978 that "we cannot transform the nature of South African society, and we will have serious problems . . . if we try" (Sal Marzullo, 1978, quoted in Sethi and Williams 2000, 12). While anti-apartheid activists argued that the code's focus on workplace conditions and desegregation could not touch the fundamental dynamics of racial exclusion and segregation, corporate leaders either claimed that their workplaces were already effectively desegregated or worried that even marginal changes would provoke conflict in their South African operations.

The gap between the code's initial demands and the goal of ending apartheid was vast. In April 1977, Union Carbide sent a self-congratulatory letter to Sullivan, describing its progress in taking down the "whites only" signs on the bathrooms in their South African offices, just a month after the first principles were published. But the letter reveals a rather limited vision of corporate reform—and inadvertently illustrates the oddly gendered character of South African racism:

> In four locations [we have] no signs. At a fifth location, the signs were taken down about a year ago without repercussions. At a sixth, removal was accomplished just last week. This accounts for all of our mining and manufacturing locations.
>
> At our head office in Johannesburg, which is our only office location, signs were removed from male toilet facilities some time ago. One sign remains on a female toilet facility. We are feeling our way with respect to this last sign because we . . . are not the only tenant in the building, and also because resistance has been evident.
>
> You can see from the above report that our signs are essentially all down. We want to keep them down, and believe the best way to accomplish this aim is to be quiet about it. (W. B. Nicholson to Sullivan, 1977, quoted in Sethi and Williams 2000, 62–63)

But keeping quiet about corporate reform proved problematic, for reasons beyond Sullivan's control. On June 16, 1976, police fired on a student demonstration in Soweto, the massive black township outside Johannesburg; the incident provoked a national uprising and attracted global attention to the situation in South Africa. Coming on the heels of the 1973 strike wave, the 1976 Soweto students' campaign stretched out into an intermittent uprising that continued over the next fifteen years as black communities protested apartheid through school boycotts, strikes and stay-aways, occasional guerrilla attacks, and other tactics designed to disrupt and undermine government control.

For debates about "good corporate citizenship," the 1976 Soweto student uprising marked the beginning of a completely new phase. In a pattern that would repeat itself regularly until Nelson Mandela's 1990 release from prison, American activists responded to news of South African protests by mobilizing in support of anti-apartheid goals on campuses, in churches, in unions, and in city councils. Each upsurge in protests inside South Africa provoked renewed energy in the American anti-apartheid movement. Within months, college students across America were asking questions about their universites' investments in companies with South African links, drawing on research provided by anti-apartheid groups, the Interfaith Center on Corporate Responsibility, and the UN Center on Transnational Corporations. By the spring of 1977, students at elite universities from Cambridge to Palo Alto were staging sit-ins in university buildings, demanding that their schools sell shares in companies with investments in South Africa or support shareholder resolutions for withdrawal.

In early 1978, Harvard University made a dramatic announcement signaling that, for the first time, a major university would consider social issues in making investments. Harvard would buy shares in companies with South African holdings only if the companies could demonstrate that their presence in South Africa benefited reform efforts. Since most major American companies had some South African ties, this policy would involve scrutiny of most of the university's investments. Over the next few years, universities, unions, pension funds, and municipalities followed Harvard's lead, adopting policies called "selective investment"—that is, retaining shares only in those companies that could demonstrate that they were promoting reform in South Africa rather than simply pursuing business as usual.

It is worth noting that Harvard's new policy did not satisfy anti-apartheid protesters—indeed, the *Harvard Crimson* (April 25, 1978) barely mentioned Harvard's dramatic policy change, emphasizing instead the university's failure to meet student demands. Massie (1997, 44) notes that "selective divestment never satisfied activists, who viewed shareholder voting and workplace reform as a diversion from the real issue: the gain both Harvard and the South African government received from American firms." Anti-apartheid protests continued to roil campuses and cities through the 1980s—until finally the federal government imposed national economic sanctions on South Africa and many of the largest companies decided to sell off their South African affiliates. It was a pattern that would repeat itself over the next decade and a half: institutions and corporations sought measures that would promote reform in South Africa without cutting economic ties, but protesters continued to reject these efforts as an inadequate response to apartheid.

Although anti-apartheid activists dismissed "good corporate citizenship" in South Africa as a superficial change, in fact selective divestment had real impact in the business world, as institutional investors and companies began to seek ways of demonstrating that their presence in South Africa could be justified. As Harvard's initial announcement acknowledged, selective divestment required some way to differentiate between "good" and "bad" companies. In 1978 universities could find only one: in March 1977, Sullivan had released his corporate code, and Harvard and other universities turned to that code as a measuring-stick against which to grade companies' behavior across the Atlantic.

Suddenly, the Sullivan Principles' monitoring system emerged as the preeminent benchmark for measuring corporate citizenship. Like Harvard, American universities, pension funds, municipalities, and state legislatures seeking to show their commitment to socially responsible investing would agree to limit their holdings in South Africa–related companies to those that could demonstrate compliance with the Sullivan Principles—a strategy that effectively forced companies to sign on to the Sullivan system and forced Sullivan and his colleagues to design and sustain a system of monitoring allowing institutional investors to determine which companies were demonstrating their "good" corporate citizenship, and which were not.

Corporations responded quickly to the institutionalized threat of stock sales, signing on to the Sullivan code and acceding to outside monitoring. In 1977, 78 signatories were reporting on their "progress" in reforming their subsidiaries in South Africa to conform to the Sullivan Principles. By 1985 that number had grown to 112 signatories, out of roughly 250 American corporations in South Africa.

Throughout this period, the Sullivan system faced constant scrutiny and criticism. As the uprising in South Africa intensified, the anti-apartheid movement in the United States intensified its pressure on corporations, forcing a constant amplification of the principles, much along the lines envisioned today in discussions of "ratcheting up" global codes of conduct—or what corporate directors decried as an unfair "moving of the goalposts" (Williams 2000b, 73). Through the first years of the program, the principles were expanded to encourage corporate support for workers' freedom of association and to increase employee participation in designing the corporate contributions to black communities required by the code. By 1985 the "amplified" Sullivan

Principles required companies to take a public stance against apartheid and actively work for the dismantlement of racial exclusion—although, as critics constantly pointed out, even the amplified principles did not prevent companies from paying taxes to the apartheid government or block sales of strategic goods to the South African military. Even amplified, the principles never satisfied critics of American investment in South Africa.

Before going on to describe the Sullivan monitoring system and its impact, three points about the Sullivan Principles are worth noting, especially as points of contrast to contemporary discussions about codes of conduct. First, the three-way relationship between the anti-apartheid movement in South Africa, the anti-apartheid movement in the United States, and corporate responses was critical to the companies' decisions to adopt corporate codes of conduct. It took concerted social movement pressure, across continents and over decades, to get corporations to change their behavior. Contemporary discussions about codes of conduct tend to treat corporate codes as free-standing, often overlooking the dynamic interaction between social movement and corporate response. Yet without social movement pressure in both South Africa and the United States, no corporations showed any interest in adopting the Sullivan Principles, and persistent movement pressure continued to be fundamental to corporations' willingness to accept a "ratcheted up" code of ethical behavior. As a journalist sympathetic to corporate dilemmas recently put it, "The effectiveness of the campaign was based on Milton Friedman's classic model of corporate responsibility, whereby external pressures on a corporation define its societal obligations, not the moral instincts arising from within. The solution in South Africa was achieved not by voluntary self-regulation, but by bashing heads " (Schoenberger 2000, 28).

Second, it is worth noting the institutional dynamic undergirding the Sullivan system. Rather than asking individual consumers to make choices based on corporate scorecards, anti-apartheid activists consistently worked through institutions to create pressure on corporate boards. Anti-apartheid organizers explicitly chose to mobilize students to focus collectively on university investments rather than ask them to examine their parents' portfolios, and corporations were far more responsive to large institutional investors' concerns than they might have been to individual shareholders' inquiries about their behavior in South Africa. Corporate accession to a code of conduct and meaningful monitoring came as a result of pressure from large institutional investors—a pattern much closer to today's collegiate licensing policies, operated through university administrators, than to individual-level decisions about buying fair trade coffee or clothes carrying social labels.

Finally, and perhaps most importantly, it is important to distinguish the underlying thrust of the anti-apartheid movement from the concerns that drive current discussions about global regulatory frameworks. Anti-apartheid protesters were dedicated to ending an entire political system, one that denied basic political rights and legalized racial oppression; they were not trying to parse detailed, technical questions around workplace improvement or even the caloric content of a "living wage." Anti-apartheid activists sought to avoid measuring the behavior of individual companies or factories, recognizing that it was virtually impossible for them to gather detailed information about specific companies' workplace behavior in South Africa. In discussions about "good corporate citizenship," activists generally explicitly refused to engage in discussions about whether one company paid better than another, or polluted less than another, focusing instead on whether companies' mere presence in South Africa upheld the regime by paying taxes or providing goods and services that supported the regime.

Bluntly, anti-apartheid activists invoked issues that were far more black-and-white than questions such as determining how to set a minimum wage in far-off countries. Delicate questions about the potential impact on employment levels were offset by South Africa's harsh reality of systemic repression and racial exclusion. Divestment activists recognized that trying to engage in detailed evaluation of individual companies' behavior would undermine the broad sense of outrage that drove the transatlantic anti-apartheid movement—a decision that stands in sharp contrast to discussions today about how best to monitor the behavior of specific companies in far-flung export-processing zones. Moreover, as Audie Klotz (1995, 466) notes, activists continually linked investments in apartheid to "support for (or at least tolerance of) racism at home," refocusing the discussion on racial oppression rather than allowing businesses to claim they had successfully integrated their South African workplaces. Although the anti-apartheid movement focused attention on corporate behavior, the underlying issues involved systematic violation of basic human rights and racial oppression. Those underlying problems—which created a context in which corporations were required by law to practice racial discrimination, support apartheid's forced migrant labor patterns, and pay taxes to a regime designed to protect white supremacy—certainly lent strength to activists' rejection of the incremental increases associated with the Sullivan monitoring system. Indeed, one might argue that the "ratcheting up" process was made possible only because activists persistently rejected Sullivan's efforts to define "good corporate citizenship." Without those pressures, the question remains open: would detailed discussions over factory life have energized activists or corporate executives enough to change corporate attitudes toward apartheid?

The Monitoring System

From 1977 until 1994, the Sullivan Principles provided a benchmark for American corporate citizenship in South Africa, representing the first and most elaborate example we have of transnational, nongovernmental corporate monitoring. Prakash Sethi and Oliver Williams (2000, 119)—two business ethicists whose partisan account based on their own involvement as advisers to Sullivan nevertheless offers remarkable insights into contemporary corporate responses—are explicit about the challenges Sullivan faced:

> The monitoring system eventually [became] the Achilles heel in, and a significant contributor to the erosion in the credibility of, the entire Sullivan Principles program. In their desire to maintain control over the monitoring system, the companies may have won the battle of information management, but they lost the war to gain public confidence and trust in the companies' claim to be playing a positive role in South Africa.

At the outset, Sullivan and the corporate executives working with him were quite conscious that they were moving into uncharted territory, yet they apparently felt little need to involve labor unions or antiapartheid activists on either side of the Atlantic in their deliberations. Several task forces, mostly comprising midlevel managers from signatory companies, spent months in 1977 thinking about how best to operationalize the principles and how best to grade corporate behavior. Initially, these task groups created self-reporting forms for companies and planned to keep all information private; they planned only to issue a composite report on signatories' progress, rather than individual company progress.

Then, in what may be the first example of corporate directors inviting outside monitors to evaluate corporate compliance with a code of conduct, Sullivan turned to Arthur D. Little (ADL), an accounting firm based in Cambridge, Massachusetts, for help in compiling a composite report to demonstrate that, overall, Sullivan signatories were trying to reform their South African operations. Soon, however, it became apparent that large institutional investors required more detailed information about specific companies: a composite report could not serve as the basis for a selective divestment strategy. Over time, ADL began to publish signatories' grades, ranging from I ("making acceptable progress") to III ("did not report"), to IV ("recent signatory"). By 1979 ADL had created a separate office to monitor Sullivan compliance. The Sullivan signatories contracted with ADL to monitor their progress, paying about $18,000 a month for ADL's monitoring; each report cost about $250,000, a fact that provoked serious complaints from signatories over the years (Massie 1997, 445; Paul 1991, 395–407).

The Sullivan framework represents the first large-scale experiment in independent monitoring. But from the outset, business ethicists and anti-apartheid activists criticized Sullivan's decision to let Reid Weedon, the head of ADL's monitoring office, make key decisions about how monitoring would proceed. Sethi and Williams (2000) argue forcefully that this decision weakened the monitoring process and undermined the principles' credibility. However, they attribute the reliance on ADL to corporate pressure, suggesting that either Sullivan did not "comprehend the implications of a weaker auditing and reporting process" or that "he was unwilling to challenge the companies on this account because he felt he would be able to use the public pulpit to raise the goalposts and thereby elicit better performance from the companies" (Sethi and Williams 2000, 120).

That question resonates today: most large corporations that do not have internal staff to monitor subcontractors' compliance with their internal code of conduct still turn to accountancy firms to do their monitoring, just as the Rev. Sullivan did. Ivanka Mamic (2004, 62), for example, found in a broad survey of codes of conduct that "a great deal of the monitoring is done by traditional financial auditing firms such as Pricewaterhouse-Coopers." In discussing the Sullivan system, critics persistently pointed out that accountants from Cambridge might not be equipped to evaluate corporate citizenship in South Africa. The ADL accountants were

> located in one space of the social universe. Arthur D. Little consultants carry around a cognitive map, which may or may not coincide with the worldview of other parties interested in and knowledgeable about South Africa. A more diverse and representative group of [monitors] might add vitality to the assignment of qualitative points (Paul 1987, 407).

ADL accountants had little background in South African issues, little training in how to monitor labor issues or workplaces, and perhaps even less training in evaluating the impact of donations to community organizations.

This problem persists, and it is frequently pointed out as a real concern in discussions of voluntary corporate codes of conduct thirty years later. Corporations are accustomed to working with auditors in monitoring internal compliance with rules; they are comfortable sharing internal company data with established accountants, while global accountancy firms have certainly been happy to take on new tasks. But as

Dara O'Rourke (2000) points out, accountants make problematic work-place monitors. They are not specialists in labor issues, and they receive no training in monitoring workplace conditions. Thus, for example, accountants generally lack the skills needed to detect toxic chemicals in the workplace, and they may not know what questions to ask about working hours and wages.

But Arthur D. Little's monitoring of Sullivan signatories suggests a prior problem, aside from questions of accountants' monitoring skills. The Sullivan experience also raises questions about who supplies the data, how it is evaluated, and with what questions in mind. Although ADL created a unit devoted solely to overseeing corporate behavior in a specific locale, the ADL monitoring office—as is normal practice in accounting firms—relied entirely on data provided by the corporations themselves, or at best, data provided by the companies and verified by their auditors. ADL did no research of its own on signatories' behavior; although ADL required signatories to confirm some data, like payroll information, with local auditors, most of the responses went directly from local South African managers to ADL, with no outside check on companies' claims. Items that might have helped investors or monitors evaluate claims about increasing black employment—data such as the number of job openings, the total number of trainees, and the total number of black employees—were entirely self-reported. In fact, compliance with only one of the principles—expenditure on corporate contributions to local community projects, such as schools or clinics—was evaluated entirely through verified data (Paul 1987, 403–12).

ADL's insularity also left managers guessing about how they could raise their grades. Throughout the lifetime of the Sullivan system, managers complained bitterly about what they considered an opaque monitoring process and about Sullivan's efforts to amplify the principles to include ever more outspoken challenges to the South African government. Managers of South African affiliates clearly felt a great deal of pressure to remain in the top Sullivan categories; although contemporary studies suggested that stock prices were not in fact gravely affected by changing Sullivan grades (Kaempfer, Lehman, and Lowenberg 1987), many multinationals began to link South African managers' bonuses to improving their Sullivan ratings (Stone 1994, 27–28). This pressure, combined with a system that emphasized self-reporting and corporate effort, created a very explicit dynamic: within five years, managers had clearly learned that the way to ensure a good Sullivan rating was to spend money on local black communities. Initially, many South African executives objected to spending money outside the factory, arguing, as one executive said, that adopting a local township school would be counterproductive, since so many black employees objected to government restrictions on what could be taught in black schools (Little, *Sixth Report*, 1982, cited in Massie 1997, 524). But as more and more American institutional investors put pressure on head offices to comply with the Sullivan system, American companies sought ways to manipulate ADL's process. As an American businessperson in South Africa remarked, "Some top officers wanted the highest rating for moral reasons, but all needed the highest rating for business reasons" (Christianne Duvall, quoted in Sethi and Williams 2000, 222).

By the mid-1980s, American corporations in South Africa had discovered that whatever opaque matrix ADL's monitors used to evaluate performance, community donations weighed heavily in it. Realizing that spending more money on black community organizations—regardless of the actual impact on community lives—was the most expedient way to raise their company's Sullivan grades, managers put their energies into philanthropy rather than workplace reforms or political challenges. By the mid-1980s, most other aspects of "good citizenship"—desegregation, affirmative action, and the like—had diminished, and signatories apparently competed with each other to pay for classrooms, ambulances, and other community goods that might raise the grade published for American stockholders.

All of this raises a key question that comes up in all discussions of local implementation of globally designed codes and monitoring. What priorities—and whose—were reflected in the monitoring program? Apparently, ADL never solicited comments from anyone in South Africa who might have worked in or with corporate signatories—not unions, not employee committees, not even recipients of corporate grants to community services. The questionnaires on which grading was based were drawn up by American accountants. Throughout the two decades the Sullivan system was in place, the grading system continued to reflect the American accountants' vision, not the realities of South African experience. One especially telling example: the ADL monitoring system never adequately reported on affirmative action in hiring or training or reflected the racial composition of companies' employees. ADL charts consistently left undefined the corporate understanding of "black" employees, a category that in South Africa can mean either only Africans or a combination of Africans, Asians, and Indians (Massie 1997, 526). With apartheid's educational segregation and the stereotypes embedded in South African racial ideology, these three groups faced very different forms of discrimination at work. Apparently, however, the ADL monitors never clarified how they expected companies to define "black" in answering questions about hiring and training, an oversight which may have allowed companies to claim great success while barely challenging racial hierarchies.

Finally, ADL's insular monitoring process never included evaluation of the companies' impact on their employees' daily lives, much less on South Africa more broadly. Although signatories' spokespeople regularly claimed that American signatories served as beacons of progress (Marzullo 1987a, 1987b), this claim was never verified; the ADL office never devised any ways to evaluate the impact of corporate efforts. In fact, it could be argued that the ADL process only gave grades for effort, not outcome, in ways that seem to undermine the entire point of monitoring. For example, despite the Sullivan code's expansion to include freedom of association, the ADL monitors never asked employees about any union experiences—surely an important source of information if you want to learn about labor practices.

Before discussing the Sullivan code's actual impact on South Africa, I want to underscore two further points relevant to contemporary discussions of international monitoring. Most corporate codes of conduct are designed to serve as yardsticks for corporate performance globally and thus explicitly lack local references. The problem, of course, is that labor problems are always deeply embedded in a local context, and a global code or global monitoring system designed to cover corporate activities around the world may miss key local problems. The remarkable fact that a code explicitly designed for South Africa could blur definitions of race in measuring the racial composition of the workforce or racial patterns in hiring is a reminder of the pitfalls involved in designing codes that appeal to American and European consumers and investors, while trying to address local problems.

But the Sullivan framework also illustrates the way in which monitors' decisions about how to measure corporate citizenship can drive company responses. Monitors' choices about which measurable indicators mattered most came to define how corporations thought about how they could do good. In South Africa, the ADL framework seems to have pushed managers simply to spend money in communities without regard for the impact of those expenditures. For local managers, making the monitors happy can easily become more important than the actual performance of their company. Unless monitors take pains to incorporate local voices and concerns—from the local meaning of race to the lived experience of labor practices—into their system of evaluation, and unless they find ways to prevent local managers from manipulating the indicators they use to measure corporate performance, the grades they give risk becoming a rubber stamp, little more than the "corporate camouflage" (Schmidt 1980) that anti-apartheid activists considered the Sullivan Principles to be.

The Impact on South Africa and Corporate Culture

In the end, what impact did the Sullivan Principles really have? I want to describe first their impact on South Africa, and then on the corporations that tried to comply with them. Although the principles' impact on South Africa may have been limited, their long-term impact on corporate culture is worth exploring more fully. The Sullivan Principles were a first step in a changing global corporate culture, as companies began to accept a measure of social responsibility and to view codes of conduct and external monitoring as reasonable ways to improve corporate performance.

Most American signatories to the Sullivan Principles started with an effort to desegregate workplaces, as the early letter from Union Carbide to Sullivan demonstrates. But even supporters of the principles were soon forced to acknowledge that South Africa's racial hierarchies remained pervasive even in the headquarters of progressive companies—managers' canteens and washrooms might have no longer been marked by "whites only" signs, but there were few black supervisors to use them. Among all of the Sullivan signatories, the percentage of supervisory staff classified black, colored, or Asian rose from 3 to 16 percent between 1977 and 1993 (Sethi and Williams 2000, 237). Of course, even these figures may be misleading; because of ADL's failure to fully define the racial categories it used in reporting on progress, these figures may well disguise persistent racial hierarchies. Certainly the vast majority of black workers remained in unskilled jobs, and there is no evidence that the signatories managed to reduce the gap between black and white average wages in this period (Bernasek and Porter 1990). Although many signatories instituted or participated in creating training programs during this period, these seem to have had little impact on the racial structure of signatory workplaces—in part because the Sullivan period was dominated by economic recession in South Africa and there was relatively little room for the levels of training or hiring that would have been required to change racial composition.

So far as we know—since the monitors never revealed how they measured compliance—the principle calling on signatories to ensure employees' freedom of association was never monitored at all. Many of the companies that consistently gained top ratings in the ADL system never recognized a union representing black workers; Hewlett Packard, for example, insisted in 1985 that because it had never recognized any unions anywhere, it should not be asked to do so in South Africa. From the point of view of South African union activists in the 1980s, Sullivan signatories were indistinguishable from other multinationals. They were no more likely than other companies to permit union stewards free movement around the plant, no more likely to implement minimum wage standards, and no less likely to call in the police in the event of a strike. Today, when asked how the Sullivan Principles affected their unionizing efforts, few South African unionists seem able even to remember what the principles were (see, for example, Bennett interview, 2004).

While a handful of moderate black unionists supported the Sullivan approach during the late 1970s, many more unionists at the time dismissed the principles as irrelevant, arguing that corporate contributions to apartheid through taxes and sales outweighed any possible benefit. By 1985, the nonracial trade union movement had unequivocally come out in support of full withdrawal (Erwin 1989, 52–56; Joffe 1989; Orkin 1987). Like many unionists today in developing countries, South African unionists understood that full economic sanctions would cut jobs for their members, but in contrast to contemporary debates about transnational companies in most developing countries, a larger goal—undermining the apartheid state—prevailed in their thinking.

On the other hand, community groups clearly benefited from Sullivan's insistence that companies should contribute to township organizations. Reflecting managers' understanding that corporate donations ranked high in ADL's scoring system, corporate contributions to community projects became the cornerstone of the Sullivan signatories' efforts. Company contributions to township schools, housing projects, and soccer teams became the main indicator of "good citizenship." From 1977 to June 1985, Sullivan companies reported that they had donated more than $15 million in the areas of health, education, community development, training, and black entrepreneurship (Alperson 1995).

It is important to recognize, however, that these contributions were never evaluated or assessed, except in dollar terms. Although the principles called on signatories to consult with employees in planning contributions to black communities, the monitoring process never attempted to measure consultation or the impact of contributions. Indeed, there is no evidence that consultation ever became an important component in local managements' thinking about what expenditures to make. Repeatedly, companies and observers complained that signatories were "throwing money" at communities without adequate planning or evaluation; there was no attempt to monitor the impact or to differentiate between the kinds of programs that were supported. Indeed, some observers pointed out that the monitors' emphasis on expenditures tended to prevent companies from exploring any unique skills they might have to offer and ways in which they might involve those skills in their community contribution; thus, for example, *Reader's Digest* apparently never contemplated including antiracist discussions in the magazine rather than, or in addition to, adopting schools or buying ambulances for black hospitals (Stone 1994).

Nevertheless, in the mid-1980s the framework began to collapse, largely because the same pressures that had prompted companies to accede to outside monitoring only intensified as anti-apartheid activists rejected the Sullivan system's underlying premises. As the South

African economy went into a tailspin, the uprising intensified and the U.S. government imposed mild economic sanctions on South Africa in 1986, corporate headquarters began to decide that remaining in South Africa was not worth the "hassle factor" involved. By late 1986, between 188 and 250 companies had pulled out, and more would follow (Spence 1998). By 1987 even Sullivan himself had apparently come to accept the argument that corporate reformism was not enough. Following Bishop Desmond Tutu's lead, in 1985 Sullivan set time limits, warning that he would call on companies to withdraw if apartheid was not fully reformed within twenty-four months. During that period, the South African government reinforced Sullivan's new stance by refusing him a visitor's visa; finally, Sullivan withdrew his support for the entire approach, arguing that the signatories' continued presence could only be interpreted as offering support to the beleaguered apartheid regime. Although corporate signatories continued to insist that they were following the Sullivan Principles, Sullivan himself called on American affiliates to withdraw (Massie 1997, 638)—testament, perhaps, to the problems inherent in trying to use workplace reform as a means of addressing broad political exclusion and repression.

South African business leaders responded angrily. By leaving, they claimed, American companies were abandoning their moral responsibility. In a remarkable statement, South African mining magnate Gavin Relly (1986) told American corporations that after decades of profit-making, they had a moral obligation to remain involved in South African reform. "The American counterparts of South African executives . . . face an awesome responsibility. Many have made good profits in South Africa for decades. But faced with lean times and a host of pressures, they are attracted to the easy option of withdrawal."

Spokespeople for American affiliates in South Africa agreed, drawing on the vocabulary of social responsibility that they had developed during their engagement with Sullivan. Business leaders who had once insisted that companies should focus on profits, now appeared to welcome the idea that international investments carried a modicum of social responsibility, arguing that Sullivan signatories had a moral obligation to remain and engage directly in social change. Instead of describing corporate goals simply in terms of profit, they used the language of moral accountability to insist on staying put. Sal Marzullo (1987a, 382), the Mobil executive who had by then served for many years as the chairman of Sullivan's Industry Support Unit, wrote: "Corporate presence is better than corporate absence. [Sullivan signatories] have begun to perceptibly change attitudes among many white South Africans who understand that fundamental structural reform and absolute equality for South Africans of all races is essential to the long-term survival of that country."

Did corporate culture really change as a result of business participation in the Sullivan system, as business ethicists today sometimes claim (Williams 2000a, 80)? Through the late 1980s, many of the businesspeople directly involved in the Sullivan process remained bitterly opposed to divestment. In 1987 a General Motors spokesperson called it "imperative" for American companies to remain to create the "basis for participation of all people in a sound economy" through corporate support for black business, employment, and training (Wilking 1987, 391). Ironically, the publication of this essay coincided with General Motors' announcement that it would sell off its South African subsidiary—a fact that probably reflected disagreement between GM's South African managers and those in its corporate headquarters. Clearly, those involved in implementing and monitoring the Sullivan system were angered by parent company decisions to leave South Africa. Even the ADL accountant in charge of independent monitoring for the Sullivan signatories weighed in; Reid Weedon claimed that the day after the local South African managing director had managed to raise his Sullivan rating from the bottom grade to the top one, his U.S. parent company announced that his affiliate had been sold to a South African conglomerate. "At his first meeting with the new owners," Weedon (1987, 401) wrote angrily, "he was told he should no longer run the company as a charitable institution and that he should cease the activities he had instituted in line with the Principles."

Supporters of the principles continued to try to sustain the system right through the mid-1990s, suggesting that South African businesses had learned to take their social responsibility seriously (Alperson 1995). But the Sullivan framework—especially the monitoring system—clearly lost steam when Sullivan resigned from the board. Oliver Williams, a business ethicist who served on the board after Sullivan's departure, bitterly describes how the rump system became essentially irrelevant as its funding, its independence, and its visibility were watered down (Sethi and Williams 2000, 353). By 1990, as the South African government moved toward negotiations with the anti-apartheid opposition, and especially by 1994, when South Africa held its first democratic elections, the Sullivan system had faded from the memories of all but those most directly involved in promoting, implementing, and monitoring it—only to reappear years later, when it would be regularly invoked as a model for encouraging corporate citizenship and monitoring multinational investment.

Conclusion: Bringing the State Back In

As corporate codes of conduct proliferate today, what lessons can we take from the Sullivan experience? This story can be interpreted in two almost diametrically opposed ways, with very different implications for contemporary debates. For those who believe that corporate culture has changed to the extent that it now accepts a degree of social responsibility in international activities—as many business ethicists and corporate spokespeople suggest today—the Sullivan process underscores the potential effectiveness of independent monitoring and public reporting, at least in the context of persistent external pressure. Even the limited external assessment and grading involved in Sullivan clearly had an impact on internal corporate dynamics and performance. The Sullivan experience offers some support for contemporary efforts to involve managers in addressing workplace conditions: getting them to think through how and why they should contribute to employees' well-being does seem to have had some impact on managerial culture, in ways that led at least some corporate officers to take social responsibility seriously. When outside pressure made it necessary, corporate headquarters managed to create rewards and punishments for individual local managers, apparently changing the way those managers thought about their firms' role in society.

Even from this perspective, however, the Sullivan system holds several cautionary notes. First, corporate visions of "good citizenship" directly reflected choices made by those who designed and monitored the code. Despite Sullivan's rhetoric of empowerment, corporate officials were much more concerned about fulfilling any aspects of social responsibility that would raise their grade than they were about involving their employees in the process or perhaps even about doing any actual good for black communities. The lack of employee involvement in the design, implementation, and evaluation of the Sullivan Principles is typical in contemporary codes of conduct. This case underscores the danger that even companies that create and comply with transnational codes of conduct may still ride roughshod over voiceless workers and communities, at least as long as the monitoring and reporting processes are as opaque and manipulable as the Sullivan system appears to have been. The Sullivan process foreshadows the persistent exclusion of the voices of employees, communities, and their representatives—as much in the design of codes as in their implementation. Corporations today may be more willing to acknowledge some responsibility for their international operations than they once were, but their codes are more likely to reflect the concerns of northern consumers than to include issues raised by employees or their representatives from different production sites around the globe.

Second, the Sullivan example underscores the importance of institutionalized social movement pressure on corporate headquarters. Neither corporate conscience nor individual consumers alone could have prompted companies to accede to a purely voluntary code of conduct.

It was anti-apartheid activists' insistence on changing large-scale institutional relationships with South Africa and church concerns about ethical investing—not individual consumer decisions—that prompted meaningful corporate responses.

This cautionary note underscores the importance of social movement pressure in processes of social change. Even in an era when individual consumers can check the Internet for new information, institutional pressure—directed through universities, municipalities, or state governments—is far more sustainable than individual choice. Like the student movement, which has prompted university administrations to scrutinize the conditions under which university logo-ed apparel is produced, activists concerned about monitoring multinationals might do well to design strategies that create sustained pressure—through investment strategies, living wage resolutions, and the like—using institutional links to corporations as the pressure point rather than focusing solely on well-intentioned individuals making choices about what to buy.

But while the Sullivan example suggests some conditions that may be necessary if external monitoring is to serve as part of enforcing labor rights, it also offers support to those who remain skeptical about the stateless approach to transnational regulation. Above all, the Sullivan system underscores just how much external pressure was required to persuade corporations to accept even moderate restrictions. Decades of activism, involving thousands of activists mobilized around a single strategy and able to work through major institutional investors, were required, first to persuade companies to accept any sense of social responsibility and then to force them to accept monitoring. And the character of the demands went far beyond workplace improvements; corporations accepted the "ratcheted up" Sullivan Principles only because activists were unyielding in their demand for full sanctions, and because activists organized that pressure through institutions far more powerful and coordinated than individual consumers could possibly have been.

In that context, it is worth noting yet again how unusual the anti-apartheid movement was, in terms of movements around transnational labor issues. Sustained activism came in response to a particularly egregious and oppressive form of racial exclusion—a systematic, overarching grievance that evoked far more sympathy internationally than the kind of individual, daily grievances that pervade factories in the developing world. In the context of South African calls for international economic sanctions, anti-apartheid activists could easily elide the moral questions involved in trade-offs between investment, jobs, and working conditions—trade-offs that pervade discussions of transnational labor regulation today as developing country activists express concern that transnational activism could undermine their countries' best hope to find some comparative advantage in the brutal competition of global trade. If the Sullivan experience shows that corporations can be persuaded to accept voluntary regulation, it also shows how difficult that persuasion can be, and what kind of persistent pressure is required to ratchet up that regulation beyond the barest minimum.

What about the stateless character of the Sullivan system? Without pressure from social movement activists, South African subsidiaries would never have acceded to independent monitoring, but it is worth noting that social movement activism was centrally focused on reconstructing the state. Anti-apartheid activism was directly linked to the failure of the South African state to include or protect its citizens; this is a pattern that will reappear in the chapters describing social movement activism in India around child labor and Guatemalan activism around labor rights. In each case, the social activism that pushed companies to accept voluntary monitoring stemmed from efforts to create more democratic, more inclusive, and more effective state institutions; in each of these cases, social movement activists sought to construct a democratic, effective state, not to replace states with civil society monitoring in perpetuity.

With Nelson Mandela's election in 1994, South Africans turned to the promulgation and enforcement of national labor law as a more effective way to protect citizens at work. South Africa's new government immediately passed strict new labor codes, with contract rules, health and safety provisions, minimum wage laws, and protections against unfair dismissals, with penalties routinely upheld in newly created labor courts. Even in the context of neoliberal economic policies, high unemployment, and the threat posed by capital mobility, South African democrats and their unionist allies viewed strengthening legal protections for citizens at work as a cornerstone of the new democratic order.

Codes of conduct and transnational campaigns did not entirely disappear after South Africa's elections, but their content and meaning were transformed. After the first election, South African businesses created new voluntary codes to offer guidance to companies undergoing rapid transformation out of apartheid (David Fig interview, 2004). Similarly, although South African labor activists sometimes sought to mobilize international consumer pressure to support workers' rights in specific settings—as, for example, when farmworker organizers asked British retailers to avoid wines from vineyards notorious for labor abuses (Oxfam 2004)—mobilizing consumer pressure served as one small component of the labor movement's much larger repertoire of tactics. Rather than depending on voluntary codes of conduct, South Africans have turned to the power of the national state (Ally 2006; Kenny 2004; Neva Makgetla interview, 2004).

For those concerned with developing nonstate transnational regulatory mechanisms, the Sullivan system—despite its widely acknowledged flaws—seems to represent a measure of success, in that corporations were pushed by external pressure to comply with codes defining "good corporate citizenship." For those who are skeptical of voluntarist regulatory schemes, however, the example underscores the limitations of an approach based on nongovernmental monitoring. In the next two chapters, I turn to two more recent examples in the hope that a comparative approach will allow some broader understanding of what works—and what does not—in independent monitoring.

Chapter 4

Social Labels, Child Labor, and Monitoring in the Indian Carpet Industry

The conditions in which India's child carpet weavers work are heartrending: emaciated young boys sit before massive looms in dark, dusty weaving sheds, their legs dangling off wooden planks into pits dug into dirt floors, working as virtual captives for brutal employers by day, sleeping in cold sheds far from their families at night. Repeatedly criticized by Indian activists and condemned by transnational organizations, the South Asian handwoven carpet industry, where starving and stunted young children work under medieval conditions, has become a global symbol of brutal child labor. Transformed in recent decades from ancient craft tradition into Dickensian export industry, the carpet industry has put thousands of uneducated children from impoverished homes to work tying endless tight knots to produce the luxurious carpets that grace the floors of middle-class homes in Europe and North America.

Against the backdrop of those emaciated faces staring up through the gloom, Rugmark's smiley-face seal stands out as an international model of social labeling, a remarkable experiment in transnational consumer activism. In response to international pressure, Indian carpet makers pay independent monitors to inspect their looms, attaching a "child-labor-free" label to carpets produced on looms where no child workers have been found. Local NGOs linked to transnational networks of activists train and support teams of inspectors who regularly monitor registered looms, removing children when they are found and punishing the weavers who employ them (Gay 1998, 84; International Labor Rights Fund 1996).

Created in the early 1990s, within ten years Rugmark had become one of the world's most widely cited examples of how social labeling could transform working conditions, a demonstration of international consumers' power over producers vying for global markets:

One of the most credible labeling programs is RUGMARK. This trail-blazing initiative certifies carpet manufacturers who meet stringent requirements to assure that no child labor is used in handmade carpets from India and Nepal. Consumer confidence in the label is gained through systematic, independent monitoring and unannounced inspections of manufacturers by nonindustry RUGMARK representatives. (Golodner 2000, 249)

A few years later, an ILO textbook on child labor echoed this praise, highlighting Rugmark as a model effort "to find a positive constructive solution of using consumer power for the protection of child rights" (International Labor Organization 2004, 256–60, 267; see also Chowdhry and Beeman 2001; Hilowitz 1998; Voll 1999). Glossy brochures describing Rugmark's success are widely available in European department stores; in Germany, one of two major markets for India's carpets, the brochures are available even in municipal information offices, reminding tourists of their obligations as ethical global consumers. The label is less well known in the United States, the other major destination for India's carpets, but even there, articles in the national media regularly describe Rugmark's efforts, often referring to thousands of children freed from servitude while reminding would-be carpet buyers to avoid carpets that do not carry the organization's "child-labor-free" seal (see, for example, Shaw 2002).

At home in India, however, Rugmark is much more controversial. By the time the program was several years old, many of the activists and organizations originally associated with Rugmark had distanced themselves from it, insisting that their involvement had been experimental, tangential, or overstated (Agnivesh 1999b; Swami Agnivesh interview, 2003; Khan 1999; Gerry Pinto interview, 2003). An early sponsor, UNICEF, quietly but officially ended its rather limited involvement with Rugmark some years after it started (Gerry Pinto interview, 2003; Ryan 2000). One of India's most prominent child labor activists, Kailash Satyarthi, continued to be associated with Rugmark, but many Indian policymakers had become so skeptical that they dropped any mention of the program in descriptions of their country's efforts to eliminate child labor (Bhargava 2003; Mishra 2000). Some of Satyarthi's former colleagues went so far as to denounce Rugmark as a misleading, misguided effort designed more to secure access to international markets than to improve the well-being of India's children (Agnivesh 1999a).

Despite its local critics, however, Rugmark is worth examining closely because it is consistently invoked as an international model. Constructed by a transnational activist network linking social activists in India with conscientious consumers abroad, Rugmark appeared to have mobilized international pressure to change labor practices in an export-oriented industry. Responding to a problem first identified by local activists, and backed by transnational networks of NGOs and church groups, Rugmark's independent monitoring has served as a widely lauded example of voluntary corporate self-regulation in the face of the Indian government's failure to enforce its own prohibitions on child labor. Weavers who eliminate child labor and submit to monitoring by independent outsiders gain privileged access to international consumers; "bad" ones are punished by losing access (International Labor Organization 2004, 206).

To a much greater extent than most ethical trading schemes, Rugmark staked its labeling program on a credible system of independent monitoring, and the hand-knotted carpet industry seems perfect for such a scheme. The Indian carpet industry has long been concentrated in a particular region, the carpet belt of Mirzapur-Varanasi; studies estimate that 70 to 80 percent of exported Indian carpets come from this area (Mishra 2000, 83; Srivastava and Raj 2000, 17), allowing monitors to travel from workplace to workplace within the region. Under Rugmark, carpet weavers agree to register their looms and submit to unannounced inspection by independent monitors, who work for and are trained by an independent NGO, initially led by Satyarthi. The NGO, in turn, is paid through funds that Rugmark collects from carpet exporters, through a voluntary levy on exported carpets. Children discovered working on a registered loom for wages (rather than working for relatives as family labor) are "rehabilitated" and given education, training, and other assistance. And there are sanctions: weavers found repeatedly in violation of child labor laws are prohibited from future participation in the Rugmark program. The setup seems ideal for successful social labeling: a single industry, a single issue, in a single region, replacing India's ambivalent enforcement of long-standing child labor laws with a more active and energetic voluntary form of corporate self-regulation.

Proponents of social labeling generally acknowledge that the approach has limitations, but Rugmark seems to fit easily within those parameters. Labeling works best when consumers sympathize with the ethical framework indicated in the label—when the label refers to a widely accepted human rights concern rather than to more contested issues. Labeling works best for goods that are identifiable and distinct going intact to the consumer; labeling works less well for less identifiable components, such as ball bearings, which are rarely sold directly to consumers. Labeling may work best when it covers luxury goods, for which demand is very elastic, than when labels are attached to goods that are considered necessities; labels may also be much more effective for products for which consumers have many choices, such as floor coverings, than for products that are more basic and less substitutable.

Finally, by offering a private regulation system to supplement ordinary state inspections, labeling suggests that participants in the labeling process are meeting a higher standard than would normally be the case with goods produced in a specific region or country; labels automatically invoke some sense of monitoring, appealing to consumers partly through a suggestion that the label is applied in good faith and reflects a sincere effort to ensure that the ethical conditions claimed in the label represent reality (Hilowitz 1998; Committee on Monitoring International Labor Standards 2004). Explicitly deploying the logic of the market, systems of social labeling hope to use consumer pressure to improve global working conditions by appealing to consumers to include questions of conscience in their purchasing choices.

Given these limitations, the export-oriented handwoven carpet industry appears to be a perfect choice for social labeling. The products—hand-knotted carpets—are distinct and identifiable, and they are not absolute necessities for consumers anywhere. Ethical consumers can easily discriminate between carpets bearing the social label and those without it; and if no ethically produced carpets are available, they can choose not to purchase any carpet at all. Asking consumers to avoid carpets produced by exploited and vulnerable children hardly calls on them to make an enormous sacrifice, and the request also offers a symbolically important contribution to Indian discussions about enforcing the country's own child labor laws.

As an issue, child labor is perhaps particularly amenable to transnational appeals. Child labor fits comfortably within the human rights framework, more easily than many labor rights violations. By the late twentieth century, childhood was widely viewed as a distinct stage of the life cycle that deserves special protection, and most consumers in advanced industrial countries regard child labor as an unacceptable moral transgression. Even in developing countries where it is more common, child labor is nevertheless widely criticized as a vestige of the past, a mark of impoverishment that limits the country's development potential by destroying children's lives and health, preventing them from gaining education while deforming their bodies through overwork.

Moreover, child labor is a very visible labor violation; it is generally considered easier to spot a child in a workplace than to inspect it for violations involving complex calculations, such as underpaid overtime wages, or unfair labor practices such as unfair dismissals. And the Indian state's failure to protect children working in the carpet weaving sheds was undeniable. India has outlawed work for children under fourteen since it gained independence in 1948—including, explicitly, child labor in the hand-knotted carpet industry, labeled a hazardous industry because of the dust and dirt in the weaving sheds. But it would be hard to deny that children continued to make up a significant share of the industry's workforce. By the mid-1980s, activists could reasonably argue that the indisputable presence of children in a hazardous industry illustrated the Indian government's apparent unwillingness or incapacity to enforce its own regulations—an unwillingness that gave extra impetus to the private, voluntary social labeling approach embodied in Rugmark.

Why did the carpet industry become the center of an international campaign, and how did international consumers create such pressure on carpet manufacturers? To what extent has independent monitoring transformed weavers' practices? In this chapter, I first describe the dynamics through which international consumer attention was mobilized and the construction of a social labeling program. Next, I turn to the monitoring system itself and describe it in relation to the industry's structure. While acknowledging Rugmark's success, I also note some limitations to its monitoring scheme. These limitations may be inherent to many social labeling schemes, raising questions about an approach that may contribute more to stimulating debate and raising global awareness than to any practical change in working conditions.

Child Labor in the Carpet Industry

Global concerns about child labor in India's carpet industry emerged almost by accident as part of a larger campaign to publicize the persistence of bonded labor relations in rural India. At a dramatic press conference in 1984, activists produced a group of recently freed children found in a series of raids on weaving sheds; these children told shocked reporters about their experiences in what the *Times of India* termed the "torture camp of Mirzapur." Children between the ages of five and twelve had been kidnapped from a village in Bihar and sold to a weaver in Uttar Pradesh, where they lived under medieval conditions until their rescue. Ill-fed, beaten, and mistreated, the children showed journalists small burn marks where their employer had prodded them with red-hot pokers if they fell asleep during sixteen-hour days at the loom; their condition could not help but provoke sympathy and outrage (Agnivesh 1999b, 148; Whittaker 1988, 5).

As carpet manufacturers immediately pointed out, child labor is a widespread problem in South Asia, and one hardly limited to carpet weaving sheds. Moreover, carpet weaving—an artisanal craft brought from Persia to northern India by the Mughal emperors in the sixteenth century—is viewed as an ancient legacy from India's past. Carpet making has long been a rural handicraft; the skills needed for tying thousands of tight knots are passed down within families, and children as young as six learn to tie knots, holding the sharp knife with which they trim the threads in one hand as they move deftly along the strings. By the age of about fourteen, it is often said, children can begin to weave on their own looms (Malhotra 1996, 29; Mishra and Pande 1996, 23)—a claim that would frame traditional carpet weaving in terms more or less consistent with India's general prohibition on paid labor before the age of fourteen.

To some observers, this description apparently renders child partici- pation in carpet weaving benign, a matter of training rather than ex- ploitation—despite the fact that since 1948 the Indian government has officially classified the carpet industry as a hazardous one in which no children can legally work. Even in the face of growing international concern, in 1996 an Indian official involved in handicraft development told an industry conference, "The nimble fingers of the children at early ages help them pick up the craft comfortably. It is also quite likely that the patience to sit at the loom for long hours and do a monotonous job can be best cultivated at this standard age" (Malhotra 1996, 29). Even in 2003, government officials sometimes still claimed that within weaving households, children usually worked in their own family's workshop, not for wages or unrelated employers (Tinoo Joshi interview, 2003).

How and why, then, was the presence of children in the carpet sheds redefined as a significant social problem? The oft-repeated official em- phasis on ancient origins tends to obscure the dramatic transformation of India's carpet industry since the early 1970s; that transformation re- configured the use of all labor, including children, on the carpet looms. Until the late twentieth century, India's carpet sales were relatively unimportant, and its exports were dwarfed by neighboring Iran's Per- sian carpets. Although weaving households in northern India pro- duced some carpets for export (often through British-owned export companies) from the late nineteenth century, their sales were limited as long as Iranian production remained steady.

But in the mid-1970s, Iranian carpet production plummeted, and In- dian carpet exporters leapt to fill the gap. Indian industry analysts of- ten attribute the decline in Iranian production to political turmoil (Mal- hotra 1996, 28), but Indian child labor activists almost invariably claim that it was the Shah's ban on child labor in the 1970s that wiped out the Persian carpet industry (Kanbargi 1988; Whittaker 1988, 11). Whatever its cause, the Iranian carpet crisis opened an opportunity for Indian ex- porters coinciding with a new Indian economic policy of looking out- ward for new export-oriented growth.

In the Iranian carpet crisis, Indian carpet exporters and the Indian government saw new possibilities for increasing exports and creating new jobs for rural workers. From 1974, when India first officially recog- nized the carpet industry as a potential source of foreign earnings, In- dian carpet exports rose steadily. In 1965 Indian carpet exports earned less than $8 million (U.S.) and made up less than 6 percent of the world's total carpet sales. These figures remained relatively steady through the mid-1970s, but in 1980 Indian carpet exports jumped to $217 million, doubling to almost 15 percent of the world's total hand-woven carpet sales. Since the mid-1980s, Indian carpet exports have hovered between 17 and 20 percent of the world's total production (Srivastava and Raj 2000, 17).

The export explosion transformed carpet production, though the structure of the industry remained relatively unchanged. Large export companies worked closely with small weaving workshops scattered through the villages, subcontracting production to local weavers and their employees. A three-tiered system had prevailed for a century: large companies, often called "importers" and often foreign-owned, provided designs and materials to local companies, known as "exporters," who then contracted with village loom-owners to produce the woven carpets. Labor-intensive weaving was concentrated in small rural households that effectively worked as subcontractors for exporters. As exports rose, more and more weavers were pulled into exporters' networks. Ironically, the persistence of this "putting-out" system reflected in part a response to earlier government regulatory efforts: during a previous export surge earlier in the twentieth century, some exporters began to move production into centralized compounds. Soon after independence, however, when the Indian government's 1948 Factories Act required larger factories to submit to regular government inspection—and when the newly independent government outlawed child labor in the "hazardous" carpet industry—most carpet production moved back out of factories and into smaller workshops and homes, where no permits were needed for looms and where Factory Act regulations did not apply (Kanbargi 1988, 95).

From India's independence, then, the carpet industry offered a classic example of home-based production for export: exporters in the 1980s brought designs and materials to loom-owners, often located in villages many kilometers distant from the export-house. Collecting the knotted carpet months later, the exporters then brought the carpets to larger workshops for finishing touches such as cleaning and trimming. Payments to loom-owners depended on carpet quality—judged primarily by the number of knots per square inch, with tighter knots increasing the carpet's value. The loom was set up in a shed, often a mud hut in back of the loom-owner's house. Generally, a plank was placed across a pit in front of the loom so that the person tying the tight, multicolored knots could sit or squat on the plank, following a design drawn on paper showing colors and knots, usually placed on the wall opposite the loom.

As countless commentators have pointed out, "weaving" is a somewhat misleading term for the process through which hand-knotted carpets are made; although the loom has threads strung across it, there is no shuttle, and carpets do not involve warp and woof. Instead, each knot is tied individually along the loom's threads. After each knot, the knotter cuts the threads off with a sharp curved knife held in the knotter's hand. Tighter knots create a higher-quality rug, for which the loom owner will earn more when he returns the finished product to the exporter. This weaving is labor-intensive and slow, and while it certainly involves skills, they are not complicated: primarily, knotters must be able to replicate the pattern, tie knots, and trim the thread—and work at a monotonous and repetitive task for hours on end. Once the carpet is knotted, it is removed from the loom for cleaning and trimming, which may be completed either in the weaver's workshop or at the factory of the exporter, who, in turn, generally sells the carpets to importers from overseas. Typically, carpet prices are set by the international market, and weavers depend on exporters for materials and access to markets.

Weavers' profits, like those of subcontractors in most global export industries, are closely linked to their ability to control labor costs. When India's hand-knotted carpet exports expanded in the late 1970s, so did the industry's labor needs. Loom-owners had always needed help from family members or hired labor to complete carpets; now expanded production obviously required new workers. Indeed, it was precisely the industry's labor-intensive character that attracted the attention of government planners looking for new export industries. Carpets offered a labor-intensive export product that could simultaneously earn foreign exchange and create employment. Small weaving workshops could be located in far-flung impoverished villages, creating a source of employment and income for households across rural India.

As the industry expanded, the government tried to help new loom-owners and new workers in the Mirzapur-Varanasi carpet belt and beyond. Despite its official depiction of carpet weaving as a cottage-based industry, the Indian government, clearly committed to a more industrial approach, set up "training centers" to increase the labor supply, moving outside the more limited family-training process to expand the number of skilled knotters available to produce this new export product. In 1975 Prime Minister Indira Gandhi inaugurated the first village training center for weavers, and by 1981 the government claimed to be sponsoring six hundred centers producing an annual total of thirty thousand trained weavers under the age of fifteen. These training centers were officially limited to children aged twelve or older, but evidence suggests that children as young as six—apparently, usually siblings of older apprentices—were sometimes admitted (Juyal 1987, 8; Kanbargi 1988; Whittaker 1988, 40).

Child labor, of course, is widespread in rural India. In the early 1990s, estimates of the number of working children under the age of fourteen ranged from 11.29 million to more than 100 million—a figure that would represent just under half of all school-age children (Gosh 2000, 21; Mishra 2000, 4). Repeated studies by Indian academics and activists point out that children who work for wages come overwhelmingly from disadvantaged households. Poor parents from lower-caste, tribal, or Muslim households are far more likely than upper-caste parents to send their children to work rather than to school (Kanbargi 1988; Thorat 1999). Many commentators conclude that the Indian state's failure to enforce child labor laws is so pervasive that it should be understood in terms of widespread elite tolerance of caste-based inequality (Wiener 1991; Gerry Pinto interview, 2003).

From the late 1970s, Indian social activists began to bring to global attention the persistence of rural conditions that belied the country's developmentalist rhetoric, revealing studied ambivalence toward rural poverty among India's elite. Many activists, including the outspoken Swami Agnivesh, publicized the persistence of bonded labor arrangements in rural areas. These arrangements frequently condemned entire households, many of them from the "unscheduled" castes, to work for nothing to repay long-standing debts, leaving poor families mired in poverty for generations. Agnivesh, leader of the Bonded Liberation Front and a prominent voice in global discussions about slavery, regularly underscored the links between poverty, bondage, and child labor: children in indebted families are especially vulnerable to exploitation, and when they are forced to work rather than attend school, they are denied educational opportunities that might permit them to find a route out of poverty (Agnivesh 1999a, 1999b; Swami Agnivesh interview, 2003).

Even aside from the government training centers, the carpet industry served as an especially dramatic illustration of government neglect. A 1985 study of the Bhadohi-Mirzapur carpet belt concluded that of the 230,000 workers in the industry, about 75,000—nearly one-third—were children aged eleven to fifteen, with some as young as seven. Most had not been trained by government training centers; many were simply hired from poor families (Juyal 1987, 31; Mishra 2000, 38; Srivastava and Raj 2000, 61). Most worked in small workshops of fewer than twelve workers; most lived at the site of the workshop, under their employer's care or control, rather than with their parents. Many were migrants, brought to the carpet belt from Bihar or other poor regions, and most came from unscheduled castes. Conditions for all workers in the industry—the long, monotonous hours, the dusty air full of lint, the dark, eye-straining weaving sheds, the cuts on fingers from the sharp knives used to cut the threads—were often exacerbated by maltreatment and malnourishment. Dispersed in small workshops that did not fall under India's Factory Act, the children received wages and worked under conditions that were not subject to any government inspection or labor code enforcement (although one study's author notes that the two larger factories included in the sample did not offer significantly better working conditions) (Juyal 1987; Kanbargi 1988, 97–99). As child labor activists pointed out, the carpet industry had explicitly been decentralized in part to make it more difficult to police; the move away from consolidation into compounds and into smaller, dispersed weaving workshops had intensified in 1948 as weavers sought to avoid inspections and restrictions legally linked to factory size. By the 1980s, the dispersion of carpet workshops and the subcontracting system in which they operated had left the industry virtually unregulated.

In the 1980s, child labor specialists regularly warned of the difficulties of policing a decentralized industry, though at least one study suggested that if looms were not to be brought together in compounds, at least they should be registered with government departments so that inspectors would know where to look (Kanbargi 1988, 107). As child labor activists have long argued, even governments committed to eliminating child labor find it difficult to police home-work and piecework; families engaged in household production are all too frequently tempted to involve children in that work. The rural workshops of India's handwoven carpet industry—spread across miles of the Indian countryside, with tens of thousands of looms located in separate households often kilometers apart—presents precisely the kind of inspection challenges against which child labor specialists warn.

Moreover, activists argued, in the carpet industry government ineptitude and inaction may have been compounded by complicity. With the government's new training centers, not only was the Indian state failing to enforce its own prohibitions on child labor, but it seemed to be actively encouraging children to work. Carpet manufacturers and spokespeople for the national government's trade ministries frequently reinforced fears of official ambivalence, suggesting that India's carpet industry required the "nimble fingers" of children if exports of high-end carpets were going to expand. Fine carpets of intricate designs required more knots per square inch, and children were said to be better able to do this work, especially if their small fingers were trained from an early age. Manufacturers suggested that efforts to enforce child labor laws would impede production, bring increased corruption into enforcement mechanisms, and even perhaps be illegal. At a 1985 workshop on the subject, the All India Carpet Manufacturers Association explicitly objected to monitoring, arguing that because the industry's small workshops were scattered in villages across the carpet belt, any attempt at "enforcement of child labor laws and the Factory Act will not be legal" (All-India Carpet Manufacturers Association, 1985, quoted in Whittaker 1988, 43). Above all, the manufacturers warned that eliminating child labor would raise labor costs, undermining the industry's international competitiveness. In 1986 a leading exporter circulated an open letter warning colleagues that efforts to help child workers might increase wages by at least 50 percent, a plan that would kill "the hen that lays the golden eggs" (V. R. Sharma, 1986, quoted in Whittaker 1988, 38).

In the early 1980s, then, Indian labor activists focused on the carpet industry because two specific aspects of state policy—the creation of government training centers explicitly oriented toward bringing children into industrial work, and government regulation that effectively blocked real oversight of the weaving sheds—provided a pernicious illustration of governmental ambivalence about child labor. The government's active efforts to promote carpet weaving, activists argued, amounted to government complicity in putting children to work in an industry long designated as especially hazardous. In a context where weavers' profits depended on reducing their labor costs, child workers were vulnerable to exploitation and abuse—especially when they worked, as they frequently did, far from their families and outside any official regulatory framework. When the president of the All-India Carpet Manufacturers Association warned that 1985 conference that proposals to raise minimum wages in the industry "on the pretext of regulating the wages of bonded child workers [would] prove suicidal to the development of the industry" (quoted in Whittaker 1988, 38), activists found confirmation for their belief that conditions for India's exploited child workers were unlikely to improve unless they could mobilize new pressures on the government and employers.

Transnational Debates over the "Rights of the Child"

In the 1980s, heated Indian debates about childhood and child labor reflected domestic concerns about the relationship between development and equality. As India shifted from a socialist-nationalist development path to a more market-oriented strategy, activists were increasingly concerned with the way market dynamics reinforced existing inequalities. But the focus on child labor in particular is best understood in the context of a larger international discussion that Indian debates both reflected and fueled. Throughout the last decades of the twentieth century, a growing international human rights movement debated the extent to which childhood represents a special phase of life, with special rights attached to it. Do child workers deserve special attention, and does the state of childhood demand special protections?

Are there universal standards defining the "rights of the child," and do these rights—defined in international conferences and promulgated through international conventions—trump local custom and practice?

Child workers in India's carpet industry gained international attention because local activists brought them to the attention of the world. But that global audience was already engaged in a much larger debate about child labor, which happened to coincide with the explosion of India's carpet industry. When Swami Agnivesh and his colleagues presented tortured Indian child weavers to the world, they were clearly part of that broader discussion.

In the 1980s, just as the Indian government sought to expand carpet exports, international experts on child labor were rethinking their entire approach. Until the 1980s, most child labor policies involved prohibition: parents who put their children to work were punished. But as international agencies worked with newly independent countries in the developing world, some of them began to ask whether these efforts merely drove child workers further out of sight. Did prohibition perhaps make children's working conditions worse by hiding them from public inspection? Perhaps instead of imposing Western cultural values, these agencies proposed, policymakers should recognize and respond to real constraints on poor families. A 1988 ILO volume on child labor, for example, clearly reflected this growing international discussion:

> It is . . . becoming accepted that because of widespread poverty and a formidable array of institutional constraints facing governments, the immediate abolition of child labor will not be possible. These obstacles have . . . led to a reassessment of the traditional approach to child labor and brought about a striking evolution in public policy, which goes beyond exclusive reliance on legislation and enforcement and encompasses short- and long-term measures in such areas as the provision of services, protection and advocacy. This shift in attitude and approach is not confined to government. Indeed, another crucial development is the increasingly important role played by non-governmental organizations in the campaign against child labor and in the protection of working children. (Baquele and Boyden 1988, 9)

By the mid-1980s, many international experts were turning away from legislative prohibitions and seeking instead to find approaches more compatible with the realities that prevented poor parents from sending their children to school: poverty, constraints on opportunities, gendered expectations, and ethnocentric assumptions about appropriate skills and curricula. Experts were beginning to look toward nongovernmental programs as alternatives to state-imposed restrictions on child work—a shift that only a few years later would be embodied in Rugmark's voluntaristic, nongovernmental approach.

Responding to this debate, the Indian government took a new look at its labor legislation and revised its child labor law to permit some kinds of paid work for children below the age of fourteen. The 1986 Child Labor (Prohibition and Regulation) Act sought to regulate the conditions and industries in which children worked with the intention of protecting vulnerable workers by bringing child labor into the open. It imposed heavier sanctions on child labor in "hazardous" industries—explicitly including the hand-knotted carpet industry, along with firecrackers, building and construction, mining, and processes involving toxic chemicals—but it acknowledged the persistence of child labor and sought to ameliorate the conditions in which children worked. The government also claimed that the new law would provide incentives for poor families to enroll children in school and that it would create employment opportunities for adults in those families (Narayan 1988).

But this "realistic" approach to child labor proved controversial, in India as well as internationally. In India many activists considered the revisions a step backwards in that government officials seemed to be accepting the idea that the children of poor families faced a different childhood, and a different future, than children of the elite (Agnivesh 1999b). Some analysts suggested that Indian officials were reconciled to child labor; perhaps the ingrained cultural tropes of caste blinded government officials from imagining that poor children could ever take advantage of educational opportunities (Gerry Pinto interview, 2003; Wiener 1991). In fact, critics insisted, children's work brought little income to their families, while their concomitant lack of education ensured persistent impoverishment (Burra 2003). As for the law's increased sanctions on child labor in "hazardous" industries, critics pointed out that the law did little to increase enforcement. "One should understand that the earlier Acts were flawed," Helen Sekar (2001, 55) wrote, "not because the penalties were too light but because they were rarely enforced." The new law made little effort to address this lack of enforcement. From this perspective, the revised law simply codified a long-standing lack of concern about the children of the poor. Inadequate enforcement of child labor laws, combined with inadequate provision of primary schools in rural areas—in the context of persistent poverty, which forced families to send young children to work for pittances—was increasingly viewed as an example of the state's active abdication of its obligations to protect young citizens rather than simply as the passive result of failure.

By the late 1980s, perceived government inaction against child labor—combined, of course, with horrifying descriptions of conditions in the carpet sheds and the state's overt ambivalence—had given the Indian carpet industry almost iconic status in the child labor debate, both domestically and internationally. Although Indian activists regularly mentioned high incidences of child and bonded labor across rural India—in agriculture, brickmaking, bidi-rolling, bangle-making, and glassware as well as carpets—activists invariably referred to a "pattern of slavery" in the carpet industry, in which small children were forced to work under brutal, dangerous conditions, often far from their families, for employers who had no concern for the children's health or well-being (Whittaker 1988).

Activists commonly acknowledged that many children working in the carpet industry were more likely to have been sent by their families to work in carpet workshops than to have been kidnapped, but parental consent—especially consent given, as it often was, as a result of a family's impoverishment and rural debt bondage—hardly made the prevalence of child labor acceptable. No government spokespeople could defend the vision of children working under the conditions that prevailed in carpet sheds: the persistent dust, dirt, and long hours, as well as the injuries caused by sharp knives and repetitive motions, hardly reflected the kind of "training opportunity" suggested by proponents of vocational training.

Shifting to a new approach, activists began to appeal to transnational organizations and networks; by seeking to protect children through transnational advocacy, they hoped to mobilize international pressure and force the national state to enforce its own rules. And global audiences responded warmly. By the late 1980s, the argument that child labor policies should reflect local realities had run head-on into a different approach based on the claim that childhood deserves special protection (Myers 2001; Tegmo-Reddy 1996). A growing chorus insisted that even poor countries should protect children from exploitation and provide them with skills and training they would need later in life, both as good development strategy and as a fundamental human right. By the mid-1980s, policymakers in international organizations were increasingly committed to creating an international standard for childhood and protecting that period of innocence as a basic human right.

Ironically, the effort to create a global standard for "the rights of the child" was juxtaposed against a very different discussion in academic circles, where many voices suggested that this trans-historical standard ignored the long history of most industrial countries, as well as the realities facing impoverished rural families and developing economies. Social historians increasingly agreed that "childhood" should be understood as a socially and culturally constructed concept created through a series of social processes and policies that were historically specific to particular times and places (Ariès 1962, 2). Social historians documented decades-long conflicts over child labor prohibitions when they were first introduced; in England, for example, poor and working-class families often viewed legal restrictions on children's work as impositions from above that denied poor households needed incomes and forced children to suffer long days at school (Lavalette 1999a, 1999b; Seccombe 1993). While few academic historians have suggested that poor children do not benefit from gaining more qualifications, they have often noted that the historical record is more complicated than straightforward prohibitionists imply.

These academic discussions failed, however, to alter the tenor of international policy discussions. By the late twentieth century, few policymakers were willing to raise their voices in defense of child labor. In the context of a discourse about "the rights of the child" within a human rights framework, child labor became increasingly stigmatized, and policymakers pointed so frequently to its prevalence in South Asia that by the early 1990s, "concerns about child labor in India and Pakistan had remained at a steady drone for more than a decade" (Klein 2002, 334; see also Gay 1998; Kreamer 2002). Some experts warned that total prohibitions would be unenforceable, as well as possibly ethnocentric; others insisted that policies should distinguish between work outside the home and work or child care done within the household, suggesting that concerns about protecting children were sometimes melded with protectionist efforts to block trade with developing countries (Baquele and Boyden 1988).

International policymakers insisted in the early 1990s that concerns over ethnocentrism should not blind governments to the long-term impact of child labor. Keeping children at work rather than in school was detrimental not only to the individual children involved but to the nation as a whole, since children who work at monotonous, repetitive tasks instead of attending school are not learning skills they could use for the future. By the late 1980s, the voices raised against a wide international consensus that childhood should be considered an inalienable right and that children need special protections seemed almost anachronistic; the focus of discussion had shifted away from local context to the responsibility of parents and governments to offer children a better future.

This shift in the human rights discourse that enshrined childhood (including access to health care and basic education and protection from abuse) as a fundamental right can be traced through the international debates and conventions of the 1970s and 1980s. Childhood was gradually elevated to the level of a human right rather than an ordinary labor grievance. Fitting into the common pattern of successful transnational campaigns, these concerns were generally expressed in terms of victimization, vulnerability and physical harm, and protection was proclaimed as a basic human right. From its inception, the International Labor Organization had called for the elimination of child labor, but its adoption of the "Minimum Age Convention" in 1973 signaled a growing commitment to the creation of an international standard. Over the next two decades, concerns about child labor became a basic trope in critiques of globalization; antiglobalization activists often stressed that a key problem with corporate globalization was that by going abroad, multinational corporations were free to avoid scrutiny in their exploitation of children.

The campaign to eliminate child labor gained support, and in 1989 the United Nations adopted the "Convention on the Rights of the Child." Although the UN convention was somewhat milder than the earlier ILO "Minimum Age Convention" in that it prohibited only hazardous labor rather than all child labor (Myers 2001), it further enshrined the idea that childhood represents a fundamental right, one not subject to cultural or geographic constraints or modifications. In 1998 the ILO included a ban on child labor as one of its four "core" labor rights, and as many analysts have noted, the ILO placed "firm political pressure" on member states to adopt the convention (Myers 2001, 47)—to the point where labor activists in some developing countries complained that the ILO often seemed more concerned about protecting underage workers than improving conditions for all the rest (Homero Fuentes interview, 2003; Neva Makgetla interview, 2004). This pressure certainly reflects the ILO's real interest in preventing the abuse of vulnerable workers, but it also appears that ILO staff started to focus on child labor because the issue had gained a great deal of international appeal.

By the late 1980s, the carpet industry had become an international target. Perhaps because local Indian activists had initially raised it as an issue—and inspired perhaps as much by apparent Indian government complicity and industry assertions of the need for "nimble fingers" as by the heartrending images of tortured, emaciated children in weaving sheds—international child labor activists used images from India's carpet belt with remarkable frequency to illustrate the plight of vulnerable and abused children. Within India, many activists pointed out that the carpet industry was not necessarily the most egregious exploiter of child labor. Local activists concerned with child labor were as likely to mention the manufacture of bidis (the hand-rolled cigarettes produced primarily for domestic Indian markets), fireworks, and bangles or farm labor as they were to mention carpets (Antony and Gayathri 2002). Internationally, however, the carpet industry attracted a disproportionate share of attention. Although the images of children behind carpet looms were clearly used as part of larger efforts against child labor (see, for example, Gay 1998), the images became so prevalent in the 1990s that many carpet industry analysts began to speak of an international conspiracy, "the result of misguided propaganda by some vested interests" (Bhattacharyya and Sahoo 1996b, 21) and "malicious propaganda" that created "much mileage" for India's competitors (Dhawan 1996, 81–82). Sometimes, more generously, they viewed the images as the result of "a mixture of protectionist intent and purpose as well as genuine humanitarian concern" (Puri 1996, 80), but carpet exporters clearly regarded these recurrent images as a threat to overseas sales.

Market-Based Policies

In the late 1990s, debates over how best to deal with child labor intersected with a debate over whether trade laws could be invoked to enforce labor standards worldwide: could international trade rules be altered to stop the race to the bottom? Ironically, many developing country labor unionists—including, prominently, many of India's leading trade unionists—have vehemently rejected efforts to link international labor standards to market access, arguing that these efforts risk hurting workers in developing countries rather than improving their situation. In South Asia, labor conditions are generally worst in labor-intensive, informal sectors of the economy, such as agriculture or services, but bans on exported goods are considered more likely to affect the formal manufacturing sector—ironically, the sector where labor laws are most likely to be enforced (Basu 2003; Hoogvelt et al. 1996). Indian unionists have continued to insist that efforts to use trade treaties in response to labor grievances could block market access for products produced in the unionized, formal sector of the economy, punishing workers in export-oriented sectors for the sins of employers in rural areas—most of whose products are destined for domestic, not international, markets (Amargit Kaur interview, 2003). Even long-time labor activist Swami Agnivesh (1999a, 32) rejects "social clauses" as an overly blunt weapon that is more likely to hurt Indian workers than to help them:

> If the "social clause" were to be applied to our Indian situation, I am sure the country could not export even a blade of grass, a grain of wheat, a leaf of tea, a piece of granite, carpet, bangle, match-box, leather goods, textiles, nothing of this sort, because of direct or indirect involvement of the unorganized labor force.

Between 1990 and 1992, however, the threat to India's exports took a very concrete form: American senator Tom Harkin (D-Iowa) introduced the Child Labor Deterrence Act to Congress, "to prohibit the importation of products that have been produced by child labor," with civil and criminal penalties for violators; this measure would have targeted precisely those products, like India's hand-knotted carpets, that depended on access to global markets. Other legislative threats loomed, particularly in Germany, which had long been a key market for India's carpets. German churches and trade unions proposed legislation to block carpets made with child labor.

Indian carpet exporters had little choice but to pay attention. Especially since their product was a luxury one for which consumers could easily find substitutes, carpet producers could have had little doubt that an international boycott of their product would immediately reduce demand. Aware of these legislative initiatives, Indian policymakers and producers began to search for alternatives, and by the early 1990s, carpet exporters were looking in earnest for ways to stave off consumer boycotts.

The origins of the proposal to institute a social label backed up by independent monitoring in the carpet region are somewhat murky; it is hard to be sure who initiated the proposal for the system that became Rugmark, or what precisely motivated the proposal. In most earlier accounts, Rugmark is described as the outcome of a joint effort by Indian activists, international organizations like UNICEF, and German church and trade union activists seeking to help reduce child labor (Hilowitz 1998; International Labor Rights Fund 1996). The Indian activist Kailash Satyarthi (1994) describes the program as the outcome of activist and consumer efforts:

> We decided to focus on the consumer market, particularly in Germany, which was the single largest purchaser of Indian carpets. We then expanded to other European markets and the United States. . . . The only success we have seen has been through consumer pressure.

In fact, the German embassy played a key role in the program's origins. Working with representatives from international organizations, social activists, and large department stores in Germany to develop a program that would prevent market closure, the German embassy's Indo-German Exporting Program, directed by Dietrich Kebschull, proposed a system of monitoring and labeling that would allow consumers to feel confident that their handwoven carpets were untainted, guaranteeing that they were produced without child labor. Rugmark's founders had two goals: to assure European consumers that their carpets were free of child labor, and to maintain India's export levels by avoiding further damage to the industry's reputation. Kebschull (1999, 193) writes that in those early negotiations,

> all parties agreed on the basic market orientation of the whole concept. Instead of pleading for bans or boycotts, it would be better to give carpet manufacturing a new promising perspective. The creation of something

like a brand name would help increase confidence and also the quality of the product. The name Rugmark was chosen after long consideration. . . . After an intensive and emotional public discussion, a general opinion emerged, that all terms reminiscent of child labor should be strictly avoided. It was intended to create something new, signifying social quality for the market, without accusing others. Therefore, the originally strongly favored name *o.k. carpets*, where o.k. would have been a German abbreviation for *ohne kinder* (without children), was dropped. The connection with children is, however, reflected in the label fixed on all carpets, which shows a smiling child's face for Rugmark, *the smiling carpet*.

Far from the stateless vision often invoked by proponents of social labeling, Rugmark appears to have originated in state policy debates—at least from the perspective of the industry, which clearly shifted to support a monitoring program in an effort to ward off state actions. The Rugmark proposal quickly gained steam as advocates argued that the Indian carpet industry offered an ideal scenario in which consumer pressure and independent monitoring might "ratchet up" working conditions.

Differences between German and U.S. responses underscore the key role that market pressures played in industries' acquiescence to independent monitoring schemes. German churches and unions continued to push for legislative bans on goods made with child labor, and staff from the German embassy worked closely with industry representatives to develop a social labeling scheme. By contrast, as the International Labor Rights Fund (1996) noted rather drily, as U.S. trade pressure waned, "enthusiasm for Rugmark by the Indian government and important segments of the carpet industry began to lag. By early 1994, American carpet importers were encouraging their suppliers to resist Rugmark, since they had become convinced that [U.S. Senator Tom Harkin's proposal to block goods made with child labor] would not gain passage."

From its inception, the system of labeling and monitoring was designed to be voluntary and self-financing, although it received initial assistance from German development funds. Exporters registered the loom-owners with whom they had subcontracted to weave carpets for the export market so that monitors could independently verify that no children had worked on the looms; exporters then contributed a levy of 0.25 percent of their export earnings to support independent monitoring and administration. Foreign buyers participating in the scheme contributed 1 percent of the import value (that is, cost, insurance, and freight) toward social projects, including schools and welfare programs, "to be established for the benefit of children and their families in the carpet belt" (Sharma and Bose 1997, 6).

Both carpet manufacturers and the German government apparently insisted that the program be self-regulating rather than state-financed or -controlled. Kebschull (1999, 204) noted that "the Government of Germany [has] repeatedly emphasized that it prefers this type of private and voluntary certification and self-effort vis-à-vis the alternative of strict and rigid government regulations." Using the social label instead of a "policing regime of fines and other punitive measures," Rugmark was designed to be "market-driven in such a way that members who still worked with child labor would no longer be able to sell their products abroad" (195). Facing the threat of international consumer boycotts, it was hoped, Indian carpet weavers' own self-interest would lead them to eliminate child labor and thereby gain the smiley-face label for the carpets they planned to export.

Initially, Rugmark tried to involve existing monitoring agencies in its efforts, most notably Société Générale Surveillance (SGS) , a Swiss quality assurance company that was already active in India. When the firm decided, however, that monitoring for the carpet industry "was not feasible," activists and carpet exporters were left to debate the exact implications of the statement (International Labor Rights Fund 1996); Rugmark's organizers then decided they would have to develop their own team. Over the next year, Rugmark gradually elaborated its own approach to monitoring, and by 1996 it had exported nearly 300,000 labeled carpets, mainly to Germany. By 2003 that figure had risen to 2.5 million carpets (Sharda Subramaniam interview, 2003).

By the end of its first decade, Rugmark had developed a straightforward monitoring system that incorporated most of the principles described as central to independent monitoring. A local nongovernmental organization trained and employed about a dozen full-time monitors, divided up into teams of two (with frequent changes of partners). Every weekday morning each pair of monitors would receive a list of six to seven looms to visit that day. Monitors were never supposed to know in advance which looms they would see. Each team traveled in a separate vehicle, visiting looms that were often thirty or sixty kilometers apart. If they found any children seated at registered looms, they were required to check whether the child was a relative of the weaver; Rugmark's rules allowed family members to weave so long as the child was over fourteen years of age and was attending some hours of school. If the child was not a relative, the inspectors would take the child with them; if the monitors could not return the child to his or her parents, the child would be taken to one of several schools run by Rugmark. In 2003 about 1,800 students reportedly were enrolled in six Rugmark schools (Sharda Subramaniam interview, 2003). Weavers, meanwhile, would be warned; repeated violations would result in nonregistration, meaning that exporters would no longer subcontract with that weaver, at least not for goods destined for export (Dietrich Kebschull interview, 2003;

Sharda Subramaniam interview, 2003). By 1999, 782 looms out of 25,347 had been found to have child workers (Sharma 2002, 5198).

While Rugmark's proponents acknowledged that they could not absolutely guarantee that Rugmark-labeled rugs were "100 percent child-labor-free" (Sharda Subramaniam interview, 2003), they insisted that the label reflected a sincere and concerted effort to guarantee consumers that the rugs were acceptable. And Rugmark's framework does contain most of the characteristics that would appear theoretically ideal for transnational labor monitoring: independent, full-time, trained monitors making unannounced and regular visits to work sites, meting out real penalties for violations. It is this kind of monitoring that has made Rugmark such a widely cited example of social labeling; it is considered to be one of the most successful programs of its kind in the world and is frequently cited as a model for other efforts to improve working conditions.

Critics of the system, however, are caustic, and they include Indian trade union specialists on child labor (Amargit Kaur interview, 2003) and Swami Agnivesh, whose attacks on his "erstwhile colleague" Kailash Satyarthi can take on a rather personal tone (Swami Agnivesh interview, 2003; Voll 1999, xiii). Rugmark's claim that it can monitor the presence of children at looms is overstated, they assert; not only does the social label reduce pressure on the carpet industry to eliminate child labor, but it ironically could increase the risk to the industry, by creating the possibility that outside investigations will prove that labels were awarded without adequate inspection to carpets that were woven by exploited child workers. First, they point out that the system offers no safeguards against the kinds of problems that labor activists have long associated with home-work: by the time a monitoring team has parked its jeep in the village and walked fifty or sixty meters into a weaving shed, any children working on the loom will have vanished, and only the adult weaver will be seen to be working on the loom. Since carpets always take weeks, sometimes months, to be completed, the children can always return after the inspection visit. The unannounced visits, critics argue, amount to little more than spot-checks that weavers can evade; the system provides no mechanism for more persistent oversight that might catch ongoing violations (Beckman 1999; Bose 1997; John P. John interview, 2003; Khan 1999).

Second, critics note, the Rugmark system is open to manipulation by participating exporters; exporters need only register looms for carpets destined for markets where the label is known or valued. While German importing companies have been supportive of the Rugmark label, often insisting on buying only carpets with the Rugmark seal, most other importers, including American ones, have been far less concerned, and exporters have clearly noticed the difference. An exporter who participated in the Rugmark scheme was remarkably open about the flexibility permitted by the Rugmark framework, although he asked for anonymity (exporter interview, 2003); though he said he always registered looms and paid the Rugmark levy on carpets destined for German import houses, he saw no reason to do so for looms working on carpets destined for other markets. Since this exporter, like many others, contracted with weavers to produce specific designs for specific import houses, it was easy to foretell which carpets were destined for Germany, and thus should be registered, and which carpets did not require registration because they were going to New York. Rugmark's levy was hardly onerous, he admitted, but he saw no reason to involve Rugmark's monitors if the consumers did not demand it.

A third question about Rugmark's framework has to do with the frequency of inspection. Although this issue has not been a major part of local criticism, it nevertheless reflects the difficulty of monitoring thousands of looms in the far-flung villages of India's carpet belt. In written reports and in interviews, Rugmark claims that each registered loom is visited three times each year by its monitors; Rugmark directors also claimed in 2003 that it had registered 30,000 looms and made about 110,000 visits per year (Dietrich Kebschull interview, 2003; Sharda Subramaniam interview, 2003).

This claim may overstate the frequency of monitoring visits, accepting Rugmark's claim that six teams of monitors each see between six and seven looms each weekday, for a maximum total of between 180 and 210 inspections each week. According to Rugmark's own figures, even under the best possible conditions, only 7,800 to 10,920 inspections could be carried out in a year. Since these figures represent almost unattainable maximums, it seems unrealistic to expect that Rugmark looms could be seen by monitors more than once every three years.

Even if monitoring is more frequent than Rugmark's data suggest, the industry's extensive networks of exporters and subcontractors, combined with the fact that the looms are relatively portable and spread throughout the villages of the carpet belt, may complicate the monitoring effort. In 1998 an ILO study concluded that manufacturers may have transferred their operations to other areas beyond Varanasi, making looms less visible and harder to monitor (Hilowitz 1998; Khan 1999). In 2003, when asked how often Rugmark inspectors actually visited his looms, the same exporter who admitted that his company selectively registered only those carpets intended for Germany winked, saying with a grin, "That's an industry secret."

The Broader Impact of Social Labeling

While critics question how much social labeling has reduced child labor in carpet weaving sheds, it is worth exploring further the broader impact of Rugmark's efforts. Even Rugmark's critics in India acknowledge that the social labeling campaign has helped to change the debate around child labor, especially in relation to the carpet industry, by prompting increased attention to the issue (K. Chandramouli interview, 2003). Instead of focusing simply on social labeling's impact on the use of child labor at registered looms, it seems worth considering the extent to which the institution of Rugmark and the discussion around its efforts have affected approaches to child labor in the carpet industry, and perhaps in India more broadly.

In India's carpet industry—as in every other independent monitoring case described in this book or elsewhere—the establishment of a new form of nonstate oversight of working conditions almost immediately prompted the creation of imitators. Carpet manufacturers immediately proposed and created several other voluntary initiatives designed to offer consumers similar reassurances that their rugs were not made with child labor. Alternative codes—including several that made little real claim to monitor looms—proliferated. Almost as soon as Rugmark began to operate, manufacturers that did not join Rugmark created their own social label, an alternative program that avoided Rugmark's effort to create a direct link between registered looms and independent monitors. In mid-1995, the Carpet Export Promotion Council created its own labeling program, Kaleen. Manufacturers were required to donate 0.25 percent of their carpet earnings (up to 2,000 rupees) to a special fund for improving the welfare of children. In return, their carpets could carry a label that read, "A portion of proceeds of this sale is going to the rehabilitation of children." Although Kaleen has a code of conduct and contracted its monitoring to an independent NGO, three years after its founding an ILO study found little evidence of its operation (Hilowitz 1998). In 2003 the program certainly existed, but its impact—aside from disbursing funds to several NGOs that run village schools—was questionable. Swami Agnivesh himself served on its board, and the director of the Carpet Export Promotion Council insisted that Kaleen's program had helped to make carpet manufacturers more aware of the need to eliminate child labor from their weaving sheds (Swami Agnivesh interview, 2003; T. S. Chadha interview, 2003), but Sharma (2002, 5199) found its monitoring program relatively ineffectual; it inspected only about 4,300 looms out of some 90,000 registered with the Carpet Export Promotion Council.

At the same time, several other voluntary programs quickly sprang up. German carpet sellers, apparently concerned about consumer responses and the threat of a declining market, responded almost instantly, developing the "Care and Fair" program in 1994. In contrast to Rugmark, the label was not attached to individual carpets but was meant for display by retailers to show consumers their commitment to ending child labor. To receive the label, German members had to contribute to several development projects in the carpet producing belt. By January 1996, Care and Fair claimed to have collected 1.4 million deutsche marks and to have funded eighteen school and health projects in India, Nepal, and Pakistan (Hilowitz 1998). Similarly, the Swiss Association for an Honest Oriental Carpet Trade, founded in 1986 by eight Swiss importers, created the "Step" label in 1995. Like Care and Fair, the Step label expressed a commitment to improving conditions for carpet workers, but rather than claiming that a specific carpet is free of child labor, it indicated that importers and manufacturers had paid a levy toward improving conditions in the carpet belt (Hilowitz 1998). Neither of these voluntary programs involved actual monitoring to prevent children from working on carpets, but proponents insisted that the programs helped their members—carpet exporters—to discourage their subcontracted weavers from employing underage workers.

Have these labeling programs reduced the incidence of child labor in the industry? A 2002 survey of looms across India suggested that labeling and monitoring may have had some impact, but not necessarily because of the labeling itself. In a careful study across different sections of India's carpet belt, Sharma (2002) found that 19 percent of just over 5,500 workers on 1,065 looms were under fourteen years of age, and that 22 percent of these children were hired workers rather than family members. Looms registered with Rugmark showed minimal differences in the use of nonfamily child labor from those registered with other programs—despite the fact that other programs did not involve independent monitoring. There was, however, some difference between looms that were registered with any program and those that were not, leading Sharma (2002, 5204) to conclude that weavers who registered their loom with any program—whether or not the program involved monitoring—might have been slightly less likely to employ child workers than weavers who failed to register their looms. On the other hand, Sharma notes that some of these differences may have been regional. Areas where programs have raised awareness about the problems involving child labor—including, of course, the threat that looms employing child labor will be shut off from the export business—seem to employ smaller percentages of nonfamily labor than areas that have not yet been exposed to this discussion or to this threat.

Nevertheless, Sharma's (2002, 5204) study does not offer much evidence that monitoring of any sort made a large difference to weavers. He concluded that "the incidence of child labor has not [been] reduced significantly as a consequence of these labeling initiatives," and added, "It can be concluded that social labeling programs and other similar initiatives to eradicate child labor at best have had a limited reach and only a marginal impact." A somewhat smaller study similarly found that voluntary monitoring programs have had relatively little impact;

limited results were confined to the geographic areas where monitors were most active, and carpet weaving outside those areas was unaffected (Srivastava and Raj 2002, 109-10).

Did Rugmark's social labeling scheme promote new attitudes toward child labor in the carpet belt, or did it simply lead to the creation of weaker imitators? Ten years after the first Rugmark labels were attached to carpets, it was almost impossible to find a handwoven carpet in the United States that did not carry some sort of label promising prospective buyers that no children had worked on the carpet. Although carpets carrying the Rugmark label were quite difficult to find in the United States—a fact that in our 2003 interviews Rugmark's directors attributed darkly and somewhat vaguely to personality conflicts in the New York office—every carpet for sale seemed to carry some other label assuring consumers that they could buy the carpet in good conscience. None of these labels, of course, were backed by any monitoring or real evidence that exporters or weavers were committed to eliminating child labor, but few American consumers were likely to be able to discriminate between labels. In Germany, Rugmark was far more visible—glossy brochures in department stores reminded consumers about the program, and the program's directors claimed that about one-third of the Indian carpets sold in Germany carried Rugmark's label (Dietrich Kebschull interview, 2003). Skeptics often dismissed labeling efforts—frequently joking that "stitching product labels could be another industry for employing children" (Basu 2003, 100)—but most activists viewed these labels with measured detachment, suggesting that perhaps labeling schemes helped increase awareness both at home and abroad of the need to reduce child labor, even if the labels had little direct impact on the problem.

But activists who agree that Rugmark's program may have increased awareness frequently insist that the labeling scheme has misled international consumers, diverting pressure that might otherwise have prompted the Indian state to provide schools and welfare programs for poor children (Basu 2003). Other Indian activists note that Rugmark's limited scope does little to attract attention to child labor in other industries, and while voicing sharp criticisms of Rugmark's school program, they question whether a program predicated on exports might not undermine efforts in other sectors (Swami Agnivesh interview, 2003). Trade unionists and government officials tend to emphasize Rugmark's lack of accountability, often contrasting NGOs—which tend to speak on behalf of victims but lack structures that would make activists accountable to those affected by their programs—with organizations that have more formal democratic structures, including unions and political parties (Amargit Kaur interview, 2003).

Conclusion

Rugmark's history seems fairly typical of the way transnational networks are constructed and illustrates some common dynamics of nongovernmental regulatory schemes and transnational activism around labor issues. First raised by local activists committed to changing national policies, the plight of child workers in India's carpet industry was initially viewed as a symbol of several local issues—particularly the failure of the Indian state to enforce its own local labor laws, its neglect of poor and lower-caste families, and its dramatic shift in development strategies in the late 1970s. The turn to an international audience certainly intensified pressure on local manufacturers to act against child labor, but it seems worth noting that local issues may be redefined in the process of making global appeals. On the global stage, the carpet industry's child workers served as a slightly different symbol, illustrating the concerns of a global campaign against child labor. Some of the issues that had originally gotten the attention of local activists disappeared from view—especially those issues linked to state policies, the provision of schools, and the empowerment of adult workers.

The specter of a ban on Indian carpets prompted almost immediate responses from local manufacturers—just as proponents of social labeling schemes would predict. As with the Sullivan Principles, however, it is worth underscoring the institutionalized character of the boycott threat. Far from relying on individual consumer choice, Indian carpet exporters responded to proposed state actions, as both the American and German governments considered laws banning imports made with child labor. Again, as in the Sullivan case, activist groups speaking for the consumers among their constituents—in this case, German trade unions and church groups—supported trade prohibitions, but the threat of state action clearly gave strong impetus to the Indian industry to act.

The decision to deploy a voluntary labeling scheme based on consumer pressures seems to have fit the carpet industry better than most, given the character of the product. True, the structure of the industry—especially the village- and home-based character of production—clearly makes it difficult to monitor looms, but the labeling process seems best suited for products that are easily identifiable and for which demand is elastic.

Given that reality, the gaps in Rugmark's monitoring program may be less important than the fact that carpet manufacturers in India can now choose between an array of alternative codes and labels, most of which carry no promise of monitoring. This proliferation may, of course, reflect new attitudes toward child workers as more and more carpet weavers demonstrate real commitment to ending child labor in their industry. Skeptics, however, might view this proliferation as evidence that most consumers, in most of the world, will not distinguish between different kinds of codes or different social labels—and most carpet manufacturers know it. While some consumers may insist on a specific label, most are far less conscious or aware of variation; even in a world linked by high-speed Internet connections, Indian exporters have learned that unless their carpet is going to a very specific market, they need not participate in Rugmark's program at all.

As I suggest in the next chapter, the voluntary character of most monitoring schemes immediately raises questions not only about the funding of monitoring schemes but also about the ability of employers to choose the level of monitoring they want to accept. While transnational campaigns may be able to insist on the implementation of some form of monitoring, decisions on the ground will matter to the process— and with voluntary programs, employers will inevitably adopt the level of monitoring that suits their needs. Some companies, of course, will be honestly committed to improving their workplaces; certainly, the Rugmark program has made some exporters and some weavers more conscious about employing children than they might otherwise have been. But others may be less conscientious. Voluntary programs may help persuade well-intentioned employers to comply with outside norms, but they clearly allow more cost-conscious, or less ethical, employers to "play for the gray," in Braithwaite's (2002) phrase—complying only as much as is required by the regulatory framework.

Just as Rugmark exporters and weavers seem quite conscious that they can manipulate the Rugmark process—registering looms only when a specific carpet is destined for a market where the social label might matter—most voluntary programs are open to manipulation on the ground. Sometimes this may be due to funding patterns; when NGOs depend on employers for funding, perhaps flexible monitoring schemes are attractive because they reach more work sites. But this flexibility is also a straightforward result of Rugmark's insistence that the program be voluntary, a choice that allows enormous slippage; no nongovernmental group, no matter how well organized or resourced, can gain access to a work site if employers do not admit them. Voluntary programs and social labeling may demonstrate real compliance in many cases, but as long as some employers can easily opt for less rigorous codes and less vigilant monitors, international networks will find it difficult to judge which labels are meaningful and which labels are simply misleading.

Finally, like the Sullivan system, Rugmark's social labeling program raises two questions: How are decisions made about which standards should be applied? And how is it decided who should make these decisions? The hostility toward the program repeatedly displayed by child labor activists, unionists, and government officials had many facets, but linking all of them was a concern about accountability, both in designing the program and in implementing the monitoring. Lacking any accountability, as well as any channel through which child workers or their families could articulate their concerns, Rugmark appeared—even to activists who sympathized with its initial goals—to be a foreign-dominated effort imposed from outside that gave Indian citizens little control over the goals, the process, or the outcome, to such an extent that critics accused the program of misdirecting and misleading international consumers rather than mobilizing their support for long-term, far-reaching change.

Alternative Approaches to Eliminating Child Labor

Before leaving this chapter, I want to touch on alternative approaches to eliminating child labor. While social labeling remains a favorite topic in discussions of transnational labor activism, child labor campaigns have generally moved in a somewhat different direction.

Increasingly, international efforts to help children in poor families have shifted to a focus on how best to provide for children's needs, rather than simply prohibiting them from work. Several efforts to ban child labor through import restrictions had mixed effects. In 1992 Bangladeshi government officials, concerned that Senator Harkin's proposed ban on goods made with child labor might hurt Bangladesh's surging garment exports, asked the ILO to help them develop a new labor inspectorate that could certify the country's factories as free of child workers. Although this program certainly removed child labor from factories, it was harshly criticized, both because ILO inspectors apparently failed to monitor other labor law violations in the same factories and because the program failed to provide other help to the impoverished children now excluded from the factories (Bissell 2003; Brooks 2005).

A few years later, a transnational campaign to eliminate child labor from soccer ball production created a more complete monitoring program involving the ILO and government inspectors in Sialkot, Pakistan. Threatened with a global consumer boycott—possibly to be coordinated by the world soccer federation, FIFA—major manufacturers agreed in December 1997 to move previously home-based stitching into large centers, where outside monitors could more easily ensure that children were not involved in the work. Since a handful of brands control nearly all soccer ball sales globally, the brands' cooperation led to a quick change in the industry—at least in Sialkot. Child labor was virtually eliminated from Sialkot's supervised centers. However, critics charge that children continue to work in their homes in Sialkot's expanding surgical instrument industry and that this work is unseen by the ILO or government inspectors (Nadvi and Kazmi 2001). In 2006 the international Global March Against Child Labor (2006) insisted that even Sialkot's soccer ball industry had escaped monitoring, claiming that major brands were now outsourcing production to small, unmonitored workshops scattered in villages outside Sialkot. In late 2006, Nike ended its contract with its Sialkot subcontractor, on the grounds that the subcontractor was no longer restricting production to the supervised central workshops. Nike planned to move its contracts for hand-sewn soccer balls to subcontractors in China and Thailand (Nike 2006).

Discussions of how best to eliminate child labor had shifted by 2005 to a focus on improving children's lives rather than on monitoring workplaces—improving children's homes, nutrition, health care, and access to education rather than simply prohibiting their wage labor, in large part because of a growing recognition that, by the early twenty-first century, even impoverished parents in developing countries view literacy and education as important skills. If primary schools are available and affordable, most parents are eager to have their children learn, and most parents welcome and comply with state policies that encourage and enable school attendance (Burra 2003; Kabeer 2003; Kabeer, Namissan, and Subrahmanian 2003a; Lieten 2002; Wazir 2002).

State policies that make primary education universally available and compulsory have already greatly reduced levels of child labor around the world, according to international agencies involved in monitoring global programs. After reviewing two decades of global progress in reducing child labor, especially in hazardous industries, the ILO's director-general concluded in 2006 that countries that have successfully reduced child labor are those that have invested heavily in universal access to primary education and in monitoring child welfare at home.

> Child labor and poverty reduction through economic development go hand in hand. The relationship is not automatic, however. The pace of child labor elimination accelerates when strategies open up "gateways of opportunity" for poor people. [Where] development efforts focus on the reduction of child poverty, when the length of compulsory education is progressively extended and when government agencies, employers, trade unions and others combine forces to enforce minimum wage employment laws and create opportunities for children to avoid the trap of premature work, especially under hazardous conditions, then progress is made in fighting child labor. (International Labor Organization 2006, 14)

In poorer countries, innovative programs involving incentives to poor families show real promise. From 1996, Brazil's innovative bolsa escola (and from 2003, its bolsa familia) program—involving a small cash payment to poor families when their children attend school regularly—demonstrated how much even a small cash payment increases enrollment. Brazil's program soon came to be viewed as a model (Gould 2003), and it is now central to most policy discussions about how to reduce child labor still further (International Labor Organization 2006). Monitoring workplaces to ensure that workers are above a minimum age is, of course, important, but the ILO's report generally concurs with what Indian child labor activists have long argued (Burra 2003): improving children's lives at home and at school is the most effective strategy for eliminating child labor. And as both Indian activists and the ILO would agree, the responsibility for programs to raise children out of poverty cannot be left to market forces but rests with national governments.

= Chapter 5 =

Constructing a Culture of
Compliance in Guatemala

The word "sweatshop" has long evoked the garment industry: poor young women bent over sewing machines in dimly lit, badly ventilated rooms, working long hours for pitiful wages. Sadly, that image is not outdated. Exposés from Los Angeles to Bangladesh regularly reveal conditions not much different from those which prevailed in New York's Triangle Shirtwaist Factory one hundred years ago. The seamy underside of globalization is revealed in clothing factories around the world, where the confluence of poverty, gendered labor markets, and racial hierarchies force workers, mainly young women, to accept conditions that give harsh meaning to the term "race to the bottom."

But clothing factories have also been central to transnational labor campaigns. Much as American consumers confronted sweatshop realities after the 1911 Triangle Shirtwaist fire, modern tales of fire, underage workers, and abuse have made the global apparel industry a primary target for labor campaigns, the site where international trade, poor working conditions, corporate images, consumer boycotts, and independent monitoring schemes all come together.

Do these campaigns illustrate the promise of stateless regulation? International consumer campaigns have certainly helped raise global awareness, placing real pressure on brand-name retailers, which have, in turn, begun to insist that their subcontractors comply with new codes of conduct. But as I demonstrate in this chapter, voluntary compliance has its limits, and consumer pressure goes only so far. Rather than bypassing national institutions, transnational campaigns may be most effective when they seek to strengthen states' capacity for protecting citizens at work. "Stateless" monitoring in Central America emerged during the cold war's waning decades as activists sought to protect citizens across the region from violence and intimidation. Especially in Guatemala, monitoring grew out of human rights activism during a long and difficult peace process; rather than viewing monitoring as a way to provide information to consumers, activists viewed it as a strategy for creating more inclusive democratic institutions at home and thus as part of a broad effort to reconstruct the state.

To a much greater extent than was true in the case of either the Sullivan Principles or Rugmark, transnational appeals in Central America reflected local voices. These campaigns were built on a base of long-term relationships, and transnational activists may have been more attuned to local histories and local dynamics. When Guatemalan labor monitoring emerged in the 1990s, it operated within a preexisting web of transnational links involving church groups, human rights organizations, indigenous groups, and labor activists as well as ordinary migrants. Existing transnational relationships allowed networks to respond flexibly to local activists and avoided many of the tensions that can complicate cross-border discussions.

Even in this case, however, transnational involvement required some reframing of workers' claims. To appeal to global audiences, workplace issues were repeatedly reframed in terms of fundamental human rights and universal concerns about protecting vulnerable victims from physical harm. Repression in Central America had long targeted labor activists—vividly illustrating the tie between labor rights and human rights—yet as Guatemala moved toward a more normalized society, transnational networks struggled to develop strategies that might mobilize international consumer pressure in support of workers facing more complicated situations.

In this chapter, I first discuss the emergence of independent monitoring in Guatemala as activists sought to create a "culture of compliance" and deepen democratization by monitoring, using information about violations to mobilize international pressure on powerful state actors and employers. But, I will argue, monitoring by "civil society" appeared not as an end in itself but as a strategy for constructing the institutions of democracy—that is, as a step toward building a democratic state. Human rights monitoring expanded to include workplace monitoring in the 1990s as export-processing zones expanded across the region. Taking advantage of open access to American markets, major brands outsourced production to cost-cutting subcontractors. In the context of a prototypical race to the bottom, human rights activists and unionists—many of them participants in preexisting transnational networks—drew on their monitoring repertoire to address new challenges.

Debates over monitoring in the global apparel industry reflect both the promise and the problems inherent to nongovernmental monitoring schemes. Guatemala's Commission for the Verification of Codes of Conduct (COVERCO), I suggest in this chapter, is as successful as any nonstate monitoring scheme in Central America and has worked hard to provide credible information about factory conditions to a broad array of transnational activists. Ironically, however, COVERCO's efforts are aimed primarily at local targets; its engagement with international audiences stems not from a desire to bypass local institutions in favor of global ones, but from a broader effort to construct a more democratic and responsive state at home.

Monitoring for Change

Guatemala's human rights networks provide an archetypal example of the transnational "human rights boomerang" process. Through the country's decades-long civil war, local groups appealed to international organizations to help change national dynamics. Facing a repressive government and a hard-line military engaged in a civil war driven by social and economic pressures, ethnic divisions, cold war tensions, and superpower meddling, Guatemalan human rights groups became adept at mobilizing international support to promote democratization at home. Especially after 1980, as government-sponsored terror in Guatemala's highland villages reached horrifying proportions, local church and civil groups grew skilled in working with international human rights networks, international agencies, and foreign governments to push the country toward peace.

The Guatemalan conflict appeared endless and intractable, from its initial phases in the 1950s, through a particularly brutal period in the early 1980s, to the negotiated transition of the mid-1990s. In the worst year, from 1981 to 1982, the army killed or "disappeared" over 100,000 of the country's citizens, 400 massacres were committed, and entire highland villages were forced to flee (Amnesty International 1987; Carmack 1988). Guatemalan society was highly polarized; the country's business and political elite viewed all opposition as guerrilla-inspired and then ruled out negotiation with any group linked to armed resistance. Only when international actors applied firm pressure to limit the options available to the country's armed factions did negotiations move past a persistent stalemate. Although the Central American Peace Accords established a framework for negotiated agreements in Nicaragua, El Salvador, and Guatemala in 1987, Guatemala's military and government continued to resist any settlement. The United Nations and powerful neighbors continued to demand a negotiated settlement, however—so much so that in 1993, when Guatemala's government seemed on the verge of suspending both negotiations and the constitution, major trading partners, including the United States, threatened to impose economic sanctions. During the next few years, repeated threats of international economic sanctions pushed Guatemala's conservative business elite to the bargaining table; in 1995 and in 1997, the Consultative Group of Donor Countries (including the United States, Europe, and international institutions) threatened to withhold major funding unless all parties accepted a final peace accord (Jonas 2000, 46 and 169 ff).

Despite these outside pressures, Guatemala's transition was slow, difficult, and interrupted by violence. Repeated attempts at negotiated accords collapsed, and even when a UN-brokered agreement was signed in 1996, neither the government nor the guerrillas seemed committed to the kind of compromise required for building peace. Kidnappings, assassinations, and attacks continued; a guerrilla faction was expelled from the negotiations for refusing to disarm, while hard-liners in Guatemala's military and business elite refused to "negotiate with terrorists," rejecting many of the reforms proposed by international agencies.

Suzanne Jonas, a highly respected analyst of Guatemala's transition process, suggests that only persistent international involvement prevented a slide back into violent conflict. The UN's verification mission (MINUGUA), she writes, represented "direct, on-the-ground, ongoing international presence in Guatemala, [which] shifted the balance of forces within the country. . . . International pressure and presence was required to overcome the convoluted, ideologically over-determined logic of Guatemalan politics, the legacy of a thirty-six year Cold War civil war" (Jonas 2000, 47, 58). To sustain negotiations and the settlement, the United Nations committed itself not only to broker the peace but to monitor it, maintaining a visible presence and involvement.

Nevertheless, domestic activists played a key role in the drawn-out peace process. From the mid-1980s, Guatemalan NGOs—especially human rights groups—were prominent supporters of political negotiations, crucially creating space for discussions that might bypass the deadlocked negotiations between the militarized state and armed guerrillas. The UN's peace-building strategy therefore revolved around incorporating these groups—often described as Guatemala's "civil society"—into the democratization process. Local church-based groups, human rights groups, unions, and indigenous groups were closely involved in the UN's efforts, first by calling attention to the violence in the countryside, then increasingly by calling for negotiation and compromise to break the stalemate. Transnational links were central to these groups' activities; outside pressure could protect local activists from arrest or worse, while local activists provided information that could inform international efforts.

During the transition, these groups from civil society remained vocal and active, and international organizations actively supported their efforts. Even in an era of neoliberal cost-cutting, international agencies recognized the importance of funding local groups to articulate citizens' concerns and monitor Guatemala's attempts to construct a democracy, rather than leaving the construction of a new state in the hands of an elite that had long demonstrated exclusionary and repressive tendencies. Local groups from Guatemala's civil society seemed to offer an alternative to the polarized split between government and guerrillas. International donors—the UN, the European Union, UNICEF, and others—supported local projects ranging from demilitarization to educational reform to new efforts to articulate the concerns of Guatemala's indigenous communities. In 1994 peace negotiators established the Assembly of Civil Society, an arena in which previously excluded social actors could articulate alternatives. MINUGUA and other international agencies worked closely with local groups to promote participation, inclusion, and the construction of new institutions that would allow "participation by historically marginalized groups" and promote "conflict resolution and consensus-building among actors with very different interests in an extremely polarized society" (Jonas 2000, 168; see also Hale 2002; Warren 1998).

Monitoring the powerful formed an essential component of this strategy. With Guatemala's long history of state repression and paramilitary activity, participation alone would not ensure democratization, while guerrilla violations might undermine the peace agreement. For those already versed in using transnational networks to pressure local actors, NGO monitoring and publicity offered a mechanism through which Guatemalan civil society could restrain those in power. When information could mobilize international pressure against domestic actors, monitoring offered a civil society–based strategy for replacing the "culture of impunity" that characterized Guatemala's armed actors with a "culture of compliance" in which both government and citizens—no matter what their social status—would learn to comply with rules designed through a democratic process and enforced across the board. Throughout Guatemala's protracted peace process, monitoring by NGOs played a key part; just as human rights groups had provided information about repeated massacres and gross violations of human rights through the 1980s, local groups monitored the gradual disarmament of the warring military and militias during the peace process.

Monitoring qua monitoring played a specific, almost unique role in Guatemala. By monitoring compliance by both government and guerrillas, voluntary groups "bore witness" and provided information to international agencies, which could then put pressure on the powerful. During the peace process, however, the targets of monitoring changed slightly. Local activists began to use similar mechanisms to create a culture of compliance in the workplace, using information and transnational linkages to protect labor rights at home.

Labor Rights: A Special Kind of Human Rights

How did labor rights enter into this process? For many of Guatemala's NGOs, the shift from monitoring human rights violations to tackling broad questions of political and economic inclusion was not a difficult one to make. Marked by extreme inequality and poverty, Guatemala is one of the poorest countries in the hemisphere. From almost any perspective, peace would require concerted efforts to promote economic development and to spread the benefits of growth beyond the country's tiny elite. Human rights abuses have often been blurred with labor rights in Guatemala's recent history, and labor issues came to the fore as these monitoring groups sought to construct a more inclusive democracy.

Throughout the transition, Guatemala's human rights activists stressed the importance of social and economic rights as well as political inclusion. In this poor country where Mayan Indians worked plantations owned by a tiny Spanish-speaking elite, human rights abuses were always closely intertwined with vivid racial and ethnic divisions, exclusion, and labor repression (Goldin 2005; Grandin 2000). In 1999 Guatemala's UN-administered Truth Commission explicitly linked the country's political violence to historical patterns of exclusion and labor control:

> Due to its exclusionary nature, the [Guatemalan] State was incapable of achieving social consensus around a national project able to unite the whole population. Concomitantly, it abandoned its role as a mediator between divergent social and economic interests, thus creating a gulf which made direct confrontation between them more likely. . . . Faced with movements proposing economic, political, social or cultural change, the State increasingly resorted to violence and terror in order to maintain social control. Political violence was thus a direct expression of structural violence. (Comision para el Esclarecimiento Historico, 1999, quoted in Organization of American States 2001, 38)

More than half of Guatemala's population is indigenous, many living in rural poverty; in 2001 about 40 percent of the population was said to earn less than one U.S. dollar a day (Organization of American States 2001, 39). Reflecting broad recognition of how poverty had contributed to Guatemala's civil war, the peace accords of the late 1990s included commitments to economic and social development and committed the new government to attend to the special needs of the country's indigenous population.[1]

Labor rights were prominently discussed in this process. Although all Guatemalans who sought to mobilize or articulate demands for inclusion and social justice had been at risk during the civil war, human rights activists noted that trade unionists in particular were repeatedly targeted by state and paramilitary forces and frequently were assassinated or disappeared. Although Guatemalan history is replete with examples of repression, attacks on unionists intensified during the civil war. In one notorious episode from the late 1970s, eight Coca-Cola workers who tried to form a union were murdered; similarly, twenty-one leaders of a national labor federation were abducted from their office in 1980. During the following period, hundreds of Guatemalan trade unionists were "disappeared" and executed by paramilitary death squads. Amnesty International (1987, 26) concluded bluntly in 1979—and repeated in 1987—that "to be a trade unionist in Guatemala is to risk one's life" (see also Davis 1988; Forster 1998; Frundt 1987).

As international human rights campaigns gained wider audiences in the United States, the repression of trade unionists in Guatemala and other parts of Central America played into a larger debate within the American labor movement over labor's support for U.S. foreign policy. After World War II, AFL-CIO leaders had tended to be more concerned about stopping Communist influence than about protecting international labor rights—a concern that repeatedly led American unionists to acquiesce in support for labor-repressive regimes, especially in Latin America.

Until the mid-1980s, the AFL-CIO channeled its involvement in Central America through the American Institute for Free Labor Development (AIFLD), a program funded by the U.S. government and frequently criticized for putting American foreign policy objectives and cold war security concerns ahead of training labor organizers (Bergquist 1996; Herod 2001; Silverman 2000; Spalding 1988). This tendency was perhaps nowhere more evident than in Guatemala. In 1954 the Central Intelligence Agency mounted a covert campaign against Guatemala's democratically elected government, providing clandestine support to block President Jacobo Arbenz's moderate efforts to limit hacienda size, restrict foreign ownership of railways and oil concessions, and mobilize urban and rural workers. American unionists failed to protest the intervention; instead, the AFL-CIO continued to promote "business unionism" in Guatemala (Schlesinger and Kinzer 1982).

In the 1980s, however, American labor activists adopted a new stance, partly in response to a general shift regarding American foreign policy, but often also at the insistence of union delegations that had visited Central America and seen firsthand the dangers faced by local unionists. Again, Guatemala offers a vivid example. In the mid-1970s, American church groups involved in discussions about socially responsible investments—including the same Interfaith Center on Corporate Responsibility that had raised concerns in the religious community about holding South Africa–related stocks (Frundt 1987, 28, 73ff)—began to raise questions about labor repression in Guatemala, especially in relation to the union drive at a Guatemalan bottling plant operating under a Coca-Cola franchise. When leading unionists were assassinated in Guatemala City in 1979, human rights groups asked unionists to join international protests, and even the U.S. embassy expressed concern (Frundt 1987, 98). Over the next several years, American and European unionists joined human rights and church groups in supporting the militant Coca-Cola workers, and the experience increased American unionists' awareness of Guatemala's broad pattern of labor repression.

As in the case of South African shareholder resolutions, it was religious denominations concerned with socially responsible investments that first brought Guatemala's human rights abuses to Coca-Cola's attention and persuaded the multinational company to pressure its Guatemalan franchiser to recognize a union (Frundt 1987, 225). But church-based human rights campaigns soon began to raise concerns among American unionists about their Central American counterparts. U.S. labor activists formed several new groups focusing on labor in Central America, including the Chicago-based U.S.-Guatemala Labor Education Project (US/GLEP) and the National Labor Committee (NLC), which was formed in the early 1980s; these groups would become leading forces in transnational campaigns to support Central American labor activists (Battista 2002).

Transnational contacts—specifically, personal visits by American unionists to the region and personal contacts between individual activists across borders—altered the way American activists understood regional repression. Especially in a context where churches and an international human rights movement were increasingly visible, participation in human rights delegations deepened American unionists' concerns about Central American repression (Battista 2002; Frundt 1998).

These personal ties clearly shaped transnational labor activism in the region. In marked contrast to both the Indian and South African examples, concern for regional labor rights emerged in a context where it was possible to construct dense personal networks. As visiting American unionists joined "fact-finding missions" to the region, they met Central American unionists across the ideological spectrum, and familiarity increased Americans' concerns for individual unionists' safety. Many Central American unionists remain wary of North American motives, even today, but frequent visits and exchanges altered the tenor of discussions within U.S. unions.

Transnational ties soon deepened beyond concern for individual unionists to support for broad social change and democratization. In 1985 an AFL-CIO resolution challenged American government policy in the region, calling for an end to U.S. support for repressive regimes (Battista 2002, 438). American unionists argued that the region's human rights record was directly related to poor working conditions. The same elite-dominated states that violated citizens' human rights, they insisted, allowed employers to exploit those citizens at work. Challenging the AFL-CIO's long history of accepting cold war alliances, unionists engaged in Central America began to argue that anti-communism could not justify government failure to protect labor rights (Battista 2002). In 1984, for example, after meeting with government officials in Guatemala, an AFL-CIO delegation reported that in Guatemala a "rationale of subversion is used to cover up attacks on the union movement. . . . The delegation believes that there is a systematic attempt to undermine free trade unionization using kidnapping and murder to intimidate workers and to instill fear of death for unionization activity" (AFL-CIO report, quoted in Amnesty International 1987, 121).

Expanding the human rights agenda to include labor rights echoed Guatemala's activists, who pointed out that their country's "culture of impunity" was perhaps nowhere more visible than in the state's failure to enforce its own labor laws. Not only did the Guatemalan government routinely restrict union activities—by banning strikes or closing unions, as well as by failing to protect union organizers from disappearances and torture by paramilitary death squads—but at a more mundane level, it failed to impose any serious consequences on employers who ignored the law. Guatemalan employers routinely flouted the country's labor code, with unfair dismissals, underpayment, and even physical abuse going unchecked. The failure to enforce labor laws was so widespread that employers sometimes refused to even acknowledge that the government had any role to play in the workplace at all. In some notorious examples, employers refused to allow labor inspectors onto plantations or to implement decisions made by the government's labor courts, turning to other branches of government for support against the Labor Ministry. When workers tried to get the government to enforce legal rights, employers could simply fail to appear at hearings, so that proceedings could drag on for years (Mancilla Garcia interview, 2003). Moreover, child labor and bonded labor remained rampant, despite legal prohibitions on both (Frundt 1998, 143).

This failure to enforce protections for workers continued long after the transition to peace was well under way. A decade after the peace process began, trade unionists and labor inspectors in Guatemala City described the government's failure to bring employers into compliance as the basic problem facing workers. Many could recount lengthy efforts to demand enforcement, noting tensions between government ministries, judicial processes dragged out by bureaucratic inaction and ineptitude, and employers avoiding compliance through legal maneuvering (José David Morales interview, 2003; Mancilla Garcia interview, 2003; José Luis Morales Perez interview, 2006; César Gatica interview, 2006).

Especially in light of the region's history, it was easy to argue that labor and human rights were intertwined; the same repression that stifled democratic opposition also prevented workers from demanding protection from unscrupulous employers. The human rights community adopted unionists' themes as it increasingly described the failure of states to enforce labor laws as a basic component of a failure to create democratic institutions or to protect vulnerable citizens from abuse. Over the next twenty years, this view became dominant, even in official human rights reports. In a section of its 2001 report devoted to concerns about the status of women in Guatemala, for example, the OAS Inter-American Commission on Human Rights noted in passing that "one reason for women's greater participation in the labor market is their growing employment in maquilas. The Commission's attention has been drawn to allegations of abuse in this sector, including extended compulsory overtime hours, poor working conditions and harassment, coupled with the lack of adequate inspection and oversight by the Ministry of Labor" (Organization of American States 2001, 222–23).

As the OAS report noted, the changing character of economic ties between North and Central America and the changing structure of the North American apparel industry during the last decades of the twentieth century had given rise to new kinds of production in the region's export-processing zones, creating new labor concerns in the process.

Apparel Companies, Maquilas, and a New Set of Labor Concerns

While most fact-finding missions to Central America in the 1980s were inspired by concerns about American foreign policy and human rights violations, visiting American union delegations noticed during their trips that many American companies were moving production south. In 1983, for example, union delegates were taken aback to discover that American government aid programs were "helping U.S. apparel manufacturers get established in El Salvador" (Krupat 1997, 65).

Although the process was almost invisible to international audiences horrified by massacres of indigenous villagers and brutal repression of human rights, Guatemala's economy was transformed through the 1980s. The United States, of course, played a key role, offering a new form of development assistance to accompany military aid. In 1982 President Ronald Reagan announced his Caribbean Basin Initiative, designed to stimulate and diversify production in Central America and the Caribbean through subsidies and incentives. Over the next few decades, countries across Central America turned to new economic strategies, seeking to attract foreign capital to export-processing zones and exporting fruits, vegetables, and apparel as well as coffee, bananas, and sugar to American markets.

Central American policymakers—often trained in the United States and persuaded that export-oriented production offered new possibilities—viewed access to American markets as a crucial new opportunity and welcomed investors who might hire their countries' low-wage workers. By the early 1990s, elites across the region had adopted a new strategy for economic growth: drawing on the language of neoliberalism and globalization, technocratic policymakers turned to what was known as "export-led development," a strategy that saw private investment in export-processing zones and other nontraditional exports as central to new patterns of growth (Babb 2001; Paige 1997; Robinson 2003).

The North American apparel industry was among the first to leap in. Indeed, North American garment manufacturers had begun to eye low-wage workers in the region with interest even before export-oriented trade became the official centerpiece of American development aid (Rosen 2002). By the early 1980s, some American producers had turned to global outsourcing; instead of seeking to block imported clothing, some companies began to move production offshore to low-wage sites. Taking advantage of a clause in American trade law encouraging overseas assembly of U.S.-made components, some American companies began to ship textiles to low-wage production sites in the Caribbean and Central America and then ship the assembled garments back to sell, duty-free, on the American market. Although Reagan's Caribbean Basin Initiative was meant to promote nontraditional agricultural exports, not apparel, by 1986 apparel made up 40 percent of the value of all goods imported from the Caribbean Basin countries to the United States (Rosen 2002, 136–40). In 1986 new American trade rules reduced tariffs on apparel sewn in Central America still further; over the next decade, total apparel imports to the United States from Central America skyrocketed, rising 584 percent between 1987 and 1997 (Bonacich and Appelbaum 2000, 57; Rosen 2002, 144–48).

What transformed an industry that had long demanded protectionist trade policies that blocked foreign garments from American stores? Why did apparel producers shift from blocking global imports to outsourcing to foreign subcontractors? Where once American brand-name companies produced clothes in wholly-owned factories within America's borders, new tariff policies and new technologies prompted apparel giants to focus on marketing and design, leaving production to smaller subcontractors producing in low-wage regions of the world. Apparel imports to America soared from less than $1 million in 1962 to more than $40 billion in 1997; by 2000, imports were estimated at 60 percent of the $101 billion American wholesale apparel market (Bonacich and Appelbaum 2000, 9).

American trade policies played a key role in the industry's restructuring. It was only when the U.S. government reduced tariffs and quotas on clothing imported from specific locations—usually, low-wage countries that the United States sought to bring into its sphere of influence—that corporate planners took advantage of new ways to cut costs. Once import duties were cut, Central America and the Caribbean Basin offered obvious attractions to corporate planners: the region was conveniently close, it offered large populations eager for work even at low wages, and local governments competed to attract major companies' attention. As new investments flooded into industrial zones from the Dominican Republic to Costa Rica, factories throughout the region competed for new contracts with major brands and retailers to produce clothing for American consumers.

By the early 1990s, the apparel industry served as the archetypal global commodity chain. Global brands concentrated on advertising and design in the wealthy markets of North America and Europe while subcontracting production out to smaller subcontractors located in export-processing zones in low-wage areas (Bair and Gereffi 2002; Gereffi 1994). As Jane Collins (2003) demonstrates in her compelling comparison of corporate strategies, cost-cutting pressures created an apparently inexorable logic. While companies like Liz Claiborne became adept at global sourcing, strategically pursuing locations privileged by the American import quota system to ensure their competitive edge, companies that tried to maintain production within the United States found themselves forced to choose between bankruptcy and globalization (see also Ross 2004; Schoenberger 2000).

The change in the industry was remarkable. For most of the twentieth century, clothes destined for American markets had been produced in the United States. By 2000, the industry had been transformed: major labels concentrated on design, advertising, and retail sales, leaving the actual sewing to subcontracted companies, which could be located anywhere in the world as long as trade policies allowed easy access to American markets. The number of garment workers in America dropped from a high of about 1.4 million workers in 1973 to fewer than 300,000 in 2004 (Murray 1995).

In 1989 the American Apparel Manufacturers' Association officially shifted its stance. Once, the industry's lobby group had represented companies that sewed clothes and sold them within the United States, but by 1989 its member companies were using factories throughout the world to sew clothes destined for American consumers, and the lobby group had become such an outspoken proponent of outsourcing that South Carolina's staunchly protectionist Senator Ernest Hollings called it the "Central American Apparel Manufacturers' Association" (quoted in Collins 2003, 52). In 1995 the International Ladies' Garment Workers' Union and the American Clothing and Textile Workers' Union abandoned their long-standing rivalry to merge their ever-shrinking memberships under a new label, the Union of Needletrades, Industrial, and Textile Employees (UNITE). In 2004, as the American apparel workforce shrank even further, UNITE merged again, this time joining the Hotel Employees and Restaurant Employees to form UNITE-HERE. Garment workers had helped shape American labor struggles early in the twentieth century, but by the early twenty-first, unionists clearly viewed the hotel, restaurant, and laundry workers—whose jobs are more geographically rooted—as more promising terrain for organizing drives.

But when American companies looked to Central America, they rarely opened their own factories. Instead, they looked for partners for subcontracting in the burgeoning maquila districts—and many of these partners were also foreigners. As Central American elites shifted to take advantage of new opportunities, embracing foreign investment and trade as an alternative to older strategies for growth, they redesigned national policies to encourage foreign investors through the creation of special "export-processing zones," offering tax breaks and subsidies and even reduced minimum wage levels to new investors. Local manufacturers often responded to these incentives by retooling factories, turning away from the domestic market, and subcontracting to American brands (Gereffi, Spener, and Bair 2002; Plankey-Videla 2004; Robinson 2003).

Local entrepreneurs were hardly the only ones racing to subcontract for the American market. Second-tier subcontractors—including, above all, small apparel manufacturers from Taiwan and South Korea facing rising labor costs at home and attracted by easier access to American markets—also responded to the new export-processing incentives. Between 1989 and 1991, at least eighty-two Korean and Taiwanese manufacturers moved to the region, investing $85 million, mainly in electronics and apparel assembly plants (Rosen 2002, 147). In 1993 about 17 percent of all apparel and electronics assembly in Costa Rica, the Dominican Republic, El Salvador, and Honduras was either Taiwanese- or Korean-owned.

Guatemala appears to have been especially favored by Korean investors. Between 1989 and 1993, Korean owners opened 55 new apparel factories in Guatemala alone; ten years later, nearly half of Guatemala's apparel exports were produced in Korean-owned factories (Robinson 2003, 168). As I show later in this chapter, these new patterns of subcontracting, often involving second-tier companies in the subcontracting chain, also gave the labor process a new racialized twist, which may have added fuel to transnational campaigns.

Campaigns Across Borders

By the early 1990s, American policymakers recognized that globalization had moved apparel factories beyond the reach of American labor law. Especially within the context of new regional trade agreements—specifically the 1994 North American Free Trade Agreement (NAFTA)—American unionists argued that a global free trade regime would alter the very basis of labor law enforcement as businesses used the threat of flight to undermine strict workplace regulation and supported the search for new strategies. Key policymakers agreed; soon after President Clinton's inauguration, then-Secretary of Labor Robert Reich announced a "no sweat" initiative, arguing that globalization demanded new regulatory approaches (Brobowsky, n.d.).

In the mid-1980s, most discussions of "runaway" shops focused on the small producers that often employed illegal immigrants within the ethnic enclaves of New York or Los Angeles. Unionists tried legal stratagems, hoping to make retailers and brand-name companies liable for violations in their subcontractors' factories through the assertion of legal "joint liability" (Bonacich and Appelbaum 2000; Wolensky, Wolensky, and Wolensky 2002). Arguing that subcontracting relationships did not absolve the brand-name company of responsibility for the workers who made goods bearing brand labels, unionists sought to make brand-name producers liable for labor law compliance—no matter who owned the factory where the production took place.

Business lobbyists suggested, by contrast, that the American response should be to deregulate work at home, to match conditions in export-processing zones. The U.S. government accepted that logic. Fearing that "overregulation" would push the entire American garment industry to move, it argued that labor law enforcement might drive away jobs. In 1992 the U.S. Department of Labor began to experiment with privatized factory monitoring in the Los Angeles garment industry, seeking to enlist manufacturers' help in getting subcontractors to comply with labor laws. The Department of Labor hoped "to walk a very fine line, attempting to 'clean up' the industry while not pushing manufacturers too far, lest they move production over the border" (Esbenshade 2004, 39).

That policy, however, was often criticized for apparently contributing to a return to sweatshop conditions, especially in immigrant enclaves in New York and Los Angeles (Ness 2003). In 1995, when an Immigration and Naturalization Service (INS) raid freed seventy-two Thai garment workers who had been kept as virtual slaves in a Los Angeles sweatshop (Nutter 1997; Proper 1997; Su 1997), the scandal revealed the impact of global restructuring and the way in which cost-cutting pressure had re-created sweatshops within the United States as well as abroad (Howard 1997). In New York and California, unionists supported state laws to hold brand-name companies liable for the conditions under which subcontracted work was performed (Bonacich and Appelbaum 2000, 109), while Labor Secretary Reich (1997, 269) threatened to shame brand-name corporations that failed to police working conditions in the factories of their subcontractors.

Nevertheless, the industry continued to move offshore, and unionists and policymakers began to argue that American workers' interests depended on improving working conditions abroad; apparel's global reach demanded a transnational regulatory framework. In 1991 the National Labor Committee—an NGO formed in the early years of American unionists' support for human rights campaigns in Central America—reported:

> The struggle for worker rights . . . in Central and South America has never been more important than it is now to the labor movement in the United States. . . . In the absence of effective worker rights in the region, increased economic integration will only exacerbate the already fierce wage competition which threatens the jobs, wages and living conditions of workers throughout the Americas. (quoted in Battista 2002, 447)

The failure of Central American states to intervene to protect worker-citizens loomed large in discussions about the "race to the bottom"—a skepticism perhaps especially warranted in Guatemala. A decade after the signing of Guatemala's peace accords, state resources for labor law enforcement were still glaringly inadequate. Even Guatemalan congressional representatives warned that without outside support—external pressure and external resources for training inspectors and facilitating inspections—Guatemala was unlikely to develop the capacity to enforce the labor laws that were on the books (Victor Hugo Toledo interview, 2005).

How weak was Guatemala's commitment to or capacity for enforcing its labor laws? In 2006—after a decade of relatively peaceful stability during which United Nations agencies had prioritized strengthening the government's capacity for labor code enforcement (Ricardo Changala interview, 2003)—Guatemala's Department of Labor national inspectorate included about three hundred labor inspectors. Of these, however, no more than fifty were usually engaged in field inspections at any given time, and for visiting thousands of work sites spread across the country, they shared a total of four old vehicles (one of which, according to inspectors interviewed in 2006, chronically malfunctioned). Inspectors who were not lucky enough to be assigned one of the three working vehicles were expected to use personal funds to take ordinary buses to work sites. Most inspectors could count on only two aids for their trips to factories: copies of Guatemala's labor code, and an identity card that announced their official right to enter the premises. Inspectors also carried forms to be filled out during the interview process, but since they lacked portable computers or any other equipment, they were forced to rely on employers to supply typewriters or computers to those filling out the forms (José Luis Morales Perez interview, 2006; César Gatica interview, 2006).

American labor law stopped at the border, but Central American states were unwilling or unable to protect their citizens. What, then, could prevent a vicious cycle in which cost-cutting pressures continued to erode working conditions across the globe? For activists, policymakers, and scholars, the most obvious answer in the 1990s lay in transnational consumer campaigns. A handful of successes underscored the strategy's promise. In the Dominican Republic in 1992, an unusually energetic and globally minded American apparel union organizer, Jeff Hermanson, deployed traditional American organizing tactics in new ways: door-to-door house visits laid the basis for a local unionizing drive. But in an innovative twist, Hermanson combined local organizing with appeals to the U.S. government, asking the U.S. trade representative to insist that the Dominican Republic reform and enforce its labor law to protect workers and unionists. In addition, Hermanson pursued what would become the dominant tactic of transnational apparel campaigns over the subsequent decade: threatening major brands with a consumer boycott, transnational activists persuaded multinational labels to push their subcontractors to negotiate with the union (Frundt 1999; Jessup and Gordon 2000, 200).

Other visions of transnational activism, however, generally drew their inspiration from human rights campaigns rather than from traditional labor organizing tactics. In 1991 Guatemalan workers at a Phillips–van Heusen (PVH) subcontractor began looking for advice and assistance in organizing a union. Supported by American unionists, they worked gradually over the next five years, initially trying to get the American government to use its trade leverage to force the government to recognize the union's existence (Frundt 1999, 98). But official recognition did not easily translate into collective bargaining rights; as Ralph Armbruster-Sandoval (2005, 39) notes, that step required leverage not only on states but also on corporate actors. In 1997 a strike broke out. Activists in Chicago's Guatemala Labor Education Project learned that PVH's chief executive officer, Bruce J. Klatsky, served on the board of Human Rights Watch—a widely respected human rights organization with a long record of monitoring and responding to Central American human rights violations (Anner 2000, 252). Activists persuaded Human Rights Watch to send an observer team, and PVH's Klatsky agreed to investigate the labor dispute. By confronting corporate directors with the uncomfortable links between past human rights violations and present labor abuses, labor activism took on an unmistakable moral insistence (Armbruster-Sandoval 2005, 47–49).

Despite its success, the Phillips–van Heusen campaign illustrated the moral quandary often faced by transnational activists. Although the union was recognized and collective bargaining successfully raised workers' wages, the factory closed less than two years later. The campaign was frequently cited as a success by activists, who saw corporate recognition of a maquila union as a key first step toward establishing labor rights in export-processing zones in Central America (Frundt 1999, 98), but its aftermath underscored the fragility of any gains. In a pattern that would become all too familiar, transnational pressure on brands and subcontractors could secure factory-by-factory victories, but subcontractors could simply close up shop to avoid negotiations. Especially in a region where most unions were legally factory-based rather than industrywide, workers lost both their jobs and their union when the factory closed.

Faced with this dilemma, few unionists abandoned state-centered reform efforts, even while they experimented with transnational consumer campaigns. During the Clinton presidency, unionists worked through the U.S. trade representative to insist on labor law reform, using promises of easier access to American markets—and threats of closure—as incentives. Guatemalan Congressional representatives resented finger-wagging lectures from the U.S. trade representative, but they passed a labor reform bill that would have allowed the Ministry of Labor to levy fines against employers found in violation of labor rights—apparently for the first time in the ministry's history (César Castillo interview, 2005). Resistance was fierce; Guatemalan politicians watered down the bill so much that by the time the bill left Guatemala's congress in 2001, when the bill foundered in the courts, few reform proponents fought to resuscitate it. Guatemala's Supreme Court ruled the new mechanism unconstitutional in 2004 (International Labor Rights Fund 2004)—underscoring, yet again, the difficulties facing labor activists in situations where even modest propositions for strengthening the capacity of the state to enforce its own laws face solid opposition.

Turning to "Stateless" Regulation

In the context of Guatemala's repeated failures to enforce its own laws, it was perhaps inevitable that activists and policymakers would turn away from the state, looking instead to stateless forms of regulation. In 1996, following several highly publicized examples of abuse and a handful of successful transnational campaigns, then-Labor Secretary Robert Reich called on leading manufacturers, unionists, and NGOs in the apparel industry to develop industrywide international standards and monitoring. Over the next two years, conflicts raged over what those standards might be and how they might be implemented. In general, brand-name companies resisted publishing the names and locations of subcontractors, suggesting that monitoring could be adequately performed by internal auditors or private accounting firms. Unionists and activist groups, on the other hand, insisted that without the threat of violations tarnishing corporate images, a voluntary code of conduct would not work. "Independent monitoring," in the eyes of most activists, would have to involve open access to workplaces by external monitors, public reports on factory conditions, and transparent funding mechanisms; internal monitoring, or monitoring by accountants responsible only to the brand-name corporation, would not suffice.

By mid-1998, Reich's effort to extend America's regulatory reach through nonstate mechanisms reached a stalemate, and what he had called an "apparel-industry partnership" split into two warring factions. The industry's largest manufacturers created what became known as the Fair Labor Association (FLA). Dominated by major apparel brands, this was an organization that promoted private monitoring of factories and voluntary corporate codes of conduct—efforts that were consistently criticized by American activists as inadequate. Outside that coalition, student groups and American unionists argued that corporations were dragging their feet, offering a weak version of monitoring in the hope of appeasing American consumers without providing adequate oversight over factory conditions. While the FLA participants stressed cooperation—arguing that international workplace monitoring could not succeed unless brands were willing to force subcontractors to allow outside monitors into their factories—critics dismissed the FLA on the grounds that internal monitoring would not provide the information needed to permit consumers to punish or reward.

In early 2000, student activists, NGOs, and unionists formed a separate organization. Rather than relying on corporate support for access to subcontractors' factories, the Workers' Rights Consortium (WRC) developed a model of monitoring that they believed would be more independent, more transparent, and, above all, more responsive to workers' complaints. Instead of trying to monitor all factories, the WRC sought to bring global attention to factory abuses, bringing egregious situations to public attention rather than providing a seal of approval. In discussions of monitoring, the WRC strategy became known as the "fire alarm" approach. Its role would be to publicize problems rather than monitor compliance (Scott Nova interview, 2004).

Student protestors demanded that university administrations across the country to sign on to the WRC and pay the membership fees that would fund the organization. But over the next few years, the debate over different approaches to monitoring continued. Both the FLA and the WRC acknowledged that monitoring across international borders was still in an experimental stage, and each new workplace intervention and each new report of grievous violations seemed to raise new challenges and issues. Within five years of their founding, both organizations had shifted somewhat. Jill Esbenshade (2004, 195) notes that the FLA had "publicly acknowledged that workers' empowerment is a central facet of code enforcement and . . . moved toward a model that mitigates companies' control of their enforcement process," while the WRC had quietly sought, and received, assistance from the FLA to gain access to Caribbean Basin factories it could not otherwise have entered. WRC executive director Scott Nova repeatedly reminds audiences that the two forms of monitoring can coexist. While the FLA monitors have the access and resources required for frequent and repeated visits to factories, the WRC can respond to workers' complaints in specific cases, offering a more independent and transparent process to workers' efforts to express their grievances (Scott Nova interview, 2004).

The debate over monitoring strategies has been widely discussed elsewhere (Esbenshade 2004; Featherstone and United Students Against Sweatshops 2002; Rodríguez-Garavito 2007; Ross 2004). Rather than rehearse the details of that discussion, I want to note three points of comparison between the Central American apparel campaigns, the Sullivan Principles debate, and the Rugmark process. First, in all three cases, monitoring and transnational regulation stemmed from consumer pressure mobilized through major institutions, not from individual consumer choices. Second, concerns over labor issues were in each case reframed as human rights concerns. Finally, a key difference between the cases demands attention. In Central America, preexisting dense networks of personal ties between transnational and local activists gave a different impetus to debates about workplace monitoring, in part because transnational activists had easy access to information about local conditions. In Central America, transnational activists built on preexisting relationships involving mutual trust and accumulated local knowledge. If in the two other cases consumer concerns tended to revolve around issues and concerns that were more global than local, the transnational discussion around Central American monitoring reflected far more direct knowledge of and engagement in local issues. Once institutional pressures were mobilized, consumer campaigns were guided by activists who understood local issues far more clearly than was the case in either the Sullivan Principles or Rugmark case; this difference, I suggest, was crucial in explaining the relative success of the transnational campaigns.

In all three cases, pressures were clearly mobilized through constituencies brought together in institutional settings rather than through individual consumer choice. In the 1990s, student activists focused on garments bearing university logos and asked university administrations to refuse to allow the university logo to appear on products made in sweatshops; just as anti-apartheid activists focused on institutional

investors, campus-based activists emphasized university-based constituencies and university-wide purchasing power.

The strategy emerged almost haphazardly in the mid-1990s; in an
early protest, student activists focused on The Gap, a national clothing
retail chain aimed specifically at the college-age market. Accounts of
teenage Central Americans working long hours for low wages were
widely disseminated; in 1996 Gap agreed to fund human rights monitors in El Salvador to investigate conditions in its subcontractors' plants
(Krupat 1997). Realizing that students offered a potent source of pressure, labor activists began to organize campus-based campaigns.

The National Labor Committee, now moving away somewhat from
its unionist origins, proved especially adept at mobilizing student audiences, bringing young Central American workers on speaking tours
and appealing to audiences of college students to show their concern
(Battista 2002; Ross 2003). Beginning at Duke University in 1999, student activists—often working with unionists—launched campus demon-
strations, protests, and sit-ins to demand that their universities adopt
codes of conduct. As a corollary, student activists insisted that their universities support the Workers' Rights Consortium, since without monitoring that was explicitly independent of corporate control, voluntary
codes of conduct were "just pieces of paper" (Featherstone and United
Students Against Sweatshops 2002, 13).

Like other transnational campaigns, campus activists tended to emphasize grievances related to physical and moral vulnerabilities rather
than collective bargaining rights. Many individual activists—including
leading figures from the National Labor Committee—had participated
in human rights groups around Central American issues, and they often drew on the same repertoire of images and tactics. Labor activists
publicized the low wages of apparel workers with vivid illustrations: a
video showing a U.S. embassy staff person describing El Salvador's
union-free export-processing zones, or a photograph of a factory
worker's pay stub, reflecting the pittance paid to make expensive
sports shoes. Like the human rights movement, activists gave specific
names to the corporate entities involved and to the victims of labor
abuses, illustrating their claims about exploitation with individual stories that tugged at their audiences' heartstrings.

Many campaigns stressed the presence of underage workers in the
maquilas rather than the equally common practices of blacklisting
union activists or delaying wages and denying severance pay. Underage workers were frequently brought on speaking tours across American campuses that stressed their vulnerability and exploitation. Discussions of working conditions often stressed the vulnerability of women
workers, who described sexual harassment and supervisors who
forced them to take contraception rather than fulfill their legal obliga-

tions regarding maternity leave, or who forced mothers to stay long hours at work, neglecting their children. Ethel Brooks's (2003, 79–82) general comment about transnational campaigns around sweatshops is perhaps more true for Central America than for anywhere else: "Tactics have relied upon the circulation of stories of abuses, visions of factories, and women's bodies. . . . Garment workers and sweatshops have become part of a circulation of signs and symbols, of virtual factories and perpetual victimhood."

While an emphasis on victimization may be common to all transnational appeals, another kind of reframing has marked most of the successful transnational mobilizations in Central America. Although few transnational activists willingly acknowledge the trend, virtually all of the labor disputes that have gained international notoriety in Central American apparel plants involve Asian employers and Central American workers. In Guatemala, at least, most activists acknowledge that workplace disputes become far more contentious when they are magnified by differences of language, workplace culture, and nationalist sentiment.

This pattern demands some attention. In her careful study of Taiwanese factories in southern Africa, Gillian Hart (2002) points out that foreign investment can alter gender dynamics at work, adding racial overtones and undermining empathy. In Taiwan, she suggests, the fact that managers may view coethnic workers as potential daughters, mothers, or wives contributes to a paternalistic workplace culture. In southern Africa, by contrast, racial and cultural differences can undermine the common understanding and human sympathies that might otherwise inflect relationships at work. Conversely, she suggests, African workers may view Taiwanese managers as the foreign "other," and the resulting lack of trust and miscommunication can compound ordinary workplace tensions.

Certainly, some of the East Asian industrialists Hart interviewed had learned to communicate and sympathize with their African employees, but, she writes,

> the majority of Taiwanese industrialists, who had come from a setting in which negotiations with women workers are conducted in the idiom of kinship and family, constructed African women as so different that they had no means at all of invoking and deploying these idioms. The anger and resentment that African women experienced is captured in the phrase I heard a number of times—namely their sense of "being treated just like animals." (Hart 2002, 191)

Similar dynamics are almost certainly at work in Central America's export-processing zones. Indeed, the complaint that employers refuse to recognize workers' basic human dignity—a complaint that may reflect cultural differences and linguistic misunderstandings as well as social difference—underlies many of the workplace conflicts that have attracted international attention (Anner 2000; Armbruster-Sandoval 2003; Frundt 1999; Jessup and Gordon 2000; Juárez Núñez 2002; Murillo and Schrank 2005; Stillerman 2003; Williams 2003).

In Central America, local and foreign employers all face pressures to cut costs and increase efficiency. Competitive pressures require subcontractors to cut costs, to increase production, and to improve quality to meet the requirements of large brand names and retailers. Undoubtedly, local Central American entrepreneurs rely on many of the same tactics that have provoked conflict in foreign-owned maquilas, from forced overtime to abusive behavior on the shop floor. Yet as Nancy Plankey-Videla (2004) notes in her insightful ethnography of a strike at a Mexican-owned subcontractor near Cuernavaca, Mexico, managers at locally owned plants may be able to deploy slightly different discursive tactics than foreign owners. Plankey-Videla observed Mexican managers asking Mexican workers to identify with their efforts, appealing to a sense of community and for support in a nationalist project. Conversely, it seems possible that local activists are more willing to target foreign employers, responding to cultural differences while minimizing local complaints about the danger of undermining long-term economic growth.

As in both the other cases described in this book, then, transnational campaigns in Guatemala tended to define issues as much in terms of their appeal to broad audiences as in terms of local concerns. But in one important respect, Guatemala's experiences differ dramatically from the way transnational campaigns elsewhere have mobilized global support. American involvement in Central America left a legacy of broad, dense contacts across borders, as well as bilingual activists and easy communication within the network. In contrast to South Africa, where most anti-apartheid activists had been refused any permission to visit, or to India, where few global child labor campaigners had long-standing ties, many labor activists were already deeply immersed in Central American work. As they took up labor issues there, transnational activists found it much easier to get information and access. Through their long histories in Central American support work, leading anti-sweatshop activists in the United States were familiar with the region and trusted by local activists, and they often understood one another with no need for translation or interpretation.

The NLC's Charles Kernaghan explicitly acknowledged the importance of his own and others' human rights networks in describing his group's activities:

> Over the years, NLC had built up deep contacts on the ground in Central
> America. They were precious, based on real trust and real faith. We were
> hooked up to labor groups, religious groups, women's organizations,
> students. We had local chapters all across the United States. It seemed
> nuts to throw it all away. (quoted in Krupat 1997, 71)

Many other anti-sweatshop activists had equally long-standing regional ties. Medea Benjamin, the energetic cofounder of the San Francisco–based Global Exchange, had long been involved in Central American support work, for example, and her knowledge of local conditions
clearly informed her anti-sweatshop activism. Similarly, the prominent
American activists Mark Anner and Jill Esbenshade both had strong
personal ties to Central America, including several years living in the
region.

Undoubtedly, these dense networks shaped the anti-sweatshop campaigns that emerged in the mid-1990s. In most cases of voluntary monitoring, codes of conduct are developed and monitored for use in global
markets, and transnational activists have little direct knowledge of or
engagement in local concerns. In contrast, the transnational networks
built up around Central America's apparel industry could draw on direct knowledge of local conditions and local actors as they tried to develop new strategies for protecting labor rights; discussions of monitoring were informed by personal relationships, and transnational
activists took pains to understand how local actors understood their
own situation.

Monitoring at Work

How has independent monitoring actually worked in Guatemala? In
contrast to both the Sullivan Principles and Rugmark, Guatemala's experiences with labor monitoring seem to offer real possibilities for improving conditions at work. Two aspects of Guatemala's experiences
stand in sharp contrast to the other cases. First, in Guatemala local activists viewed independent monitoring not as an alternative to oversight by state institutions but rather as a key part of trying to strengthen
and democratize them. In South Africa, Sullivan monitored compliance
with rules that directly contradicted local state policy; in India, Rugmark's inspections were offered as an alternative to inadequate state
enforcement. Both these examples reflect a sense of state failure, and
both schemes turned away from the state in the search for solutions. By
contrast, Guatemalan activists viewed civil society involvement in
monitoring as part of building a new "culture of compliance"—a
process they viewed as part of a larger effort to construct a democratic
state, not to bypass it. Second, and perhaps equally importantly, non-

governmental monitoring was developed in the context of already established ties between local and transnational activists, whose ongoing contacts helped sustain the possibility that "naming and shaming" violators would have a real impact on sales in the United States and elsewhere.

Guatemalan activists were among the first to organize local efforts to monitor corporate codes of conduct in the apparel industry. By the late 1990s, NGOs were already monitoring progress and providing information to international audiences about human rights violations. It was a very short step to monitoring corporate subcontractors, especially those located in the export-processing industrial areas around Guatemala City. The mission statement of one of the most visible of these new groups, the Commission for the Verification of Codes of Conduct (COVERCO), explicitly invokes broad concerns about constructing a "culture of compliance" as a counterweight to Guatemala's long tradition of elite impunity. In a situation where the Guatemalan state has been unable, or unwilling, to enforce its own labor code, COVERCO was founded in 1997 to strengthen enforcement.

COVERCO's founders included labor activists and human rights activists with long and respected records of involvement in Guatemala's struggles over the previous decades. Homero Fuentes, COVERCO's founding executive director, had been a well-known student and labor activist in the 1980s and 1990s, including a term as a visible leader in Guatemala's militant bankworkers' union. As COVERCO emerged, even unionists who distrusted the concept of independent monitoring expressed high regard for Fuentes' integrity and vision (José David Morales interview, 2003). Reflecting the importance of transnational ties in Guatemala, COVERCO's founding president, Dennis Smith, had worked through the 1980s as an American human rights activist living in Guatemala, with strong links to American church groups involved in Central American social justice campaigns. Other staff members included mainly activists who had participated in civil society monitoring efforts of the 1980s and 1990s, and who viewed their work for COVERCO as a logical extension of earlier efforts to bring peace and democracy to their country.

COVERCO explicitly links its decision to monitor and publicize labor abuses to the larger project of monitoring Guatemala's reconstruction. Its mission statement succinctly summarizes its rationale:

In 1996, Peace Accords put an end to thirty-six years of bloody civil war and removed a major obstacle to foreign investment in Guatemala. While many civil society organizations had emerged to advocate for peace and human rights, labor rights had still been largely unaddressed. It was clear, however, that Guatemala's growing export sectors and the working conditions in those sectors would play a major role in determining future social and economic conditions in Guatemala.

COVERCO was founded in 1997 by a group of labor, human rights and religious leaders in Guatemalan civil society who saw an urgent need to address this void. Their objective was clear: to work towards establishing the rule of law and a culture of compliance with labor rights in Guatemala. (COVERCO 2005)

Much of COVERCO's work has involved broad research projects on working conditions in specific sectors, including the coffee-growing sector, sugarcane plantations, and bananas (Schrage 2004). In the apparel industry, COVERCO has undertaken several monitoring projects in relation to specific factories, generally in Guatemala City's maquila zone, usually when a brand responds to transnational pressure to hold its local subcontractors accountable to a corporate code of conduct.

For factories, COVERCO's monitoring program is highly detailed, reflecting international "best practice" as well as sincere efforts by the organization to ensure transparency, integrity, and balance. The organization accepts monitoring projects only if they are scheduled to last a minimum of eighteen months, and it turns down requests for short-term "certifications" or seals of approval. The staff insists on repeated, frequent, unannounced visits by trained monitors, and that staff is accountable to COVERCO rather than to either employers or workers. Monitors visit factories in groups and meet with workers off-site to reduce intimidation or employer retaliation. Above all, COVERCO insists on transparency: its reports are posted on the Internet, for both corporate managers and transnational activists to see.

COVERCO's staff is highly respected, and even Guatemalan trade unionists who generally express deep reservations about independent monitoring—arguing that it can undermine workers' organizations by replacing workers' voices with those of NGO staff members—recognize that COVERCO's monitoring efforts are more consistent, more independent, and more transparent than those of most NGOs.

What ensures that independent monitors retain their integrity? To some extent, COVERCO's reputation stems from the people who work there—its ability to negotiate its independence may simply reflect the personal integrity of staff members, most of whom, like Fuentes, are committed individuals with long histories of involvement in labor struggles. But COVERCO also includes some distinctive features. First, COVERCO took pains to ensure its independence from corporate clients; although COVERCO was primarily funded during its first five years of existence through contracts with major exporters, it also received funding from various U.S. development agencies and from independent labor NGOs in the United States. Second, and perhaps even more importantly, COVERCO is closely linked to networks of transnational activists, who keep a close eye on labor conflicts in Guatemala. Frequent contacts and exchanges of information and persistent questioning from American unionists and transnational activists give COVERCO an unusual degree of independence from corporate clients through its ability to involve American labor groups in its discussions. Even critical Guatemalan unionists grudgingly acknowledge that COVERCO's efforts have helped mobilize outside pressure in support of workers' struggles (José David Morales interview, 2003).

COVERCO's staff members are open about the limits to their efforts. A small, relatively underfunded NGO, the group can monitor only a tiny handful of sites—hardly Guatemala's entire apparel industry. Given their insistence on repeated, unannounced visits and long-term monitoring programs, COVERCO's staff can only cover a handful of factories at a time. Further, COVERCO's monitors depend on brand-name companies' permission for access to factories: unless these companies insist, subcontractors need not admit COVERCO to the premises or show them their records. Despite COVERCO's efforts to avoid financial dependence on the major brands, its access to subcontractors' factories depends on the involvement of these companies—and when they insist that NGOs demonstrate evenhandedness and independence, embattled workers and unionists are likely to be disappointed, since the NGO cannot side with workers in ongoing workplace conflicts (José David Morales interview, 2003).

COVERCO's leaders are acutely aware that they will never be able to monitor every factory in Guatemala, not only because staff and funding are limited, but also because they will never have access to most factories. Large multinational companies that are concerned about protecting their brand's image may force subcontractors to accept voluntary monitoring, but most companies are less vulnerable to boycotts, and more cavalier. Equally seriously, if COVERCO discovers code violations at a subcontractor's factory, the NGO has few mechanisms other than persuasion to prevent its client—usually, the brand-name corporation—from simply ending its contract with the problematic subcontractor. On its own, the monitoring group cannot prevent the brand from simply walking away from a dispute. Although COVERCO has been careful to work only with brand-name representatives who seem genuinely committed to improving conditions in their Guatemala subcontractors' factories, COVERCO has no mechanism other than moral suasion to keep brands engaged in a problematic situation. In the worst-case scenario, a brand-name company's decision to abandon a subcontractor removes outside pressure and leaves militant workers without jobs—a possibility of which COVERCO staff members are all too aware (Homero Fuentes interview, 2005). Unless the Guatemalan state or international unions step in, the monitoring group has little power to intervene.

COVERCO's most widely discussed experience of factory monitoring reveals both the strengths of its approach and the limits of independent monitoring. In 2003 workers at two closely related, Korean-owned apparel factories managed to gain recognition for their union—one of only a small handful of recognized unions in Guatemala's maquila sector. With support from a multinational brand, COVERCO was closely involved in monitoring the subcontractor, and the NGO's staff persuaded the multinational brand to intervene repeatedly. But the workplace situation was tense. Although the unionized workers clearly looked to COVERCO's representatives for protection, it was often difficult for the monitors to be sure how best to proceed—especially when some of the workers' claims involved events outside the workplace, such as attacks on a worker's family members by masked men (ChoiSim/Simatex workers collective interview, 2003).

COVERCO's leadership faced a difficult dilemma: repeated violations of the multinational's code could result in a termination of the factory contract, perhaps pushing the subcontractor to file for bankruptcy. Guatemalan law limits unions to individual enterprises, so if the factory filed for bankruptcy, the workers' union would be effectively decertified. Even if the factory were to reopen under a new name, workers would be fired, and the organizing drive would have to begin all over again—this time almost certainly without COVERCO's monitors in attendance (ChoiSim/Simatex workers collective interviews, 2003).

In this case, however, COVERCO found an informal alternative: by directing transnational activists' attention to the situation, COVERCO helped stimulate an international campaign involving transnational activist networks in Washington and Geneva. When these larger networks, including the international clothing workers union, focused on the situation, the Guatemalan government was embarrassed to the point where the Ministry of Trade threatened to withdraw the subcontractor's export license—effectively using the state's control over market access to enforce compliance (Rodríguez-Garavito 2005a).

In contrast to most transnational campaigns, international pressure in this case focused on the subcontractor, not the brand, and it involved threats about market access made by the exporting state rather than the importing one. The strategy was remarkably effective: three years later, the ChoiSim union was still in existence, one of the longest-surviving maquila workers' unions in Central America.

But the ChoiSim saga also illustrates what is perhaps COVERCO's most serious constraint. As a private NGO, COVERCO can monitor factories only when the employer grants permission, which usually comes when a multinational brand insists on compliance. But most companies are less concerned about image, and most brands do not seek out the most reliable monitors. In early 2005, a representative of Guatemala's business federation pointed to broad variation in the way American corporations view labor rights, attributing this variation to companies' views of their customers and to the threat that scandal might reduce their market share. Companies aimed at American students, like The Gap, may want to demonstrate good citizenship, but companies that aim at more price-conscious consumers—say, Wal-Mart—are less likely to care. From the perspective of the company—for which the important variable is the target market, not conditions at the workplace—a privatized, voluntary system of codes of conduct and monitoring allows it to set its own "comfort level" in terms of monitoring (Guido Richi interview, 2005).

This perspective is clearly reflected in the proliferation of monitoring options for Guatemala's employers, which can choose the level of monitoring that suits their needs. Just as Indian carpet manufacturers have developed less stringent alternatives to Rugmark's monitoring teams, apparel manufacturers in Guatemala have generally *not* chosen COVERCO to monitor subcontractors. Instead, the apparel industry's organizing council, VESTEX, publishes its own code of conduct (in Korean, English, and Spanish) and has created a new dispute resolution center—alternatives both to the traditional labor courts and to a separate new dispute resolution center created by the Ministry of Labor with funding from USAID.

In this context—where Guatemala's business associations continue to reject labor law reform and companies can choose the code of conduct and the kind of monitoring they want to accept—independent monitoring acts as a temporary substitute rather than an alternative to state enforcement of labor laws. Recognizing the limits of private enforcement, therefore, COVERCO has participated energetically in several training programs for Ministry of Labor inspectors, drawing on its monitoring experiences to strengthen the state inspectorate (Homero Fuentes interview, 2006; Rodríguez-Garavito 2007). As long as Guatemala fails to pass or implement labor laws to protect its citizens or to allocate adequate resources for inspection and enforcement, COVERCO views its monitoring efforts as a stopgap measure. But COVERCO clearly acknowledges the limits of its efforts, much like the Indian activists concerned with child labor; COVERCO insists that, in the end, the best way to protect workers would be by strengthening state enforcement of a national labor code.

Conclusion

Independent monitoring in Guatemala must be viewed against the backdrop of the country's painful history. In the aftermath of a long civil war, monitoring emerged as local activists sought to reconstruct their society's "culture of impunity" as part of a larger effort to reconstruct the relationship between state and citizens. In contrast to those who view independent monitoring as a step toward stateless regulation, COVERCO's staff view their efforts as helping to build a local state, not to replace it. While it certainly engages in transnational campaigns—working with transnational groups, pressing corporate brands to gain access to local factories, publicizing information on the Internet—COVERCO's main goals are nevertheless local, focused on strengthening state capacity to intervene on behalf of vulnerable citizens at work.

This focus on local state-building does not diminish the contribution of dense transnational network ties. But it is important to note that in Guatemala's case transnational networks are unusually responsive to local concerns. First, frequent contact and trust have given most foreign activists great sympathy for, and understanding of, local concerns. Second, local activists are more sympathetic to transnational efforts; based on their experiences in human rights campaigns during the civil war, local labor activists view foreign pressure as a viable strategy for engaging the Guatemalan state. The region's painful history has created strong personal relationships and trust, while activists' ability to share information and perspectives across borders also gives unusual depth to transnational discussions.

But as COVERCO staff members are the first to acknowledge, independent monitoring has a limited reach when the only pressure involved is the threat of consumer boycotts. A voluntary system gives corporations wide latitude. As codes and monitors proliferate in Guatemala, companies can choose the level of monitoring that their customers demand—and no independent monitor, however transparent and honest, can prevent the construction of monitoring schemes that offer corporate cover rather than compliance.

As I argue in the next chapter, COVERCO's clear understanding of the limitations of privatized, voluntary codes underscores a deafening silence in discussions about stateless regulation. Instead of seeing independent monitoring as an effort to bypass the state or unions or to create a global regulatory process, labor activists in Guatemala tend to see workplace monitoring in terms of a small building block, part of the effort to construct a democratic Guatemala. Ironically, COVERCO's monitoring efforts are aimed not at creating new processes but at building a society in which voluntary regulatory schemes will become irrelevant.

When the Guatemalan state can provide trained labor inspectors with adequate resources and enforcement mechanisms to protect workers and citizens, creating the kind of atmosphere that allows workers to represent themselves through unions and collective bargaining processes, NGOs will be able to turn their attention away from monitoring workplaces to monitoring how well democratic institutions of governance protect Guatemalan citizens.

═ Chapter 6 ═

Citizenship at Work

To allow the market mechanism to be the sole director of the fate of human beings and their natural environment . . . would result in the demolition of society. . . . No society could stand the effects of such a system . . . unless its human and natural substance as well as its business organization was protected from the ravages of this satanic mill.

Karl Polanyi (1944/2001)

This study began with some rather straightforward questions. What are the characteristics of successful consumer-based campaigns? How have transnational activists managed to persuade corporations to accede to the independent monitoring of workplace codes of conduct, and what has been their impact? By comparing widely cited transnational interventions, I sought to discover some common characteristics that would help explain the success of some of these campaigns. How do activists persuade corporations to cooperate? What kinds of issues attract international audiences? What kinds of campaigns prompt companies to try to prove they are "good corporate citizens" and submit to independent monitors?

Despite important differences, similar patterns emerged—from the organization of consumer pressures to the way issues have been framed to the ways in which threats of market closure push global brands to accede to monitoring. But the comparison of these "successful" examples raises other questions. Thus, after summarizing the common patterns that seem to help explain relative success of campaigns, I go on to discuss common features of the monitoring schemes themselves, looking at the promise and limitations of "stateless regulation." While transnational campaigns have been successful in making global consumers aware of the human costs of cheap labor, even the most widely praised monitoring schemes are plagued by significant limitations—limitations that may be inherent in the very structure of stateless enforcement mechanisms.

In the concluding section, I turn to the implications of these findings. What lessons do they hold for transnational strategies to improve workers' lives? If cost-cutting pressures push corporations into a race to the bottom, what kinds of transnational advocacy might counterbalance those pressures so as to strengthen states' willingness and ability to intercede and protect citizen-workers from the "ravages of this satanic mill"? Transnational campaigns have generally asked corporations to support new monitoring schemes, bypassing inadequate state enforcement; given the limitations inherent in privatized voluntary monitoring schemes, however, I suggest that transnational campaigns might create more lasting protections for citizens at work if they reconceptualize their targets, seeking instead to strengthen democratic states and their capacity to enforce national labor laws.

Organizing Consumer Pressure

The three transnational labor campaigns discussed in this book display some striking similarities. First, there are obvious parallels in patterns of consumer mobilization. In each case, successful consumer pressure was organized through institutions rather than through individual purchases. Although many transnational campaigns invoke the threat that individual consumers will boycott products, the empirical evidence is instructive: each of these cases successfully attracted corporate attention when activists backed demands for "good corporate citizenship" with institutional pressure, either pressure for new laws blocking products from lucrative markets or pressure in terms of institutional purchases. The Sullivan Principles, of course, relied most heavily on institutional investors—individual shareholders were never even asked to follow ethical guidelines—but both the Rugmark system and the apparel industry monitoring processes are also the result of university and church involvement in global trade debates.

Groups and institutions—universities, churches, even municipal buying programs—appear to have been far more effective than an individual's "silent choice, made alone, in the aisle of a crowded supermarket" (Jasper 1997, 264). Social movement theorists suggest that individuals respond to minor grievances experienced collectively more easily than they are able to act on more serious grievances experienced in isolation (Piven and Cloward 1977), and perhaps a similar dynamic is at play in institutional consumption choices. Perhaps it is easier for participants brought together in a large institution to create a collective identity as consumers and to develop a common sense of moral accountability. More immediately, however, companies and politicians certainly respond faster to aggregated demands; large purchasers can have an immediate impact on corporate profits, and institutional decisions to boycott companies attract more publicity. When the moral concerns of activists are magnified by the purchasing power of large institutional buyers or investors, and when large institutions publicly reject a company's ethical stance, corporations are far more likely to agree to accede to new regulatory demands.

Framing Issues to Mobilize Global Support

What kinds of issues mobilize institutional pressures on corporate headquarters, creating that sense of moral accountability that lies at the heart of consumer-based campaigns? In each of these cases, transnational campaigns focused less on workplace violations than on much larger patterns of human rights concerns—appealing to global audiences on basic issues of human dignity and worth, underscoring the physical violence, repression, and discrimination that prevailed in the systems by which companies were profiting. Apartheid in South Africa, child labor in India, or Guatemala's "culture of impunity"—in each of these cases transnational networks argued that companies were complicit in degrading workers' human rights at the broadest and most visible level. Activists stressed issues that could be presented in stark terms—racist oppression, exploitation of children, legacies of human rights violations and repression—thereby infusing the daily minutiae of labor grievances with the moral weight of universal concerns.

Of course, the relative success of these examples may reflect how corporate executives respond to appeals rather than activists' reframing. Perhaps transnational appeals based on human rights violations are more successful because corporate executives are more likely to be moved by activists' appeals when they involve the protection of innocent victims from egregious abuse. Accustomed as they may be to rationalizing low wages or cost-cutting, corporate directors may find it more difficult to reconcile human rights violations with their own moral consciences when the specific violations cry out for a moral response.

Yet whatever the explanation, the similarity in framing begs the question: In reframing local issues, do transnational appeals disempower local voices? If local activists seek transnational support, can they insist on local priorities rather than stressing grievances that violate universal norms and invoke fundamental human rights, the protection of vulnerable victims, or basic human dignity? As the Sullivan Principles' confusion over racial identity illustrates, there is always the danger that local issues will be mistranslated; similarly, Indian activists fear that Rugmark's focus on export industries undermines their efforts to push government officials to improve conditions for all Indian children.

In Guatemala, where even government officials sometimes describe external campaigns as necessary to push the government to enforce labor law, tensions between local unionists and NGO organizers reflect profound concerns about NGOs, delicately poised between national and transnational agendas. Global codes of conduct may reflect universal standards, but do they reflect the priorities of local workers? Do they strengthen channels of communication at work? Do they protect workers from victimization by abusive employers? Most transnational activists recognize the pitfalls inherent in stressing victimization over voice and the danger that global codes will reinterpret local priorities, yet as trade unionists in each of these cases insist, even well-intentioned transnational networks find it difficult simultaneously to respond to local workers' concerns and to mobilize the kind of global support that will get the attention of global brands.

Building Trust

Perhaps the most striking difference between these three cases lies in the extent to which local and global activists responded to one another and in the way transnational campaigns responded to, and reflected, concerns articulated by local activists. Anti-apartheid activists generally dismissed Sullivan's monitoring process as "corporate camouflage," and Indian child labor activists were clearly divided over Rugmark's efforts. South Africa under apartheid illustrates the dangers of extreme distance: South African visa policies meant that Sullivan monitors operated without any oversight by skeptical transnational activists, while local activists dismissed the code of conduct as one that more clearly reflected American concerns—and American racial ideologies—than those of local South African workers. The Rugmark activist networks involved closer ties and more consistent contact, and efforts to police the carpet industry's use of children were prompted by local activists, not outside corporate directors. However, Rugmark's efforts to design a voluntary code for the carpet industry were marked by strong disagreements: local activists worried that a narrow focus on carpets might distract from larger efforts to change Indian national policy toward poor and lower-caste children. Personality conflicts played some role in these disagreements, but the underlying tension seems to have revolved around the way local activists prioritized appeals to global audiences compared to claims against the national state.

In contrast to both these examples, Central American campaigns built on preexisting relationships across borders. Central American activists had already turned to international pressure as a way to influence local dynamics, and transnational activists were already familiar with local concerns. Over the years of Central America's wars, frequent contact had laid some basis for trust and friendship. Consistent contact and dense ties permit easy discussion within networks; local activists play a much larger role in defining issues, articulating local concerns, and helping interpret and disseminate information. Frequent visits and cross-border contacts help transnational activists better understand the local context and the challenges facing monitors on the ground—especially problems of access, funding, and accountability.

Constraints on Independent Monitors

In reality, how well does independent monitoring work? In each of the cases described in this book, three constraints loomed large: problems of access, resources, and accountability persistently impeded monitors' ability to offer reliable or consistent information about workplace conditions or to share that information with transnational networks and consumers. Even in cases where transnational activists and monitors worked together closely enough to avoid some of the distrust that has plagued many monitoring schemes, NGO monitors recognized that their ability to deploy international pressure to intervene in specific work sites remained sharply limited—by factors that may be inherent to stateless monitoring efforts.

Access presents the most glaring problem for all NGOs. The ability to disseminate credible information about specific work sites requires access to work sites, but independent monitors can only enter premises when employers grant them permission. State inspectors, of course, can legally insist on access, but independent monitors cannot pry open doors that have been shut in their faces.

The problem of gaining access to problematic work sites plagues every voluntary monitoring scheme, limiting the kind of evidence that monitors can request and the way visits are scheduled and carried out. Sullivan's monitors simply relied on evidence provided by companies; Rugmark's monitors visited only registered looms and, as a result, often saw only those carpets that exporters believed might need the label. Even COVERCO could gain access to subcontractors' factories only when brand-name companies were willing to make that access a condition of the contract. If a local subcontractor chose to slam the door, COVERCO had to appeal to the brand for help—and if the brand decided to end its contract, either because of frustration over bad publicity or because the product didn't meet its requirements, COVERCO had no mechanisms to help workers at all.

Financial constraints posed another persistent problem to each of the monitoring schemes discussed in this book. NGOs everywhere are perennially short of funds, trained staff, and other resources; the typical structure of an activist organization does not include a membership base or compulsory funding system for salaries or training. When NGOs decide to embark on consistent monitoring programs, their first challenge is inevitably to locate a funding source; not coincidentally, each of the "successful" examples of monitoring described in this book involved some effort to tax employers through a voluntary levy.

Asking companies to fund the monitoring systems that are supposed to report workplace violations to international consumer groups creates real dilemmas; as long as companies can choose their own labor codes and their own monitors, small, underfunded NGOs will be tempted to avoid conflictual situations. In voluntary systems, where employers can seek out and fund monitors whose reports are less stringent, the temptations are obvious. Not coincidentally, in the three cases discussed in this book, there was a clear correlation between financial dependence and tensions with local activists who questioned monitors' integrity; the fact that COVERCO continues to win grudging respect from local unionists may well be tied to its success in attracting some outside funding, beyond corporate levies.

But even COVERCO, whose integrity is widely respected, faces persistent questions about accountability and representation. Local monitors may see their work as aiding workers, but few monitoring groups have found it easy to include workers in strategic decisions. None of the groups described in this book created mechanisms through which workers could hold monitors accountable for errors or misjudgments or challenge monitors' findings. The dilemma may be inherent in the very concept of "independent monitoring": if monitoring groups want to maintain their credibility in the eyes of employers, they may find they have no choice but to distance themselves from workers and their representatives. Monitoring groups like COVERCO may take great pains to ensure that workers can speak freely to monitors, but if NGOs become too responsive to workers' local concerns, employers are likely to see them as biased and untrustworthy.

Importantly, it is precisely the stateless and voluntary nature of these independent monitoring programs that underlies each of these persistent constraints. Because NGOs cannot insist on access to the workplace, companies can choose their monitors. Because NGOs cannot demand funds, they are dependent on voluntary funding sources—and often end up asking for funding from the very companies they expect to monitor. That dependence, in turn, may make NGOs reluctant to appeal for consumer pressure—since, of course, the threat of boycotts may prompt brand name companies to break their contacts with both sub-contractors and monitors, moving production to less-fraught sites as a way to end consumer pressure. And because NGOs need to demonstrate their independence to the companies they hope to inspect, they often avoid including workers' representatives in their decisionmaking process. The limits to independent monitoring are painfully obvious to everyone involved on the ground: even moderately successful monitoring programs spawn pale imitators, and companies threatened by global consumer pressure can simply seek weaker monitors. Instead of an upwardly ratcheting spiral, in which companies seek to meet ever-more-stringent standards in a globally competitive context, voluntary regulation seems far more likely to produce a race to the bottom in monitoring as well as in production. As codes and monitoring schemes proliferate, even well-intentioned global consumers are likely to be confused. Under a voluntary system, it is employers, not workers, who have choices. When monitoring groups appear too friendly to workers, or too willing to report minor violations, employers can fund a different monitoring group—a more "independent" NGO—and global audiences are unlikely to spot the difference.

Expanding Citizenship

A paradox lurks at the heart of independent monitoring schemes. Most activists, policymakers, and scholars involved in global discussions agree that the best protections for labor rights would be those that empower workers, allowing them to demand compliance with locally negotiated work rules, either in the form of democratically designed national labor laws or locally negotiated contracts. Yet most transnational campaigns mobilize global pressure against corporations, deploying consumer pressure to enforce companies' compliance with universal standards—not to strengthen workers' voices.

Campaigns that target employers—the brand-name companies vulnerable to "naming and shaming" by ethical consumers—rarely consider whether their strategies contribute to expanding citizenship or enable workers to articulate their grievances or concerns. Many transnational campaigns have been remarkably effective in publicizing the conditions in which people in far-off communities live and work and in persuading companies to acknowledge some responsibility for the conditions in which their products are made; campaigns that alert global audiences to abusive working conditions arouse public concern about the "ravages of the satanic mill." But the impact of voluntary codes of conduct on activists' real goal—empowering workers and stopping competition from eroding working conditions everywhere—may be more questionable.

In this concluding section, I return to the comparison sketched in chapter 2 between human rights campaigns and labor strategies to suggest that an alternative strategy would focus on how best to change the behavior of states toward corporations rather than the behavior of corporations toward sub-contractors. Rather than working within the logic of corporate globalization, treating companies as the only powerful actors, perhaps transnational campaigns could follow Polanyi's approach: Could transnational social movements press states across borders to protect the labor rights of their own citizens, even in a world of global competition? Could transnational campaigns act as a counterweight to threats of capital flight and provide support for labor law enforcement instead of accepting a race to the bottom as inevitable?

States are, of course, central to the realities of labor activism. Like human rights campaigns, even campaigns called "stateless" involve states as well as corporate headquarters and NGOs. Corporations respond when powerful states threaten to close off market access—and transnational labor activists invoke those threats much as human rights activists have invoked powerful states' policy tools to promote human rights reforms around the world. Credible threats of state sanctions have been central in persuading companies to accept responsibility for improving working conditions—and even more important in persuading companies to submit to external monitoring.

But transnational labor activists often overlook states' centrality to the long-term enforcement of labor rights. Treating weak states as enemies rather than as potential allies, they tend to reify the extent to which global pressures have "thinned" national states. Ironically, by abandoning any hope that state regulatory action could be strengthened, transnational labor campaigns may further undermine states' potential to protect rights in the long run. Instead of trying to make do with voluntary schemes, perhaps transnational activists should focus their efforts on shoring up weak states, reinforcing national institutions rather than trying to replace them with even weaker NGOs. Could strategies be found that might strengthen states' capacity to inspect worksites for labor law violations, to insist that employers follow national labor codes, to enforce health and safety rules, or even to protect worker-citizens who try to negotiate with employers on their own behalf?

Human rights campaigns have tended to be less cavalier about the role of the state, and about the potential capacity of state mechanisms for protecting individuals over the long run. Of course human rights campaigns target local states, since local states are generally either perpetrators or enablers of abuse. Much as local activists tend to frame labor issues in terms of state failure, offering evidence of state complicity in labor abuse, human rights campaigns frame abuse in terms of states' refusal or inability to protect vulnerable citizens. But human rights activists also seek to re-create state institutions and strengthen protections for civil rights—recognizing that the best long-term protection for human rights would be the creation of viable democratic institutions. Many local labor activists similarly insist that their most viable strategies involve strengthening government agencies' capacity to intervene at work. Human rights campaigns generally view stable democratic institutions as the best way to prevent future violations of citizens' human rights; similarly, while recognizing that their governments have often protected elite interests in the past, local labor activists describe democratic institutions—energetic national enforcement agencies, backed by law, provided with adequate resources to do their jobs, paid enough to prevent corruption and responsible to local communities— as the way to create more viable protections for workers in the long run.

In the long run, states offer more effective instruments for intervening at work than even well-intentioned NGOs. In contrast to voluntarist monitoring groups—even those backed by mobilized consumer campaigns—state inspectors can legally insist on access to the workplace and enforce compliance with standards defined by national law; they stand in a very different relation to workplaces and to employers, with legal sanctions backing their enforcement efforts. Labor analysts writing about industrialized countries regularly note that voluntarist regulatory systems work only when they are backed by threats of state enforcement to prevent "bad" employers from undercutting "good" ones (Braithwaite and Drahos 2000; Esbenshade 2004); conversely, reduced state protection of labor rights is widely considered a key factor in explaining declining union strength (Clawson 2003; Fantasia and Voss 2004; Milkman 2006). Campaigns demanding state enforcement of workplace standards often serve as a starting point for mobilizing broad support around labor issues, as workplace grievances become redefined as struggles around the character of citizenship and inclusion (Gordon 2005). In the cases described in this book, local activists rarely dismissed the potential power of states to help improve working conditions; instead, local activists generally described their long-term goals in terms of making states more protective of and responsive to the concerns of poor and vulnerable citizens. In South Africa under apartheid, anti-apartheid activists sought to replace the apartheid regime with a democratic state; in India and Guatemala local activists viewed state failures to protect workers as a facet of the larger state failure to protect poor and vulnerable citizens. As the Indian labor journalist John P. John (quoted in Labour File 2005) succinctly puts it, "Labor rights are an integral part of Indian democracy. If you take away that, you are taking away a part of . . . democracy."

Strategies aimed at strengthening state institutions—especially those that train inspectors who can carry out regular inspections and enforce national labor law through a legal industrial relations framework—would echo the historical experience, described by Polanyi and others, of communities mobilizing to demand state intervention to protect human beings from brutal employers or abuse driven by competitive market pressures. Throughout the history of industrial capitalism, social movements and political reformers have turned to national states to enact and enforce pragmatic regulations, including trade rules, factory legislation, and programs for the poor. Polanyi (1944/2001, 79–80) writes that, "while on the one hand markets spread all over the face of the globe . . . on the other hand a network of measures and policies was integrated into powerful institutions designed to . . . resist the pernicious effects of a market-controlled economy. Society protected itself against the perils inherent in a self-regulating market system."

Skeptics point to the problems that plague existing national labor relations programs, especially underfunded and weak labor departments in which corruption is rampant or where employers can refuse to permit inspectors on sites without fear of consequences. But can these institutions be strengthened by simply ignoring them? Could transnational campaigns instead seek to strengthen the capacity of state institutions to protect workers' rights by providing training and resources and bringing pressure to bear on relevant state actors? Where state enforcement is weak, voluntary systems are likely to be even weaker, and even the most successful transnational campaigns are unlikely to prevent abuse. By contrast, when states take clear action against abusive employers, their impact can be immediate—as, for example, when foreign pressure persuaded the Guatemalan Ministry of Exports to step in to protect a fragile union in the ChoiSim factory, as described in chapter 1.

On their own, labor inspectors cannot end abuses at work. But energetic national labor inspectors can make a real difference, even in the context of global competition. In post-apartheid South Africa, for example, new labor legislation and an active labor inspectorate have certainly changed the status of labor rights, and most employers realize that failure to meet their legal obligations to workers will incur real penalties. Even when governments are explicitly committed to attracting investors by offering a cheap and reliable labor supply, there is ample evidence that energetic government officials can sometimes force foreign investors to respect local laws and workers' dignity. Ching Kwan Lee (1998, 60–61), in her rich ethnography of an export-processing zone in southern China, is skeptical about the Chinese state, but nevertheless describes local labor officials responding to workers' complaints and forcing foreign-owned companies to end abusive practices. Similarly, Dara O'Rourke (2004) suggests that in Vietnam, when state inspectors respond to workers' and communities' complaints, they can force foreign employers to comply with national laws.

Could transnational pressures be deployed to strengthen state intervention and shore up the capacity and commitment of local labor departments? In Guatemala, COVERCO's efforts clearly point in this direction. Drawing support from dense transnational networks and bringing pressure to bear on Guatemalan officials however it can, COVERCO seeks to strengthen institutional capacity and push government officials to respect and protect labor rights. Could transnational pressure strengthen the capacity and will of government agencies?

Andrew Schrank (2006) writes that the government of the Dominican Republic responded to external pressure by quietly enacting new labor laws, funding and training a more effective labor inspectorate, and providing these inspectors with new powers. Backed by a labor minister who points to outside pressure when employers complain about the costs, that new inspectorate has begun to intervene in previously unregulated workplaces, enforcing labor laws even in export-processing zones once notorious for waiving the country's basic legal standards (see also Jessup and Gordon 2000; Piore and Schrank 2006).

The Dominican Republic's apparent new commitment to enforcing national law suggests that transnational campaigns focused on states rather than brands could prompt policymakers to view the protection of citizens as an important goal, counterbalancing the desire to attract new investors at any cost. In contrast to the vision embodied in stateless regulatory schemes, government labor inspectors can demand access to factories and insist on enforcing basic labor laws, and they are paid by the government rather than by the corporations they are expected to monitor. Schrank (2005) argues that the Dominican Republic's new labor inspectorate—with higher salaries meant to reduce the likelihood of corruption, better training so as to increase professional commitment to catching violators, hopes for promotion and potential career ladders within the inspectorate, and an oversight system that promises to remove incompetent or corrupt inspectors—could make a real difference, countering the global market-driven race to the bottom with state legislation and enforcement at work.

Clearly, strategies to build state capacity involve complicated choices. Polanyi's double movement was located primarily within borders, as national communities mobilized to demand regulatory action; external pressure on national policy must take more complicated and roundabout routes. Can transnational campaigns provide leverage and resources to policymakers trying to strengthen labor law enforcement? Perhaps activists, policymakers, and scholars should reconsider the widespread view that corporations are more vulnerable to global pressure than states. Instead of boycotting brands, transnational strategies might look for tactics to push governments to strengthen labor law enforcement.

Several campaigns in the late 1990s and early 2000s illustrate the possibilities of such strategies, although they also illustrate potential complications. In Sialkot, Pakistan, transnational campaigns raised the specter of global boycotts when children were found sewing soccer balls in cottage-based production; in response, global brand-names supported ILO teams working with government inspectors to shift all soccer-ball production into central work-sheds where government inspectors could check workers' ages. Similarly, when U.S. policymakers threatened to block imports from Bangladesh because children worked in its garment factories, Bangladesh invited the ILO to provide special inspectors to check for underage workers. Finally, global pressure persuaded the Cambodian government to enact new labor laws and invite the ILO to help create a factory inspectorate to monitor its fast-growing garment industry (Becker 2005).

To be sure, these cases also offer support for skeptics. In Pakistan, soccer-ball production has moved out of the Sialkot region, beyond the limited purview of the ILO-trained inspectorate, and children continue to sew soccer balls just outside the city (Global March 2006; Montero 2006; Nadvi and Kazmi 2001). In Bangladesh, ILO inspectors pay regular visits to apparel factories, but critics charge that the sole focus on underage workers allows other labor violations to go unnoticed (Brooks 2005). In Cambodia, the new labor inspectorate operates in a context of widespread corruption, and Cambodia's efforts to advertise "sweat-free" clothing have been met by raised eyebrows among activists familiar with working conditions there.

Despite these criticisms, these examples provide some support for the possibility that transnational campaigns might effectively put pressure on states to police working conditions rather than relying on corporate consciences and voluntary codes. By pushing states to enforce their own laws and helping to strengthen national capacity for workplace intervention, transnational campaigns could deploy global pressure to deepen, rather than thin, national state capacity.

That shift—from seeking to create stateless regulation to strengthening state enforcement—might open new space for workers to articulate their own concerns. Well-intentioned NGOs may listen carefully to workers, but the very structure of independent monitoring groups reduces the likelihood of accountability. Especially when they depend on corporate donors for funding and when they are monitoring compliance with a global code of conduct aimed to satisfy far-off consumers, NGOs find it difficult to give workers any real voice. By contrast, even in contexts where states are not particularly democratic or accountable, most governments offer some channels through which citizens can make claims or appeal decisions. Historical and contemporary evidence suggests that even authoritarian states can enforce limits on working hours, regulate working conditions, or make sure that employers pay minimum wages (Cook 2006). Could transnational campaigns push national governments to protect their citizens even in a world of global competition?

In marked contrast to stateless approaches, state-centered strategies hold out some promise—however tentative—that transnational campaigns might help expand democratic citizenship. Even in a globally integrated world, efforts to build state capacity might also help strengthen workers' voices at work. Again, there is some precedent for this approach. In his classic essay on citizenship, T. H. Marshall (1950/1992) argued that definitions of political citizenship first began to expand when states protected workers from employer retaliation, allowing workers to organize at work and to press their claims against both employers and national governments. Although Marshall's essay is widely cited today (Somers 2005), relatively few scholars note the key role that his account assigns to protective factory legislation. For Marshall, protective legislation enforced by active state inspectors served as a crucial first step—protected at work, citizens could mobilize to demand further state support in other arenas (Goldberg 2007).

Much as Polanyi suggested that social movements would call on states to regulate the relations between employers and citizens, constructing a more humane capitalism, Marshall argued that protection for workers' rights laid the foundation for political movements demanding social change and democratization beyond the factory. By the end of the nineteenth century, Marshall (1950/1992, 15–26) wrote, "the factory code had become one of the pillars in the edifice" of democratic participation, providing a framework within which workers could demand further protection and representation. Protective legislation at work, for Marshall, created space in which workers could organize to make further demands on the state, redefining and expanding the meaning of citizenship.

Since the early 1970s, transnational activists have focused their efforts on changing corporate attitudes, appealing to global consumers to demand that companies acknowledge corporate social responsibility for workers and communities. But transnational campaigns do not easily translate into expanded citizenship; the privatized regulatory schemes linked to voluntary codes of conduct seem limited in both execution and possibility. For activists involved in transnational campaigns around labor rights, raising broad public awareness of working conditions around the world is an obvious first step toward creating a global regulatory scheme, and transnational campaigns have gained some leverage—especially when mobilized consumer groups have worked together with importing states to raise a credible threat of market closure.

But instead of focusing that pressure on employers alone, perhaps transnational campaigns should shift their efforts to strengthening the institutions of democratic citizenship. Instead of working within the logic of global competition, could transnational campaigns work within the logic of citizenship? When transnational labor campaigns seek to strengthen workers' voices, creating channels for articulation and collective representation—rather than simply publicizing the worst kinds of abuses—they are in a better position to help construct new visions of citizenship, create new possibilities for voice and participation, and strengthen labor rights for workers across borders.

= Notes =

Chapter 2

1. Ironically, such productivity-based strategies may often weaken organized labor in the medium term by reducing unions' ability to build broad alliances outside the workplace. The language of competitiveness and productivity is a narrow one, undermining labor's ability to develop collective demands, collective identity, or collective action; it narrows labor's perspective by mirroring the logic of the market and emphasizing productivity over solidarity. Over the past century, labor movements have repeatedly been forced to recognize that while they claim to speak in the name of the working class, their members represent only a core of employed, often relatively privileged workers, not a larger working class whose jobs may be far more precarious. Historically, unions have managed the resultant tension—between representing the immediate interests of their members and representing the interests of all workers—by appealing to the state to protect labor rights, prevent employers from replacing militant workers with cheaper ones, and provide a social security net that benefits all citizens. Invoking citizenship rights and state involvement in the workplace, then, has been a recurrent theme in labor struggles for most of the past century. Where demands for full citizenship provided an inclusionary strategy through which unions could avoid narrowly representing members' interests, union strategies that narrow their membership base risk undermining support outside the workplace.

Chapter 3

1. An earlier version of this chapter appeared in *Politics and Society* (September 2003).

Chapter 5

1. Even the International Monetary Fund (IMF) acknowledged that Guatemala's government had failed to provide basic services for the country's rural, largely indigenous majority. In 1997, at a time when the IMF was asking most borrower governments to cut state expenditures, IMF executive director Michel Camdessus visited Guatemala specifically to ask for tax reforms, seeking to ensure that internal funding would be provided to support the targets for growth and social spending laid out in the accords—although, as Jonas (2000, 17) notes, Guatemala's business leaders continued to resist an increased tax burden.

═ References ═

Adams, Julia, Elisabeth Clemens, and Ann Shola Orloff, eds. 2005. *Remaking Modernity: Politics, History, and Sociology*. Durham, N.C.: Duke University Press.

Adler, Genn, and Eddie Webster, eds. 2000. *Trade Unions and Democratization in South Africa, 1985–1997*. New York: St. Martin's Press.

Agnivesh, Swami. 1999a. "A Critique of Selective Western Interventions and WTO." In *Against Child Labor: Indian and International Dimensions and Strategies*, edited by Klaus Voll. New Delhi: Mosaic Books.

———. 1999b. "Indian Child Labor: Historical-Contemporary Review and Worsening Civilizational Crisis." In *Against Child Labour: Indian and International Dimensions and Strategies*, edited by Klaus Voll. New Delhi: Mosaic Books.

Ali, Karamat. 1996. "Social Clauses and Workers in Pakistan." *New Political Economy* 1(2): 269–73.

Ally, Shireen. 2006. "'Maid' with Rights: The Contradictory Citizenship of Domestic Workers in Post-Apartheid South Africa." PhD diss., University of Wisconsin at Madison.

Alperson, Myra. 1995. *Foundations for a New Democracy: Corporate Social Investment in South Africa: How It Works, Why It Works, Who Makes It Work, and How It's Making a Difference*. Johannesburg: Ravan Press.

Alston, Phillip. 2006. "'Core Labor Standards' and the Transformation of the International Labor Rights Regime." In *Social Issues, Globalization and International Institutions*, edited by Virgina A. Leary and Daniel Warner. Boston, Mass.: Martinus Nuhoff Publications.

Amnesty International. 1987. *Guatemala: The Human Rights Record*. London: Amnesty International Publications.

Anner, Mark. 2000. "Local and Transnational Campaigns to End Sweatshop Practices." In *Transnational Cooperation Among Labor Unions*, edited by Michael Gordon and Lowell Turner. Ithaca, N.Y.: Cornell University/ILR Press.

Antony, Piush, and V. Gayathri. 2002. "Child Labor: A Perspective of Locale and Context." *Economic and Political Weekly* (December 28): 5186–9.

Ariès, Phillippe. 1962. *Centuries of Childhood*. Translated by Robert Baldick. New York: Vintage Books.

Armbruster-Sandoval, Ralph. 2003. "Globalization and Transnational Labor Organizing: The Honduran Maquiladora Industry and the Kimi Campaign." *Social Science History* 27(4): 551–76.

————. 2005. *Globalization and Cross-Border Solidarity in the Americas: The Anti-Sweatshop Movement and the Struggle for Social Justice.* New York: Routledge Press.

Arthurs, Harry. 2004. "Private Ordering and Workers' Rights in the Global Economy: Corporate Codes of Conduct as a Regime of Labor Market Regulation." In *Labor Law in an Era of Globalization: Transformative Practices and Possibilities*, edited by Joanne Conaghan, Richard Fischl, and Karl Klare. Oxford: Oxford University Press.

Ayres, Ian, and John Braithwaite. 1992. *Responsive Regulation: Transcending the Deregulation Debate.* Oxford: Oxford University Press.

Babb, Sarah L. 2001. *Managing Mexico: Economists from Nationalism to Neoliberalism.* Princeton, N.J.: Princeton University Press.

Bain, Carmen. 2006. "Standards for Whom? Standards for What? The Regulation of Agricultural Labor in Chile and Its Gendered Effects." Paper presented to the American Sociological Association Meetings. Montreal, Quebec, August 2006.

Bair, Jennifer, and Gary Gereffi. 2002. "NAFTA and the Apparel Commodity Chain: Corporate Strategies, Interfirm Networks, and Industrial Upgrading." In *Free Trade and Uneven Development: The North American Apparel Industry After NAFTA*, edited by Gary Gereffi, David Spener, and Jennifer Bair. Philadelphia, Pa.: Temple University Press.

Bandy, Joe, and Jennifer Bickham Mendez. 2003. "A Place of Their Own? Women Organizers in the Maquilas of Nicaragua and Mexico." *Mobilization: An International Journal* 8(2, June): 173–88.

Bandy, Joe, and Jackie Smith, editors. 2003. *Coalitions Across Borders: Transnational Protest and the Neoliberal Order.* Lanham, Md.: Rowman and Littlefield.

Baquele, Assefa, and Jo Boyden. 1988. "Child Labor: Problems, Policies, and Programs." In *Combating Child Labor*, edited by Assefa Baquele and Jo Boyden. Geneva: International Labor Organization.

Bartley, Tim. 2003. "Certifying Forests and Factories: States, Social Movements, and the Rise of Private Regulation in the Apparel and Forest Products Fields." *Politics and Society* 31(3, September): 433–64.

Basu, Kaushik. 2003. "International Labor Standards and Child Labor." In *Child Labor and the Right to Education in South Asia: Needs Versus Rights?* edited by Naila Kabeer, Geetha B. Namissan, and Ramya Subrahmanian. New Delhi: Sage Publications.

Battista, Andrew. 2002. "Unions and Cold War Foreign Policy in the 1980s: The National Labor Committee, the AFL-CIO, and Central America." *Diplomatic History* 26(3, Summer): 429–51.

Becker, Elizabeth. 2005. "Low Cost and Sweatshop Free." *New York Times*, May 12.

Beckman, Marc. 1999. "Success and Limitations of Social Labeling Against Child Labor in the Carpet Industry." In *Against Child Labor: Indian and International Dimensions and Strategies*, edited by Klaus Voll. New Delhi: Mosaic Books.

Bender, Daniel, and Richard Greenwald, editors. 2003. *Sweatshop USA: The American Sweatshop in Historical and Global Perspective.* New York: Routledge.

Bender, Thomas, editor. 1992. *The Anti-Slavery Debate: Capitalism and Abolition-*

ism as a Problem in Historical Interpretation. Berkeley, Calif.: University of California Press.

Bergquist, Charles. 1996. *Labor and the Course of American Democracy.* London: Verso Press.

Bernasek, Alexandra, and Richard C. Porter. 1990. *Private Pressure for Social Change in South Africa: The Impact of the Sullivan Principles.* Discussion paper 125. Ann Arbor, Mich.: University of Michigan, Center for Research on Economic Development (August).

Bhargava, Pramila. 2003. *The Elimination of Child Labour: Whose Responsibility?* New Delhi: Sage Publications.

Bhattacharyya, B., and L. Sahoo, editors. 1996a. *The Indian Carpet Industry: Evolving Concerns, Prospects, and Strategies.* New Delhi: Indian Institute of Foreign Trade/Global Business Press.

———. 1996b. *Carpet Industry: Prospects and Perspectives.* New Delhi: Indian Institute of Foreign Trade.

Bickham Mendez, Jennifer. 2005. *From the Revolution to the Maquiladoras: Gender, Labor, and Globalization in Nicaragua.* Durham, N.C.: Duke University Press.

Biersteker, Thomas J. 1995. "The 'Triumph' of Liberal Economic Ideas in the Developing World." In *Global Change, Regional Response: The New International Context of Development,* edited by Barbara Stallings. Cambridge: Cambridge University Press.

Bissell, Susan. 2003. "The Social Construction of Childhood: A Perspective from Bangladesh." In *Child Labor and the Right to Education in South Asia: Needs Versus Rights?* edited by Naila Kabeer, Geetha B. Namissan, and Ramya Subrahmanian. New Delhi: Sage Publications.

Blanpain, Roger, editor. 2000. *Multinational Enterprises and the Social Challenges of the Twenty-first Century: The ILO Declaration on Fundamental Principles at Work, Public and Private Corporate Codes of Conduct.* The Hague and Boston: Kluwer Law International.

Blashill, John. 1972. "Proper Role of U.S. Corporations in South Africa." *Fortune* (July): 49.

Blowfield, Mick. 1999. "Ethical Trade: A Review of Developments and Issues." *Third World Quarterly* 20(4, August): 753–70.

Bonacich, Edna, and Richard Appelbaum. 2000. *Behind the Label: Inequality in the Los Angeles Garment Industry.* Berkeley, Calif.: University of California Press.

Boris, Eileen. 2003. "Consumers of the World Unite! Campaigns Against Sweating, Past and Present." In *Sweatshop USA: The American Sweatshop in Historical and Global Perspective,* edited by Daniel Bender and Richard Greenwald. New York: Routledge Press.

Bose, Tarun. 1997. Untitled study of child labor and social labeling in the carpet industry. New Delhi: Center for Education and Communication.

Braithwaite, John. 2002. "Rewards and Regulation." *Journal of Law and Society* 29(1, March): 12–26.

Braithwaite, John, and Peter Drahos. 2000. *Global Business Regulation.* Cambridge: Cambridge University Press.

Brobowsky, David. n.d. "Creating a Global Public Policy Network in the Apparel Industry: The Apparel Industry Partnership." Case study for UN Vision

Project on Global Public Policy Networks. Accessed at www.globalpublic policy.net, January 18, 2007.

Bronfenbrenner, Kate, and Robert Hickey. 2004. "Changing to Organize: A National Assessment of Union Strategies." In *Rebuilding Labor: Organizing and Organizers in the New Union Movement*, edited by Ruth Milkman and Kim Voss. Ithaca, N.Y.: Cornell University/ILR Press.

Brooks, Ethel. 2003. "The Ideal Sweatshop: Transnational and Gender Protest." In *Sweatshop USA: The American Sweatshop in Historical and Global Perspective*, edited by Daniel Bender and Richard Greenwald. New York: Routledge Press.

———. 2005. "Transnational Campaigns Against Child Labor: The Garment Industry in Bangladesh." In *Coalitions Across Borders: Transnational Protest and the Neoliberal Order*, edited by Joe Bandy and Jackie Smith. Lanham, Md.: Rowman and Littlefield.

———. 2007. *Unraveling the Garment Industry: Transnational Organizing and Women's Work*. Minneapolis, Minn.: University of Minnesota Press.

Brown-Thomson, Karen. 2002. "Women's Rights Are Human Rights." In *Restructuring World Politics: Transnational Social Movements, Networks, and Norms*, edited by Sanjeev Khagram, James V. Riker, and Kathryn Sikkink. Minneapolis, Minn.: University of Minnesota Press.

Brysk, Alyson, and Gershon Shafir, eds. 2004. *People Out of Place*. New York: Routledge Press.

Bullert, B. J. 2000. "Progressive Public Relations, Sweatshops, and the Net." *Political Communication* 17: 403–7.

Burra, Neera. 2003. "Rights Versus Needs: Is It in the 'Best Interest of the Child'?" In *Child Labor and the Right to Education in South Asia: Needs Versus Rights?* edited by Naila Kabeer, Geetha B. Namissan, and Ramya Subrahmanian. New Delhi: Sage Publications.

Candland, Chris, and Rudra Sil. 2001. "The Politics of Labor in Late-Industrializing and Post-Socialist Economies: New Challenges in a Global Age." In *The Politics of Labor in a Global Age*, edited by Chris Candland and Rudra Sil. Oxford: Oxford University Press.

Carmack, Robert M., ed. 1988. *Harvest of Violence: The Maya Indians and the Guatemalan Crisis*. Norman, Okla.: Oklahoma University Press.

Charnovitz, Steve. 2000. "The International Labor Organization in Its Second Century." In *Max Planck Yearbook of United Nations Law*, vol. 4, edited by Armin von Bogdandy and Rudiger Wolfrum, with Christianne Phillip. Leiden, Netherlands: Martinus Nuhoff Publications. Accessed at http://www .mpil.de/shared/data/pdf/pdfmpunyb/charnovitz_4.pdf.

Chowdhry, Geeta, and Mark Beeman. 2001. "Challenging Child Labor: Transnational Activism and India's Carpet Industry." *Annals of the American Academy of Political and Social Sciences* 575(May): 158–75.

Clawson, Dan. 2003. *The Next Upsurge: Labor and the New Social Movements*. Ithaca, N.Y.: Cornell University/ ILR Press.

Cohen, Lizabeth. 2003. *A Consumers' Republic: The Politics of Mass Consumption in Postwar America*. New York: Alfred A. Knopf.

Collins, Jane. 2003. *Threads: Gender, Labor, and Power in the Global Apparel Industry*. Chicago, Ill.: University of Chicago Press.

Commission on Global Governance. 1995. *Our Global Neighborhood*. Report of the Commission on Global Governance. Oxford: Oxford University Press.

Committee on Monitoring International Labor Standards, National Research Council, National Academy of Science. 2004. *Monitoring International Labor Standards*. Washington: The National Academies Press.

Compa, Lance. 2000. "The Promise and Perils of 'Core' Labor Rights in Global Trade and Investment." Unpublished paper, Cornell University.

———. 2001. "Wary Allies." *The American Prospect* 12(12, July): 181-97.

Compa, Lance, and Tashia Hinchliffe Darricarrere. 1996. "Private Labor Rights Enforcement Through Corporate Codes of Conduct." In *Human Rights, Labor Rights, and International Trade*, edited by Lance Compa and Stephen Diamond. Philadelphia, Pa.: University of Pennsylvania Press.

Compa, Lance, and Stephen Diamond, editors. 1996. *Human Rights, Labor Rights, and International Trade*. Philadelphia, Pa.: University of Pennsylvania Press.

Connor, Tim. 2001. *Still Waiting for Nike to Do It: Nike's Labor Practices in the Three Years Since CEO Phil Knight's Speech to the National Press Club*. San Francisco, Calif.: Global Exchange.

Cook, Maria Lorena. 2006. *The Politics of Labor Reform in Latin America: Between Flexibility and Rights*. University Park, Pa.: Pennsylvania State University Press.

Cooper, Frederic. 1996. *Decolonization and African Society: The Labor Question in French and British Africa*. New York: Cambridge University Press.

Cortright, David, and George Lopez, eds. 1995. *Economic Sanctions: Panacea or Peacebuilding in a Post–Cold War World?* Boulder, Colo.: Westview Press.

COVERCO. 2005. "Mission Statement." Accessed at http://www.coverco.org .gt/eng/about_us/#History, April 20, 2007.

Cowie, Jefferson. 1999. *Capital Moves: RCA's Seventy-Year Quest for Cheap Labor*. Ithaca, N.Y.: Cornell University/ILR Press.

Danaher, Kevin. 1984. *In Whose Interest? A Guide to U.S. –South Africa Relations*. Washington: Institute for Policy Studies.

Davis, David Brion. 1992. "What the Abolitionists Were Up Against." In *The Anti-Slavery Debate: Capitalism and Abolitionism as a Problem in Historical Interpretation*, edited by Thomas Bender. Berkeley, Calif.: University of California Press.

Davis, Jennifer. 1995. "Sanctions and Apartheid: The Economic Challenge to Discrimination." In *Economic Sanctions: Panacea or Peacebuilding in a Post–Cold War World?* edited by David Cortright and George Lopez. Boulder, Colo.: Westview Press.

Davis, Shelton. 1988. "Sowing the Seeds of Violence." In *Harvest of Violence: The Maya Indians and the Guatemalan Crisis*, edited by Robert Carmack. Norman, Okla.: Oklahoma University Press.

Della Porta, Donatella, Hanspeter Kriesi, and Dieter Rucht, eds. 1999. *Social Movements in a Globalizing World*. New York: St. Martin's Press.

Dhawan, R. K. 1996. "Export Promotion Policies and Programs for Carpet Industry." In *Carpet Industry: Prospects and Perspectives*, edited by B. Bhattacharyya and L. Sahoo. New Delhi: Indian Institute of Foreign Trade/Global Business Press.

Dion, Douglas. 1998. "Evidence and Inference in the Comparative Case Study." *Comparative Politics* 30(2, January): 127–45.

Erwin, Alec. 1989. "Why COSATU Has Supported Sanctions." In *Sanctions Against Apartheid*, edited by Mark Orkin. Cape Town, South Africa: David Phillips.

Esbenshade, Jill. 2003. "Leveraging Neo-Liberal 'Reforms': How Garment Workers Capitalize on Monitoring." Paper presented to the American Sociological Association meetings. Atlanta, Ga., August 2003.

———. 2004. *Monitoring Sweatshops: Workers, Consumers, and the Global Apparel Industry*. Philadelphia, Pa.: Temple University Press.

Evans, Peter. 1997. "The Eclipse of the State? Reflections on Stateness in an Era of Globalization." *World Politics* 50(1): 62–87.

———. 2000. "Counter-Hegemonic Globalization: Transnational Networks as Political Tools for Fighting Marginalization." *Contemporary Sociology* 294(January): 230-41.

Fantasia, Rick, and Kim Voss. 2004. *Hard Work: Remaking the American Labor Movement*. Berkeley, Calif.: University of California Press.

Featherstone, Liza, and United Students Against Sweatshops. 2002. *Students Against Sweatshops*. London: Verso Press.

Feld, Werner J. 1980. *Multinational Corporations and UN Politics: The Quest for Codes of Conduct*. New York: Pergamon Press.

Flanagan, Robert J., and William B. Gould IV, editors. 2003. *International Labor Standards: Globalization, Trade, and Public Policy*. Stanford, Calif.: Stanford University Press.

Forster, Cindy. 1998. "Reforging National Revolution: Campesino Labor Struggles in Guatemala, 1944–1954." In *Identity and Struggle at the Margins of the Nation-State*, edited by Aviva Chomsky and Aldo Lauria-Santiago. Durham, N.C.: Duke University Press.

Frank, Dana. 1999. *Buy American: The Untold Story of Economic Nationalism*. Boston, Mass.: Beacon Press.

Freeman, Carla. 2000. *High Tech and High Heels in the Global Economy: Women, Work, and Pink-Collar Identities in the Caribbean*. Durham, N.C.: Duke University Press.

Frundt, Henry. 1987. *Refreshing Pauses: Coca-Cola and Human Rights in Guatemala*. New York: Praeger.

———. 1998. *Trade Conditions and Labor Rights: U.S. Initiatives, Dominican and Central American Responses*. Gainesville, Fla.: University Press of Florida.

———. 1999. "Cross-Border Organizing in the Apparel Industry: Lessons from Central America and the Caribbean." *Labor Studies Journal* 24(1, Spring): 89–106.

———. 2005. "Movement Theory and International Labor Solidarity." *Labor Studies Journal* 30(2): 19–40.

Fuchs, Frieda. 2005. "The Effects of Protective Labor Legislation on Women's Wages and Welfare: Lessons from Britain and France." *Politics and Society* (December): 595–635.

Fung, Archon, Dara O'Rourke, and Charles Sabel. 2001. *Can We Put an End to Sweatshops?* Boston, Mass.: Beacon Press.

Gay, Kathlyn. 1998. *Child Labor: A Global Crisis*. Brookfield, Conn.: Millbrook Press.

Gereffi, Gary. 1994. "The Organization of Buyer-Driven Commodity Chains." In *Commodity Chains and Global Capitalism*, edited by Gary Gereffi and Miguel Korzeniewicz. Westport, Conn.: Greenwood Press.

Gereffi, Gary, and Miguel Korzeniewicz, editors. 1994. *Commodity Chains and Global Capitalism*. New York: Praeger.

Gereffi, Gary, David Spener, and Jennifer Bair, eds. 2002. *Free Trade and Uneven Development: The North American Apparel Industry After NAFTA*. Philadelphia, Pa.: Temple University Press.

Global March Against Child Labor. 2006. "World Cup Campaign 2006." Accessed at http://www.globalmarch.org/campaigns/worldcupcampaign/worldcup2006.php3.

Goldberg, Chad. 2007. *Citizens and Paupers: Relief, Rights, and Race, from the Freedmen's Bureau to Workfare*. Chicago, Ill.: University of Chicago Press.

Golden, Miriam, and Jonas Pontusson, eds. 1992. *Bargaining for Change: Union Politics in North America and Europe*. Ithaca, N.Y.: Cornell University/ILR Press.

Goldin, Liliana. 2005. "Labor Ideologies in the International Factories of Rural Guatemala." *Latin American Perspectives* 32(5): 59–79.

Golodner, Linda F. 2000. "The Apparel Industry Code of Conduct: A Consumer Perspective on Social Responsibility." In *Global Codes of Conduct*, edited by Oliver Williams. Notre Dame, Ind.: University of Notre Dame Press.

Gordon, Jennifer. 2005. *Suburban Sweatshops: The Fight for Immigrant Rights*. Cambridge, Mass.: Belknap Press of Harvard University Press.

Gordon, Michael. 2000. "The International Confederation of Trade Unions: Bread, Freedom, and Peace." In *Transnational Cooperation Among Labor Unions*, edited by Michael Gordon and Lowell Turner. Ithaca, N.Y.: Cornell University/ILR Press.

Gordon, Michael, and Lowell Turner, eds. 2000. *Transnational Cooperation Among Labor Unions*. Ithaca, N.Y.: Cornell University/ILR Press.

Gosh, Ruma. 2000. "Child Labor: Issues and Concerns." Reprinted in National Resource Center on Child Labor, *Child Labor in India: An Overview*, rev. 2nd ed. New Delhi: V. V. Girl National Labor Institute/ILO–IPEC (International Program on the Elimination of Child Labor), 2001.

Gould, William B., IV. 2003. "Labor Law for a Global Economy: The Uneasy Case for International Labor Standards." In *International Labor Standards: Globalization, Trade, and Public Policy*, edited by Robert Flanagan and William B. Gould IV. Stanford, Calif.: Stanford University Press.

Grandin, Greg. 2000. *The Blood of Guatemala: A History of Race and Nation*. Durham, N.C.: Duke University Press.

Greenwald, Richard. 2005. *The Triangle Fire, the Protocols of Peace, and Industrial Democracy in Progressive-Era New York*. Philadelphia, Pa.: Temple University Press.

Greider, William. 1997. *One World, Ready or Not: The Maniac Logic of Global Capitalism*. New York: Simon & Schuster.

Guidry, John, Michael Kennedy, and Mayer Zald. 2000. *Globalizations and Social*

Movements: Culture, Power, and the Transnational Public Sphere. Ann Arbor, Mich.: University of Michigan Press.

Gupta, Ahkil. 1998. *Postcolonial Developments: Agriculture in the Making of Modern India.* Durham, N.C.: Duke University Press.

Guthman, Julie. 2004. *Agrarian Dreams: The Paradox of Organic Farming in California.* Berkeley, Calif.: University of California Press.

Hale, Charles. 2002. "Does Multiculturalism Menace? Governance, Cultural Rights, and the Politics of Identity in Guatemala." *Journal of Latin American Studies* 34: 485–524.

Hart, Gillian. 2002. *Disabling Globalization: Places of Power in Post-Apartheid South Africa.* Berkeley, Calif.: University of California Press.

Hartman, Laura, Denis Arnold, and Sandra Waddock. 2003. "Rising Above Sweatshops: An Introduction to the Text and to the Issues." In *Rising Above Sweatshops: Innovative Approaches to Global Labor Challenges,* edited by Laura Hartman, Denis Arnold, and Richard Wokutch. Westport, Conn.: Praeger.

Hartman, Laura, Denis Arnold, and Richard Wokutch, editors. 2003. *Rising Above Sweatshops: Innovative Approaches to Global Labor Challenges.* Westport, Conn.: Praeger.

Held, David, and Mathias Koenig-Archibugi, editors. 2003. *Taming Globalization: Frontiers of Governance.* Cambridge: Polity Press.

Heller, Patrick. 1999. *The Labor of Development: Workers and the Transformation of Capitalism in Kerala, India.* Ithaca, N.Y.: Cornell University/ILR Press.

Herod, Andrew. 2001. *Labor Geographies: Workers and the Landscapes of Capitalism.* New York: Guilford Press.

Hilowitz, Janet. 1998. *Labeling Child Labor Products: A Preliminary Study.* Geneva: International Labor Organization. Accessed at http://www.ilo.org/public/english/standards/ipec/publ/policy/papers/labelling/index.htm.

Hochschild, Adam. 2005. *Bury the Chains: Prophets and Rebels in the Fight to Free an Empire's Slaves.* New York: Houghton Mifflin.

Hoogvelt, Ankie, Christopher Candland, Denis McShane, Keramat Ali, Stephanie Barrientos, and Ngail-lim Sum. 1996. "Debate: International Labor Standards and Human Rights." *New Political Economy* 1(2): 259–82.

Howard, Allan. 1997. "Labor, History, and Sweatshops in the New Global Economy." In *No Sweat: Fashion, Free Trade, and the Rights of Garment Workers,* edited by Andrew Ross. London: Verso.

Howse, Robert. 1999. "The World Trade Organization and the Protection of Workers' Rights." *Journal of Small and Emerging Business Law* 3(1). Accessed at http://www.lclark.edu/org/jsebl/vol3nol.html.

Human Rights Watch. 2000. *Unfair Advantage: Workers' Freedom of Association in the United States Under International Human Rights Standards.* Accessed at http://www.hrw.org/reports/2000/uslabor/.

International Labor Organization. 1997. *World Labor Report, 1997–1998: Industrial Relations, Democracy, and Social Stability.* Geneva: ILO.

———. 1998a. *ILO Declaration on Fundamental Principles and Rights at Work.* Geneva: ILO (June 28).

———. 1998b. *Forced Labor in Myanmar (Burma).* Report of the Commission of Inquiry Appointed Under Article 26 of the Constitution of the International

Labor Organization to Examine the Observance by Myanmar of the Forced Labor Convention, 1930 (no. 29). Geneva: ILO (July 2).

———. 2001. *Factory Improvement Program: Management and Corporate Citizenship Program.* Geneva: ILO.

———. 2003. *Employment and Social Policy in Respect of Export Processing Zones.* Governing Body, GB 286/ESP/3. Geneva: ILO (March).

———. 2004. *Child Labor: A Textbook for University Students.* Accessed at www.ilo.org/public/english/standards/ipec/publ/download/pol_textbook _2004.pdf, October 11, 2004.

———. 2006. *The End of Child Labor: Within Reach.* Report of the director-general to the ninety-fifth session of the International Labor Conference. Geneva: ILO.

International Labor Rights Fund. 1996. *Rugmark After One Year.* Washington: ILRF (October). Accessed at http://www.laborrights.org, May 10, 2006.

———. 2004. "Petition to Review Guatemala's Country Eligibility Under the Generalized System of Preferences (GSP) for Violation of Internationally Recognized Workers' Rights." Presented to the chairman of the GSP Subcommittee, Office of the U.S. Trade Representative, December 13, 2004. Accessed at http://www.laborrights.org, June 7, 2005.

Jasper, James. 1997. *The Art of Moral Protest: Culture, Biography, and Creativity in Social Movements.* Chicago, Ill.: University of Chicago Press.

Jenkins, Rhys. 2002. "Political Economy of Codes of Conduct." In *Corporate Responsibility and Labor Rights: Codes of Conduct in the Global Economy*, edited by Rhys Jenkins, Ruth Pearson, and Gill Seyfang. London: Earthscan.

Jenkins, Rhys, Ruth Pearson, and Gill Seyfang, editors. 2002. *Corporate Responsibility and Labor Rights: Codes of Conduct in the Global Economy.* London: Earthscan.

Jessup, David, and Michael Gordon. 2000. "Organizing in Export-Processing Zones: The Bibong Experience in the Dominican Republic." In *Transnational Cooperation Among Labor Unions*, edited by Michael Gordon and Lowell Turner. Ithaca, N.Y.: Cornell University/ILR Press.

Joffe, Hillary. 1989. "The Policy of South Africa's Trade Unions Towards Sanctions and Disinvestment." In *Sanctions Against Apartheid*, edited by Mark Orkin. Cape Town, South Africa: David Philips.

Jonas, Susanne. 2000. *Of Centaurs and Doves: Guatemala's Peace Process.* Boulder, Colo.: Westview Press.

Juárez Núñez, Huberto. 2002. *Rebelion en el Greenfield.* Puebla, Mexico: Benemérita Universidad Autónoma de Puebla, Dirección General de Fomento Editorial/AFL-CIO.

Juárez Núñez, Huberto, and Steve Babson, eds. 1998. *Confronting Change: Auto Labor and Lean Production in North America.* Detroit, Mich.: Wayne State University/Benemérita Universidad Autónoma de Puebla.

Juyal, B. N. 1987. *Child Labor and Exploitation in the Carpet Industry.* New Delhi: Indian Social Institute.

Kabeer, Naila. 2003. "Deprivation, Discrimination, and Delivery: Competing Explanations for Child Labor and Educational Failure in South Asia." In *Child Labor and the Right to Education in South Asia: Needs Versus Rights?* edited by Naila Kabeer, Geetha B. Namissan, and Ramya Subrahmanian. New Delhi: Sage Publications.

Kabeer, Naila, Geetha B. Namissan, and Ramya Subrahmanian 2003a. "Needs Versus Rights? Child Labor, Social Exclusion, and the Challenge of Universalizing Primary Education." In *Child Labor and the Right to Education in South Asia: Needs Versus Rights?* edited by Naila Kabeer, Geetha B. Namissan, and Ramya Subrahmanian. New Delhi: Sage Publications.

———, editors. 2003b. *Child Labor and the Right to Education in South Asia: Needs Versus Rights?* New Delhi: Sage Publications.

Kaempfer, William, James Lehman, and Anton Lowenberg. 1987. "Divestment, Investment Sanctions, and Disinvestment: An Evaluation of Anti-apartheid Policy Instruments." *International Organization* 41(3, Summer): 457–73.

Kahn, E. J., Jr. 1979. "Annals of International Trade: A Very Emotive Issue." *The New Yorker* (May 14): 117–53.

Kanbargi, Ramesh. 1988. "Child Labor in India: The Carpet Industry of Varanasi." In *Combating Child Labor*, edited by Assefa Baquele and Jo Boyden. Geneva: ILO.

Kaplinsky, Raphael. 1993. "Export-Processing Zones in the Dominican Republic: Transforming Manufactures into Commodities." *World Development* 21(11): 1851–65.

———. 1995. "Technique and Management: The Spread of Japanese Management Techniques to Developing Countries." *World Development* 23(1): 57–71.

———. 2005. *Globalization, Poverty, and Inequality.* Cambridge: Polity Press.

Kapstein, Ethan. 1999. *Sharing the Wealth: Workers and the World Economy.* New York: Norton.

Kebschull, Dietrich. 1999. "Philosophy and Achievements of the 'Rugmark' Labeling Approach." In *Against Child Labor: Indian and International Dimensions and Strategies*, edited by Klaus Voll. New Delhi: Mosaic Books.

Keck, Margaret, and Kathryn Sikkink. 1998. *Activists Beyond Borders: Advocacy Networks in Transnational Politics.* Ithaca, N.Y.: Cornell University Press.

Kenny, Bridget. 2004. "Divisions of Labor, Experiences of Class: Changing Collective Identities of East Rand Food Retail Sector Workers Through South Africa's Democratic Transition." PhD dissertation, University of Wisconsin at Madison.

Khagram, Sanjay, James V. Riker, and Kathryn Sikkink. 2002. *Restructuring World Politics: Transnational Social Movements, Networks, and Norms.* Minneapolis, Minn.: University of Minnesota Press.

Khan, Shamshad. 1999. "Community Participation Eliminates Child Labor." In *Against Child Labor: Indian and International Dimensions and Strategies*, edited by Klaus Voll. New Delhi: Mosaic Books.

Khor, Martin. 1994. "The World Trade Organization, Labor Standards, and Trade Protectionism." *Third World Resurgence* 45: 30–34.

Kidder, Thalia. 2002. "Networks in Transnational Labor Organizing." In *Restructuring World Politics: Transnational Social Movements, Networks, and Norms*, edited by Sanjeev Khagram, James V. Riker, and Kathryn Sikkink. Minneapolis, Minn.: University of Minnesota Press.

Klein, Naomi. 2002. *No Logo*, 2nd ed. London: Picador Press.

Klotz, Audie. 1995. "Norms Reconstituting Interests: Global Racial Equality and U.S. Sanctions Against South Africa." *International Organization* 49(3, Summer): 451–78.

Koo, Hagen. 2001. *Korean Workers: The Culture and Politics of Class Formation.* Ithaca, N.Y.: Cornell University/ILR Press.

Kreamer, Christopher. 2002. *The Carpet Wars.* New York: HarperCollins.

Krupat, Kitty. 1997. "From War Zone to Free Trade Zone: A History of the National Labor Committee." In *No Sweat: Fashion, Free Trade, and the Rights of Garment Workers,* edited by Andrew Ross. London: Verso.

Labour File. 2005. "Assault on Honda Workers: A Citizens' Committee Inquiry Report." *Labour File* (September).

Langille, Brian. 1999. "The ILO and the New Economy: Recent Developments." *International Journal of Comparative Labor Law and Industrial Relations* 15(3): 229–58.

Lavalette, Michael. 1999a. "The Changing Form of Child Labor Circa 1880–1918: The Growth of 'Out of School Work.'" In *A Thing of the Past? Child Labor in Britain in the Nineteenth and Twentieth Century,* edited by Michael Lavalette. Liverpool: Liverpool University Press.

———, editor. 1999b. *A Thing of the Past? Child Labor in Britain in the Nineteenth and Twentieth Century.* Liverpool: Liverpool University Press.

Leary, Virginia A. 1996. "The Paradox of Workers' Rights as Human Rights." In *Human Rights, Labor Rights, and International Trade,* edited by Lance Compa and Stephen Diamond. Philadelphia, Pa.: University of Pennsylvania Press.

Lee, Ching Kwan. 1998. *Gender and the South China Miracle: Two Worlds of Factory Women.* Berkeley, Calif.: University of California Press.

Levy, Margaret, and April Linton. 2003. "Fair Trade: A Cup at a Time?" *Politics and Society* 31(3): 407–32.

Lieten, G. K. 2002. "Child Labor in India: Disentangling Essence and Solutions." *Economic and Political Weekly* (December 28): 5190–95.

Lipietz, Alain. 1987. *Mirages and Miracles: The Crisis in Global Fordism.* Translated by David Macey. London: Verso.

London, Jonathan. 2003. "The Economic Context: Grounding Discussions of Economic Change and Labor in Developing Countries." In *Rising Above Sweatshops: Innovative Approaches to Global Labor Challenges,* edited by Laura Hartman, Denis Arnold, and Richard Wokutch. Westport, Conn.: Praeger.

Malhotra, Vinod. 1996. "Indian Carpet Industry: Prospects and Perspectives." In *Carpet Industry: Prospects and Perspectives,* edited by B. Bhattacharyya and L. Sahoo. New Delhi: Indian Institute of Foreign Trade/Global Business Press.

Malkki, Liisa. 1994. "Citizens of Humanity." *Diaspora* 3(1): 41–68.

Mamic, Ivanka. 2004. *Implementing Codes of Conduct: How Businesses Manage Social Performance in Global Supply Chains.* Geneva: International Labor Organization/Greenleaf Publishing.

Mannon, Susan. 2003. "Our Daily Bread: Constructing Households, Constructing Labor Markets." PhD dissertation, University of Wisconsin at Madison.

Marshall, T. H. 1950/1992. "Citizenship and Social Class." In *Citizenship and Social Class,* edited by T. H. Marshall and Tom Bottomore. London: Pluto Press.

Marzullo, Sal. 1987a. "Corporations: Catalyst for Change." In *The South African Quagmire*, edited by Prakash Sethi. Cambridge, Mass.: Ballinger Press.

———. 1987b. "American Business in South Africa: The Hard Choices." In *Business and Society*, edited by Prakash Sethi and Cecilia M. Falbe. Washington: Lexington Books.

Massie, Robert Kinloch. 1997. *Loosing the Bonds: The United States and South Africa in the Apartheid Years*. New York: Doubleday.

McCann, Michael W. 1994. *Rights at Work: Pay Equity Reform and the Politics of Legal Mobilization*. Chicago, Ill.: University of Chicago Press.

McKay, Stephen C. 2006. *Satanic Mills or Silicon Islands: The Politics of High-Tech Production in the Philippines*. Ithaca, N.Y.: Cornell University/ILR Press.

McMichael, Philip. 2000. *Development and Social Change*, 2nd ed. Thousand Oaks, Calif.: Pine Forge Press/Sage Publications.

Milkman, Ruth. 1997. *Farewell to the Factory: Auto Workers in the Late Twentieth Century*. Berkeley, Calif.: University of California Press.

———. 2006. *L.A. Story: Immigrant Workers and the Future of the U.S. Labor Movement*. New York: Russell Sage Foundation.

Milkman, Ruth, and Kim Voss, editors. 2004. *Rebuilding Labor: Organizing and Organizers in the New Union Movement*. Ithaca, N.Y.: Cornell University/ILR Press.

Mishra, G. P., and P. N. Pande. 1996. *Child Labor in Carpet Industry*. New Delhi: A.P.H. Publishing Co.

Mishra, Lakshmidhar. 2000. *Child Labor in India*. Oxford: Oxford University Press.

Mitchell, John, editor. 1998. *Companies in a World of Conflict: NGOs, Sanctions, and Corporate Responsibility*. London: Earthscan Publications/Royal Institute of International Affairs.

Montero, David. 2006. "Nike's Dilemma: Is Doing the Right Thing Wrong?" *Christian Science Monitor*, December 22, 2006.

Moody, Kim. 1997. *Workers in a Lean World: Unions in the International Economy*. London: Verso.

Moran, Theodore. 2002. *Beyond Sweatshops: Foreign Direct Investment and Globalization in Developing Countries*. Washington: Brookings Institution Press.

Morano, Roy. 1982. *The Protestant Challenge to Corporate America: Issues of Corporate Social Responsibility*. Ann Arbor, Mich.: University of Michigan Research Press.

Murillo, M. Victoria, and Andrew Schrank. 2005. "With a Little Help from My Friends: Partisan Politics, Transnational Alliances, and Labor Rights in Latin America." *Comparative Political Sciences* (38)8: 971-99.

Murray, Jill. 2003. "The Global Context: Multinational Enterprises, Labor Standards, and Regulation." In *Rising Above Sweatshops: Innovative Approaches to Global Labor Challenges*, edited by Laura Hartman, Denis Arnold, and Richard Wokutch. Westport, Conn.: Praeger.

Murray, Lauren. 1995. "Unraveling Employment Trends in Textiles and Apparel." *Monthly Labor Review* 118(8, August). Accessed at http://www.bls.gov/opub/mlr/1995/08art6abs.htm.

Mutersbaugh, Tad. 2002. "The Number Is the Beast: A Political Economy of Organic-Coffee Certification and Producer Unionism." *Environment and Planning* 34: 1165–84.

Myers, William. 2001. "The Right Rights? Child Labor in a Globalizing World." *Annals of the American Academy of Political and Social Sciences* (May): 38–55.

Nadvi, Khalid, with Sajid Kazmi. 2001. "Global Standards and Local Responses." Paper for the Institute for Developmental Studies workshop "The Impact of Global and Local Governance on Industrial Upgrading." Brighton, February 13–17.

Narayan, Ashok. 1988. "Child Labor Policies and Programs: The Indian Experience." In *Combating Child Labor*, edited by Assefa Baquele and Jo Boyden. Geneva: International Labor Organization.

National Resource Center on Child Labor. 2001. *Child Labor in India: An Overview*, revised 2nd edition. New Delhi: V. V. Giri National Labor Institute/ILO–IPEC (International Program on the Elimination of Child Labor).

Nelson, Lisa. 2000. "Who Speaks for the Trees? Consideration for Any Transnational Code." In *Global Codes of Conduct: An Idea Whose Time Has Come*, edited by Oliver F. Williams. Notre Dame, Ind.: University of Notre Dame Press.

Ness, Immanuel. 2003. "Globalization and Worker Organization in New York's Garment Industry." In *Sweatshop USA: The American Sweatshop in Historical and Global Perspective*, edited by Daniel Bender and Richard Greenwald. New York: Routledge Press.

Nike. 2006. "Nike Ends Orders with Soccer Ball Manufacturer." Press release, November 20, 2006. Accessed at http://www.nike.com/nikebiz/news/pressrelease.jhtml?year=2006&month=11&letter=l, January 11, 2007.

Nimtz, August. 2002. "Marx and Engels: The Prototypical Transnational Actors." In *Restructuring World Politics: Transnational Social Movements, Networks, and Norms*, edited by Sanjeev Khagram, James V. Riker, and Kathryn Sikkink. Minneapolis, Minn.: University of Minnesota Press.

Nutter, Steve. 1997. "The Structure and Growth of the Los Angeles Garment Industry." In *No Sweat: Fashion, Free Trade and the Rights of Garment Workers*, edited by Andrew Ross. London: Verso Press.

Olsen, Elizabeth. 2002. "United Nations: Labor Monitor to Go to Myanmar." *New York Times*, March 23.

Ong, Aihwa. 1987. *Spirits of Resistance and Capitalist Discipline: Factory Women in Malaysia*. Albany, N.Y.: State University of New York Press.

Organization of American States (OAS). Inter-American Commission on Human Rights. 2001. *Fifth Report on the Situation of Human Rights in Guatemala*. Washington: OAS General Secretariat.

Orkin, Mark. 1987. *Divestment, the Struggle and the Future: What Black South Africans Really Think*. Johannesburg: Ravan Press.

———, ed. 1989. *Sanctions Against Apartheid*. Cape Town: David Philips.

O'Rourke, Dara. 2000. "Monitoring the Monitors: A Critique of PricewaterhouseCoopers Labor Monitoring," September 28. Accessed at nature.berkeley.edu/orourke/PDF/pwc.pdf.

———. 2003. "Outsourcing Regulation: Analyzing Nongovernmental Systems of Labor Standards and Monitoring." *Policy Studies Journal* 31(1): 1–29.

———. 2004. *Community-Driven Regulation: Balancing Development and the Environment in Vietnam.* Cambridge, Mass.: MIT Press.

Oxfam. 2004. *Trading Away Our Rights: Women Working in Global Supply Chains.* Oxford: Oxfam. Accessed at http://www.oxfam.org.uk/what_we_do/issues/trade/trading_rights.htm.

Paige, Jeffrey. 1997. *Coffee and Power: Revolution and the Rise of Democracy in Central America.* Cambridge, Mass.: Harvard University Press.

Paul, Karen. 1987. "The Inadequacy of Sullivan Reporting." In *The South African Quagmire*, edited by Prakash Sethi. Cambridge, Mass.: Ballinger Press.

———. 1991. "U.S. Companies in South Africa." In *Up Against the Corporate Wall: Modern Corporations and Social Issues of the Nineties.* Edited by S. Prakash Sethi and Paul Steidlmeier. Englewood Cliffs, N.J.: Prentice Hall.

Picciotto, Sol. 2002. "Reconceptualizing Regulation in the Era of Globalization." *Journal of Law and Society* 29(1, March): 1–11.

Piore, Michael J., and Andrew Schrank. 2006. "Trading Up: An Embryonic Model for Easing the Human Costs of Free Markets." *Boston Review* (September–October). Accessed at http://bostonreview.net/BR31.5/pioreschrank.html.

Piven, Frances Fox, and Richard Cloward. 1977. *Poor People's Movements: Why They Succeed, How They Fail.* New York : Pantheon Books.

Plankey-Videla, Nancy. 2004. "It Cuts Both Ways: The Unintended Consequences of Lean Production in a Mexican Garment Factory." PhD diss., University of Wisconsin at Madison.

Polanyi, Karl. 1944/2001. *The Great Transformation: The Political and Economic Origins of Our Time.* Foreword by Joseph Stiglitz, introduction by Fred Block. Boston, Mass.: Beacon Press.

Posner, Michael, and Justine Nolan. 2003. "Can Codes of Conduct Play a Role in Promoting Workers' Rights?" In *International Labor Standards: Globalization, Trade, and Public Policy*, edited by Robert Flanagan and William B. Gould IV. Stanford, Calif.: Stanford University Press.

Posthuma, Anne. 1995. "Japanese Techniques in Africa? Human Resources and Industrial Restructuring in Zimbabwe." *World Development* 23(1): 103–16.

Prasad, Monica, Howard Kimeldorf, Rachel Meyer, and Ian Robinson. 2004. "Consumers of the World Unite: A Market-Based Response to Sweatshops." *Labor Studies Journal* (Fall): 57-79.

Proper, Carl. 1997. "New York: Defending the Union Contract." In *No Sweat: Fashion, Free Trade, and the Rights of Garment Workers*, edited by Andrew Ross. London: Verso Press.

Puri, Lakshmi. 1996. "Market Access Challenges for Indian Exporters in the Post-Uruguayan Round." In *Carpet Industry: Prospects and Perspectives*, edited by B. Bhattacharyya and L. Sahoo. New Delhi: Indian Institute of Foreign Trade/Global Business Press.

Raworth, Kate. 2004. "When Buying Clothes, Measure Their Ethics for a Good Fit." *Guardian Weekly* (March 11–17): 23.

Reich, Robert. 1997. *Locked in the Cabinet.* New York: Alfred A. Knopf.

Relly, Gavin. 1986. "The Costs of Disinvestment." *Foreign Policy* 63(Summer): 131-46.

Rivoli, Pietra. 2005. *The Travels of a T-Shirt in the Global Economy: An Economist*

Examines the Markets, Power, and Politics of World Trade. New York: John Wiley and Sons.

Robinson, William. 2003. *Transnational Conflicts: Central America, Social Change, and Globalization.* London: Verso Press.

Rodman, Kenneth. 1994. "Public and Private Sanctions Against South Africa." *Political Science Quarterly* 109(2, Summer): 313–34.

Rodríguez-Garavito, César. 2005a. "Global Governance and Labor Rights: Codes of Conduct and Anti-Sweatshop Struggles in Global Apparel Factories in Mexico and Guatemala." *Politics and Society* 33(2, June): 203–33.

———. 2005b. "Nike's Law: The Anti-Sweatshop Movement, Transnational Corporations, and the Struggle over International Labor Rights in the Americas." In *Law and Globalization from Below: Towards a Cosmopolitan Legality,* edited by Boaventura de Sousa Santos and César Rodríguez-Garavito. Cambridge: Cambridge University Press.

———. 2007. "Sewing Resistance: Global Production, Transnational Organizing, and Global Governance in the U.S.-Caribbean Basin Apparel Industry (1990-2005)." PhD dissertation, University of Wisconsin at Madison.

Rodrik, Dani. 1999. "Democracies Pay Higher Wages." *Quarterly Journal of Economics* 114(3, August): 707–38.

Rosen, Ellen. 2002. *Making Sweatshops: The Globalization of the U.S. Apparel Industry.* Berkeley, Calif.: University of California Press.

Ross, Andrew, ed. 1997. *No Sweat: Fashion, Free Trade, and the Rights of Garment Workers.* London: Verso Press.

———. 2003. "The Rise of the Second Anti-Sweatshop Movement." In *Sweatshop USA: The American Sweatshop in Historical and Global Perspective,* edited by Daniel Bender and Richard Greenwald. New York: Routledge.

Ross, Robert. 2004. *Slaves to Fashion: Poverty and Abuse in the New Sweatshops.* Ann Arbor, Mich.: University of Michigan Press.

Rudra, Nita. 2005. "Are Workers in the Developing World Winners or Losers in the Current Era of Globalization?" *Studies in Comparative International Development* 40(3, Fall): 24–64.

Rueschemeyer, Dietrich, Evelyne Huber Stephens, and John D. Stephens. 1992. *Capitalist Development and Democracy.* Chicago, Ill.: University of Chicago Press.

Ruggie, John Gerard. 1998. *Constructing the World Polity: Essays on International Institutionalization.* New York: Routledge.

———. 2003. "Taking Embedded Liberalism Global: The Corporate Connection." In *Taming Globalization: Frontiers of Governance,* edited by David Held and Mathias Koenig-Archibugi. Cambridge: Polity Press.

Ryan, Missy. 2000. "Child Labor as an Issue Comes of Age." *National Journal* 32(18, April 29): 1367–8.

Sampson, Anthony. 1987. *Black and Gold: Tycoons, Revolutions, and Apartheid.* London: Hodder and Stoughton.

Santoro, Michael. 2003. "Philosophy Applied I: How Nongovernmental and Multinational Enterprises Can Work Together to Protect Global Labor Rights." In *Rising Above Sweatshops: Innovative Approaches to Global Labor Challenges,* edited by Laura Hartman, Denis Arnold, and Richard Wokutch. Westport, Conn.: Praeger.

Santos, Boaventura de Sousa, and César Rodríguez-Garavito, editors. 2005. *Law and Counter-Hegemonic Globalization: Toward a Cosmopolitan Legality*. Cambridge: Cambridge University Press.

Satyarthi, Kailash. 1994. "The Tragedy of Child Labor." Interview in *Multinational Monitor* 16(10, October 1994). Accessed at http://www.multinational monitor.org/hyper/issues/1994/10/mm1094_07.html, May 13, 2006.

Schlesinger, Stephen, and Stephen Kinzer. 1982. *Bitter Fruit: The Untold Story of the American Coup in Guatemala*. New York: Doubleday.

Schmidt, Elizabeth. 1980. *Decoding Corporate Camouflage: U.S. Business Support for Apartheid*. Washington: Institute for Policy Studies.

Schoenberger, Karl. 2000. *Levi's Children: Coming to Terms with Human Rights in the Global Marketplace*. New York: Atlantic Monthly Press.

Schrage, Elliot. 2004. *Promoting International Worker Rights Through Private Voluntary Initiatives: Public Relations or Public Policy?* Iowa City, Iowa: University of Illinois Center for Human Rights.

Schrank, Andrew. 2005. "Professionalization and Probity in the Patrimonial State: Labor Law Enforcement in the Dominican Republic." Paper presented to the MIT/Sloan IWER (Institute for Work and Employment Research) seminar series, Cambridge, Mass, February 8, 2005.

———. 2006. "Labor Standards and Human Resources: A Natural Experiment in an Unlikely Laboratory." Paper presented to the Latin American Studies Association meetings, Puerto Rico, March 2006.

Seccombe, Wally. 1993. *Weathering the Storm: Working-Class Families from the Industrial Revolution to the Fertility Decline*. London: Verso.

Seidman, Ann, and Neva Seidman. 1977. *South Africa and U.S. Multinational Corporations*. Westport, Conn.: Lawrence Hill and Co.

Seidman, Gay. 1994. *Manufacturing Militance: Workers' Movements in Brazil and South Africa, 1970–1985*. Berkeley, Calif.: University of California Press.

Sekar, Helen. 2001. "The Child Labour (Prohibition and Regulation) Act, 1986, and its Implementation." In National Resource Center on Child Labor, *Child Labor in India: An Overview*, revised 2nd edition. New Delhi: V. V. Giri National Labour Institute with ILO–IPEC.

Sethi, S. Prakash. 2000. "Gaps in Research in the Formulation, Implementation, and Effectiveness Measurement of International Codes of Conduct." In *Global Codes of Conduct: An Idea Whose Time Has Come*, edited by Oliver F. Williams. Notre Dame, Ind.: University of Notre Dame Press.

Sethi, S. Prakash, and Cecilia M. Falbe, editors. 1987. *Business and Society*. Washington: Lexington Books.

Sethi, S. Prakash, and Paul Steidlmeier, editors. 1991. *Up Against the Corporate Wall: Modern Corporations and Social Issues of the Nineties*. Englewood Cliffs, N.J.: Prentice-Hall.

Sethi, S. Prakash, and Oliver F. Williams. 2000. *Economic Imperatives and Ethical Values in Global Business: The South African Experience and International Codes Today*. Boston, Mass.: Kluwer Academic Press.

Shafir, Gershon. 2004. "Citizenship and Human Rights in an Era of Globalization." In *People Out of Place*, edited by Alyson Brysk and Gershon Shafir. New York: Routledge.

Shaiken, Harley. 1995. "Lean Production in a Mexican Context." In *Lean Work:*

Empowerment and Exploitation in the Global Auto Industry. Detroit, Mich.: Wayne State University Press.

Shamir, Ronen. 2004. "The De-Radicalization of Corporate Social Responsibility." *Critical Sociology* 30(3): 670–89.

Sharma, Alakh. 2002. "Impact of Social Labeling on Child Labor in the Carpet Industry." *Economic and Political Weekly* (December 28): 5198–204.

Sharma, Mukul, and Tarun Bose. 1997. "Indian Carpet with a Smiling Face." *Labor File* 3(1 and 2, January and February): 5–15.

Shaw, Terri. 2002. "Child Labor Worries." *Newsday*, April 4.

Sikkink, Kathryn. 1993. "Human Rights, Principled Issue-Networks, and Sovereignty in Latin America." *International Organization* 47(3, Summer): 411–41.

———. 2002. "Restructuring World Politics: The Limits and Asymmetries of Soft Power." In *Restructuring World Politics: Transnational Social Movements, Networks, and Norms*, edited by Sanjeev Khagram, James V. Riker, and Kathryn Sikkink. Minneapolis, Minn.: University of Minnesota Press.

Silver, Beverly J. 2003. *Forces of Labor: Workers' Movements and Globalization Since 1870.* Cambridge: Cambridge University Press.

Silverman, Victor. 2000. *Imagining Internationalism in American and British Labor, 1939–1949.* Urbana, Ill.: University of Illinois Press.

Singh, Ruma Gosh, Nikhil Raj, and Helen R. Sekar. 2002. *Hard Labour at a Tender Age: Child Labour in the Home-Based Industries in the Wake of Legislation.* New Delhi: V.V. Giri National Labour Institute.

Slaughter, Anne-Marie. 2004. *A New World Order.* Princeton, N.J.: Princeton University Press.

Smith, Jackie, and Hank Johnston, editors. 2002. *Globalization and Resistance: Transnational Dimensions of Social Movements.* New York: Rowman and Littlefield.

Somers, Peggy. 1993. "Citizenship and the Place of the Public Sphere: Law, Community, and Political Culture in the Transition to Democracy." *American Sociological Review* 58(5): 587–620.

———. 1999. "The Privatization of Citizenship: How to Unthink a Knowledge Culture." In *Beyond the Cultural Turn: New Directions in the Study of Society and Culture*, edited by Victoria E. Bonnell and Lynn Hunt. Berkeley, Calif.: University of California Press.

———. 2005. "Citizenship Troubles: Genealogies of Struggle for the Soul of the Social." In *Remaking Modernity: Politics, History, and Sociology*, edited by Julia Adams, Elisabeth Clemens, and Ann Shola Orloff. Durham, N.C.: Duke University Press.

Southall, Roger, editor. 1988. *Trade Unionism and the New Industrialization of the Third World.* London: Zed Press.

Spalding, Hobart. 1988. "U.S. Labor Intervention in Latin America: The Case of the American Institute for Free Labor Development." In *Trade Unionism and the New Industrialization of the Third World*, edited by Roger Southall. London: Zed Press.

Spence, J. E. 1998. "South Africa: A Case Study in Human Rights and Sanctions." In *Companies in a World of Conflict: NGOs, Sanctions, and Corporate Responsibility*, edited by John Mitchell. London: Earthscan Publications/Royal Institute of International Affairs.

Srivastava, Ravi, and Nikhil Raj. 2000. *Children of Carpet Looms: A Study of Home-Based Production of Carpet in Uttar Pradesh*. New Delhi: V. V. National Girl Labor Institute.

———. 2002. "Knots that Tie Up Children in Mirzapur: A Study of Child Labour in the Carpet Industry of Uttar Pradesh." In *Hard Labour at a Tender Age: Child Labour in the Home-Based Industries in the Wake of Legislation*, edited by Ruma Gosh Singh, Nikhil Raj, and Helen Sekar. New Delhi: V.V. Giri National Labour Institute.

Stallings, Barbara. 1995. "The New International Context of Development." In *Global Change, Regional Response: The New International Context of Development*, edited by Barbara Stallings. Cambridge: Cambridge University Press.

Stiglitz, Joseph. 2003. *Globalization and Its Discontents*, 2nd ed. New York: Norton.

Stillerman, Joel. 2003. "Transnational Activist Networks and the Emergence of Labor Internationalism in the NAFTA Countries." *Social Science History* 27(4, Winter): 577–601.

Stone, Philip. 1994. "Exit or Voice? Lessons from Companies in South Africa." In *Ethics and Economic Affairs*, edited by Alan Lewis and Karl-Erik Warneryd. New York: Routledge.

Su, Julie. 1997. "El Monte Thai Garment Workers: Slave Sweatshops." In *No Sweat: Fashion, Free Trade, and the Rights of Garment Workers*, edited by Andrew Ross. London: Verso Press.

Talbot, John. 2004. *Grounds for Agreement: The Political Economy of the Coffee Commodity Chain*. Lanham, Md.: Rowman and Littlefield.

Tarrow, Sidney. 2005. *The New Transnational Activist*. New York: Cambridge University Press.

Tegmo-Reddy, Leyla. 1996. "The ILO and Child Labor (with Special Reference to Child Labor in the Indian Carpet Industry)." In *The Indian Carpet Industry: Evolving Concerns, Prospects, and Strategies*, edited by B. Bhattacharyya and L. Sahoo. New Delhi: Indian Institute of Foreign Trade/Global Business Press.

Tendler, Judith. 2002. "Small Firms, the Informal Sector, and the Devil's Deal." *IDS Bulletin* 33: 3.

Thompson, E. P. 1963. *The Making of the English Working Class*. New York: Vintage Press.

———. 1975. *Whigs and Hunters: The Origins of the Black Act*. New York: Pantheon Press.

Thorat, Sukhadeo K. 1999. "Poverty, Caste, and Child Labor in India: The Plight of Dalit and Adivasi Children." In *Against Child Labor: Indian and International Dimensions and Strategies*, edited by Klaus Voll. New Delhi: Mosaic Books.

University of Maryland. Program on International Policy Attitudes (PIPA). 2000. *Americans on Globalization: A Study of Public Attitudes* (March). Accessed at "Americans and the World," http://www.americans-world.org/digest/global_issues/intertrade/laborstandards.cfm.

U.S. Department of Labor. Office of Public Affairs (OPA). 1998. "Statement of U.S. Labor Secretary Alexis M. Herman on the Apparel Industry Partnership." Press release, November 3, 1998. Accessed at http://www.dol.gov/opa/media/press/opa/archive/opa98440.htm, November 13, 2006.

Voll, Klaus, editor. 1999. *Against Child Labor: Indian and International Dimensions and Strategies*. New Delhi: Mosaic Books.

Von Holdt, Karl. 2000. "From the Politics of Resistance to the Politics of Reconstruction? The Union and Ungovernability in the Workplace." In *Trade Unions and Democratization in South Africa, 1985–1997*, edited by Glenn Adler and Eddie Webster. New York: St. Martin's Press.

Waddock, Sandra. 2002. *Leading Corporate Citizens: Vision, Values, Value-Added.* New York: McGraw-Hill.

Warren, Kay. 1998. *Indigenous Movements and Their Critics: Pan-Mayan Activism in Guatemala.* Princeton, N.J.: Princeton University Press.

Wazir, Rekha. 2002. "'No to Child Labor, Yes to Education': Unfolding of a Grassroots Movement in Andhra Pradesh." *Economic and Political Weekly* (December 28): 5225–9.

Webster, Eddie, and Glenn Adler. 2000. "Consolidating Democracy in a Liberalizing World: Trade Unions and Democratization in South Africa." In *Trade Unions and Democratization in South Africa, 1985–1997*, edited by Glenn Adler and Eddie Webster. New York: St. Martin's Press.

Weedon, Reid. 1987. "The Evolution of Sullivan Principle Compliance." In *The South African Quagmire*, edited by Prakash Sethi. Cambridge, Mass.: Ballinger Press.

Weisband, Edward. 2000. "Discursive Multilateralism: Global Benchmarks, Shame, and Learning in the ILO Labor Standards Monitoring Regime." *International Studies Quarterly* 44: 643–66.

Wells, Don. 1998. "Building Transnational Coordinative Unionism." In *Confronting Change: Auto Labor and Lean Production in North America*, edited by Huberto Juárez Núñez and Steve Babson. Detroit, Mich.: Wayne State University/Benemérita Universidad Autónoma de Puebla.

Whittaker, Alan, ed. 1988. *India's Carpet Boys: A Pattern of Slavery.* London: Anti-Slavery Society.

Wiener, Myron. 1991. *The Child and the State in India: Child Labor and Education Policy in Comparative Perspective.* Princeton, N.J.: Princeton University Press.

Wilking, Lou. 1987. "Should U.S. Corporations Abandon South Africa?" In *The South African Quagmire*, edited by Prakash Sethi. Cambridge, Mass.: Ballinger Press.

Williams, Heather. 2003. "Of Labor Tragedy and Legal Farce: The Han Young Factory Struggle in Tijuana, Mexico." *Social Science History* 27(4): 525–50.

Williams, Oliver F. 2000a. "A Lesson from the Sullivan Principles: The Rewards for Being Proactive." In *Global Codes of Conduct: An Idea Whose Time Has Come*, edited by Oliver Williams. Notre Dame, Ind.: University of Notre Dame Press.

———, editor. 2000b. *Global Codes of Conduct: An Idea Whose Time Has Come.* Notre Dame, Ind.: University of Notre Dame Press.

Wolensky, Kenneth, Robert Wolensky, and Nicole Wolensky. 2002. *Fighting for the Union Label: The Women's Garment Industry and the ILGWU in Pennsylvania.* University Park, Pa.: Pennsylvania State University Press.

World Bank. 1996. *World Development Report 1995: Workers in an Integrating World.* Oxford: Oxford University Press/World Bank.

World Trade Organization. 1996. "Draft Singapore Ministerial Conference." Ministerial Conference, December 9–13, Singapore. Accessed at http://www.wto.org/English/thewto_e/minist_e/wtodoc_e.html, May 15, 2007.

Selected Websites

Rugmark Foundation: www.rugmark.org

Nepal Rugmark Foundation: www.nepalrugmark.org

Comisión para la Verificación de Códigos de Conducta (COVERCO): http://www.coverco.org.gt

International Labor Organization, "Export-Processing Zones, by Sector": http://www.ilo.org/public/english/dialogue/sector/themes/epz/stats.htm

Government Documents

India, Government of, Ministry of Textiles. Carpet Export Promotion Council. 2002. "Note on Kaleen Labeling System" (mimeo). New Delhi: Government of India.

————. Ministry of Textiles. 2002. "Note on Child Labor in the Carpet Industry" (mimeo). New Delhi: Government of India (October).

United Nations System's Operation in India. 1998. "Position Paper on Child Labor." New Delhi: International Labor Organization area office for India and Bhutan on behalf of the UN System in India.

Interviews

Jane Bennett, Johannesburg, March 2004.

David Fig, Johannesburg, May 2004.

Hewlett-Packard spokesperson, Davis, Calif., May 1985.

Neva Makgetla, Johannesburg, March 2004.

Scott Nova, San Francisco, Calif., August 2004.

Interviews in New Delhi and Agra

Swami Agnivesh. 7 Jantar Mantar Rd., New Delhi, January 8, 2003.

Praveen Bansal, Bansal Carpets, Agra, January 11, 2003.

T. S. Chadha, executive director, Carpet Export Promotion Council, New Delhi, January 10, 2003.

K. Chandramouli, joint secretary to the Ministry of Labor, New Delhi, January 13, 2003.

Dr. Mohatir Dubey, president, Council for Social and Economic Development. Offices of the council, New Delhi, January 7, 2003.

John P. John, New Delhi, January 9, 2003.

Tinoo Joshi, development commissioner (handicrafts), Ministry of Textiles. New Delhi, January 8, 2003.

Amargit Kaur, New Delhi, January 9, 2003.

Dr. Dietrich Kebschull, director, Indo-German Export Promotion Council (IGEP). New Delhi, January 7, 2003.

S. B. Mohaptra, secretary to the Government of India, Ministry of Textiles, New Delhi, January 8, 2003.

Gerry Pinto, UNICEF, New Delhi. January 13, 2003.

Sharda Subramaniam, deputy director, Indo-German Export Promotion Council. Offices of the IGEP, German House, New Delhi, January 7, 2003.

Interviews in Guatemala

Alejandro Argueta, adviser to the Labor Ministry, Guatemala City, January 2005.

Irene Barrientos, international affairs coordinator, Unsitragua (Unión Sindical de Trabajadores de Guatemala), Guatemala City, May 2003.

Rodolfo Batres, manager of investment in Guatemala, Ministry of Economy, Guatemala City, January 2005.

Lucy Bautista, monitor for COVERCO, Guatemala City, May 2003.

César Castillo, Vice-Minister of Labor and Social Prevision, Guatemala City, January 2005.

Ricardo Changala, United Nations Verification Mission (MINIGUA). May 2003.

ChoiSim/Simatex workers collective interviews, Villa Nueva, May 22, 2003.

Sonia Figuero, director of Social Prevision, Ministry of Labor. January 2005.

Homero Fuentes, coordinador, COVERCO, Guatemala City, 2003 to 2006.

César Gatica, labor inspector, Social Prevision, Ministry of Labor, Guatemala City, May 22, 2006.

Eda Gaviola and Floridalma Contreras, activists with CALDH (Centro de Acción Legal y Derechos Humanos), Programa de Derechos de las Mujeres, Guatemala City, May 2003.

Teresa Guillermo, VESTEX (Comisión de Vestuarios y Textiles), Guatemala City, May 2003.

Carlos E. De Icaza, International Affairs, Regional Program of Labor Market Modernization, SIECA (Secretaria de Integración Económica de Centroamericana (Secretary for Central American Economic Integration), Guatemala City, January 2005.

Carlos Enrique Mancilla Garcia, CUSG (Confederación de Unidad Sindical de Guatemala), Guatemala City, May 2003.

José David Morales, general secretary, FESTRAS (Federación Sindical de Trabajadores de la Alimentación Agro-Industria y Similares de Guatemala), Guatemala City, May 2003.

José Luis Morales Perez, labor inspector, Social Prevision, Ministry of Labor, Guatemala City, May 22–23, 2006.

Abby Nájera interviews, Guatemala City, May 2003, January 2005, May 2006.

Robert Perillo, U.S./Labor Education in the Americas Project, Guatemala City, May 2003.

Laura Podolsky, STITCH, Guatemala City, May 2003.

Guido Richi, Labor Commission, CACIF (Comité Coordinador de Asociaciones Agrícolas, Comerciales, Industriales, y Financieras), Guatemala City, January 2005.

Dennis A. Smith, president, COVERCO, Guatemala City, May 2003.

Roberto Tobar and Wendy Tobar, COVERCO, Guatemala City, January 2005.

Víctor Hugo Toledo, congressman and chair of Comisión de Previsión y Seguridad Social, Guatemala Congress, Guatemala City, January 2005.

Gabriel Zelada Ortiz, CEADEL (Centro de Estudios y Apoyo al Desarrollo Local), Guatemala City, May 2003.

= Index =